Trustworthy Compilers

WILEY SERIES ON
QUANTITATIVE SOFTWARE ENGINEERING

Larry Bernstein, *Series Editor*

The Quantitative Software Engineering Series focuses on the convergence of systems engineering and software engineering with emphasis on quantitative engineering trade-off analysis. Each title brings the principles and theory of programming in-the-large and industrial strength software into focus.

This practical series helps software developers, software engineers, systems engineers, and graduate students understand and benefit from this convergence through the unique weaving of software engineering case histories, quantitative analysis, and technology into the project effort. You will find that each publication reinforces the series goal of assisting the reader with producing useful, well-engineered software systems.

Published titles:

Trustworthy Systems through Quantitative Software Engineering
Lawrence Bernstein and C. M. Yuhas

Software Measurement and Estimation: A Practical Approach
Linda M. Laird and M. Carol Brennan

Web Application Design and Implementation: Apache 2, PHP5, MySQL, JavaScript, and Linux/UNIX
Steven A. Gabarro

Trustworthy Systems for Quantitative Software Engineering
Larry Bernstein and C. M. Yuhas

Software Measurement and Estimation: A Practical Approach
Linda M. Laird and M. Carol Brennan

World Wide Web Application Engineering and Implementation
Steven A. Gabarro

Managing the Development of Software-Intensive Systems
James McDonald

Trustworthy Compilers
Vladimir O. Safonov

Trustworthy Compilers

Vladimir O. Safonov
St. Petersburg University

A John Wiley & Sons, Inc., Publication

Published by John Wiley & Sons, Inc., Hoboken, New Jersey
Published simultaneously in Canada

For general information on our other products and services or for technical support, please contact our Customer Care Department within the United States at (800) 762-2974, outside the United States at (317) 572-3993 or fax (317) 572-4002.

Wiley also publishes its books in a variety of electronic formats. Some content that appears in print may not be available in electronic formats. For more information about Wiley products, visit our web site at www.wiley.com.

Library of Congress Cataloging-in-Publication Data:

ISBN 978-0-470-50095-8

Printed in the United States of America

10 9 8 7 6 5 4 3 2 1

To Adel, my beloved wife and my dear trustworthy friend.

Contents

Preface

This book presented to the readers is my second book published by John Wiley & Sons publishing company—thanks for such a wonderful opportunity to publish!

My first Wiley book [1] issued in 2008 covers aspect-oriented programming and its use for trustworthy software development.

First, let me explain the allegorical meaning of the picture on the front cover of the book—a view of a *rostral column*, an architectural monument at the center of St. Petersburg in Neva embankment, designed by Jean-Francois Thomas de Thomon in 1810. When accompanying a compiler development team from Sun around St. Petersburg in 1994, I realized and told my guests that the rostral columns can be considered an allegory of modern compiler architecture. The *foundation* (*pillar*) of the column symbolizes trustworthy *common back-end* of a family of compilers for some platform (e.g., Scalable Processor ARChitecture [SPARC]), and the *rostra* relying on the column (according to ancient tradition, the *rostra* should be *front parts* of the defeated enemy's ships) depicts compiler *front-ends*—FORTRAN, C, Pascal, Modula, and so on, developed for that hardware platform.

This trustworthy compilers book is the result of many years of my professional experience of research and commercial projects in the compiler development field. I was as fortunate as to work with great people and companies on compiler development: in the 1970s to 1980s—with my Russian colleagues on developing compilers for the Russian "Elbrus" [2] supercomputers; in the 1990s—with Sun Microsystems on developing Sun compilers; and since 2003—with Microsoft on its Phoenix [3] technology for compiler development. The results of these collaborations are presented in my book.

Also, the book summarizes many years of my experience in the university, teaching compilers—my courses and seminars on trustworthy compiler development I have been teaching at St. Petersburg University [4], taken and passed by about a hundred students each year. Each of the chapters of the book is supplied by practical examples and exercises on the topics considered in the chapter. So, the book can be used as a textbook for university teaching trustworthy compilers. In addition, the book companion Web page on my personal Web site, http://www.vladimirsafonov.org/trustworthycompilers, contains resources related to the book for compiler teachers.

Two questions may arise as an immediate reaction to the title of the book: "Why *compilers* again" and "Why *trustworthy* compilers?" The first question implies that, during the 50-year history of programming languages and compiler development, since the first version of FORTRAN designed in 1957, there have been so many compiler books issued that it may seem doubtful to publish just one more. The second question was asked by my colleague from the U.S.A. when I visited Microsoft's Trustworthy Computing Curriculum Seminar in Redmond in April 2006: At first glance, compilers, unlike, for example, networking or operating systems, don't seem to be suitable for trustworthy computing approach, though in this book, we show that the concept of trustworthy compiler does make sense, and analyze and advise how to accomplish it in compiler development practice.

In the book, we prove that even in such a well-studied area as compilers, there is still an opportunity for original results, efficient algorithms, and interesting research and development.

My book introduces and analyzes the concept of a *trustworthy compiler* and the principles of trustworthy compiler development, and provides an analytical overview of other promising research works in this area.

One of the most important goals of my book is to present my own efficient algorithms (faster than those in the Dragon Book [5], which I consider the "bible of compilers") for various phases of compilation, especially for semantic analysis—lookup, evaluation of semantic attributes, type evaluation, and type-checking. Some of those algorithms are patented by my four U.S. compiler patents sponsored by Sun Microsystems in the 1990s, due to my joint compiler projects with Sun. Some others were implemented before, in our compiler projects for "Elbrus." What may attract the special interest of the readers is that I explain and teach my compiler development techniques using examples of *real compilers* (in particular, the Sun Pascal compiler we were responsible for in the 1990s, and our compilers for "Elbrus" we developed in the 1980s), rather than inventing any kind of simplified language and its "toy" compiler, as many other compiler textbooks do. Our point in this respect is as follows: A real compiler project is the best way to practically acquire compiler knowledge.

In the book, we pay a lot of attention to novel kinds of compilation—*just-in-time* (*JIT*) compilation and *ahead-of-time* (*AOT*) compilation, characteristic of modern software development platforms, Java and .NET—that were actually invented long before. It appears that right now, there are no textbooks or monographs on this subject, though JIT compilation is especially important and still has a lot of things to be invented and improved. Hopefully, our book helps to fill in this gap.

In the book, we cover a number of modern compiler development tools—ANother Tool for Language Recognition (ANTLR), CoCo/R, SableCC, and many others.

As another novel compiler development area, in the book, we consider *graph compilers*, related concepts such as *graph grammars*, and graph compiler and editor development tools such as *DiaGen*.

To summarize the novel features of the book, we should say it is mostly practically oriented and tool-oriented, unlike many other, more theoretical compiler books. This is quite natural since the book is written by a compiler development professional and practitioner who participated in many research and commercial compiler projects.

Here is an overview of the book content.

Chapter 1 is an introductory chapter. It defines the concept of a *trustworthy compiler* and the related concept of a *verifying compiler* by Hoare, and shows their importance in modern compiler development. Basic compiler notions related to phases of compilation are summarized. Specifics of compilation for the novel Java and .NET platforms are explained. History of compiler development is summarized, including compiler development in the U.S.S.R. and in Russia, which is probably not familiar enough to English-speaking readers of the book—compiler experts and students. Then, we summarize compiler development technologies, including both traditional front-end/back-end compiler architecture and bootstrapping, and our own novel compiler development technology—technological instrumental package (TIP) technology [2] protected by U.S. and Russian patents.

As well known, many compiler books start with the theory of lexical analysis and finite-state automata; many books on programming languages start with the "hello world" application as well. In this regard, *Chapter 2* is nontraditional and novel. It puts the proper accent on the whole book by considering the concept of trustworthy and verifying compilers, and by analyzing some modern approaches to these concepts—*verifying* compilers by Hoare, *verified* compilers by Leroy, Microsoft's approach to trustworthy compilers—the *Spec#* system based on the C# extension by formal specifications in design-by-contract style. Problems for further research in this direction are outlined.

Chapter 3 is a description of *lexical analysis*, the first phase of compilation. Alongside with traditional issues such as theoretical model of lexical analysis, we present our own approaches and methods—efficient algorithm to distinguish between identifiers and keywords; our structure of identifier table implemented in many of our compilers; and practical recipes on the efficient implementation of lexical analyzer. The most important part of the chapter considers the trustworthy aspects of lexical analysis.

Chapter 4 covers *parsing*, probably the most widely described and taught phase of compilation, but, again, from a trustworthy approach viewpoint. We summarize *error recovery* techniques used in parsing—the basis of making this compilation phase trustworthy. We consider parsing from a practical viewpoint and offer our own algorithms of lookahead and error recovery to enhance the classical recursive descent method, still used in many compilers. Then, we describe bottom-up and specifically LR [5] parsing and pay attention to efficient error recovery techniques used in Sun Pascal compiler, which extend traditional *yacc* features. We cover *generalized parsing* as a novel approach to parsing.

Chapter 5 covers *semantic analysis and typing* and is one of the key chapters of the book. We consider in detail our own novel efficient algorithms of semantic analysis, typing, and intermediate representation of the source program; our efficient organization of compiler tables; our efficient lookup algorithm; and our methods of representing and evaluating semantic attributes we used in a number of compilers, including Sun Pascal. We explain the implementation of those methods using Sun Pascal compiler as an example. Our work on the refurbishment of Sun Pascal using the methods described in the chapter resulted in a compiler front-end speed-up of four times, and the publishing of four U.S. software patents—these results prove the applicability of the methods considered.

Chapter 6 is a kind of renovation for another well-known topic—*compiler optimization*. We consider optimizations from the viewpoint of their trustworthiness and analyze some typical bugs in optimizers related to simplified "C-like" view on the implementation of programming languages. As an example of a modern approach to optimizations, we summarize Sun Studio compilers and their optimization techniques. Modern software development platforms, Java and .NET, pose new optimization problems to compiler developers, in particular—optimizations during JIT compilation; these are also covered in this chapter. Later, in Chapter 10, we cover optimizations in Microsoft Phoenix compiler development toolkit.

Chapter 7 is devoted to *code generation*—the concluding phase of compilation. We consider this phase, alongside with the problem of *runtime data representation* in compilers. We show how to implement data types and structures—records, arrays, objects, and so on—and how to generate a code accessing them and their components. Instead of using any abstract or imaginary model of object code, we explain the basics of Reduced Instruction Set Computer (RISC) and SPARC, and the principles of code generation for various kinds of language constructs using Sun Studio compilers. The chapter also covers such code generation-related issues as generation of debugging information and optimization during code generation (based on SPARC hardware platform).

Chapter 8 covers classical and modern approaches to *runtime*—tools and environment to support trustworthy execution of a program code generated by a compiler. We consider the tasks to be solved by a language runtime and the relationships between the language runtime and the operating system. The novel content of the chapter is presented in the sections on principles and architecture of *JIT compilers*, inherent parts of Java and .NET platforms. JIT compiler works at runtime and compiles each first called method from an intermediate code (Java *bytecode* or .NET common intermediate language code—*Common Intermediate Language* [*CIL*], or *Microsoft.NET Intermediate Language* [*MSIL*]) to a native code of the target platform. We consider JIT compilers in Java and .NET and, as an example, describe our research project on adding profiler-based optimizations into a JIT compiler for an academic version of .NET—*Rotor*.

As a new and prospective kind of compilers, in *Chapter 9*, we summarize *graph compilers* that use, as the source code of the program to be compiled, its graph-based representation, rather than the traditional source code—a text containing high-level language constructs—and compile them to other graphs or to some object code. Graph compilers are used for *visual programming*—in the electronics industry and a variety of other problem areas. We summarize related theoretical concepts, such as *reserved graph grammars*, *layered graph grammars*, and so on, and tools for developing graph compilers and graph editors, such as *DiaGen*.

Chapter 10 is, to our knowledge, the first detailed description in scientific literature of one of the most promising compiler development toolkits— *Microsoft Phoenix*. Phoenix is an optimizing compiler back-end development toolkit, with multiple, extensible set of target object platforms (including ×86/×64 and .NET). Our team has been one of the first academic users of Phoenix since 2003. In particular, we use Phoenix in our Aspect.NET project [1]. In Chapter 10, we describe in detail the principles of Phoenix, its architecture, internal representations of programs in Phoenix, its optimizations, the ways how to extend the set of Phoenix target platforms by a new one, and methods of organization of *Phoenix-based tools*—compilers, code browsers, and analyzers. We present our Phoenix project—*Phoenix-FETE frontend development kit* targeted to Phoenix—and summarize our other Phoenix projects.

The *Conclusions* summarize the content of the book and outline further perspectives of trustworthy compilers.

We recommended the following order of reading. Chapters 1–8 should be read in their textual order, since they cover successive phases of compilation. The concluding Chapters 9 and 10 can be read in arbitrary order, in case the readers are interested in the particular compilation issues and tools described, although the content of those chapters implies that the reader is familiar with the basics of compilers and compilation. An experienced compiler developer can read any of the chapters of personal interest in any order.

As an important resource for teaching compilers using this book as a textbook, we provide *exercises* for each chapter.

Also, as online companion to the book, university teachers can use the compiler teaching resources available on our personal Web site: http://www.vladimirsafonov.org/trustworthycompilers.

The curricula of our "Trustworthy Compilers" course are available for compiler teachers at the Microsoft Academic Web site [4] and we hope will be a helpful addition to the book material.

As an experienced compiler teacher, I am sure that compiler development is as a fundamental discipline in teaching computer science and software engineering as mathematical analysis, set theory, and algebra in teaching mathematics. So, please study, teach, and develop trustworthy compilers with the help of this book.

VLADIMIR O. SAFONOV

St. Petersburg University

Acknowledgments

Thanks a lot to the great people I have been fortunate to meet and work with during all my compiler projects. Their school and practical recipes are of greatest value for me as a compiler expert. They are, in chronological order:

Dr. Svyatoslav S. Lavrov, corresponding member of the Russian Academy of Sciences, my scientific advisor and teacher, the author of the first ALGOL compiler in the U.S.S.R., and the leader of Russian school of informatics, who passed away in 2004;

Dr. Vladimir M. Pentkovsky who worked for many years at the Institute of Precise Mechanics and Computer Engineering of Russian Academy of Sciences (IPMCE RAS), Moscow, was the author of the EL-76 programming language, and the leader of compiler projects for "Elbrus" computers; the person who greatly helped to the success of our university compiler projects for "Elbrus" described in the book; now with Intel;

Dr. Igor V. Pottosin, one of the greatest compiler developers and optimization theorists and teachers in Russia who worked at Novosibirsk Institute of Informatics Systems of RAS for many years, and passed away in 2001;

Dr. Boris K. Martynenko, professor of our university department who taught me, as well as many other students of our university school, his very interesting compiler university course in the 1970s;

Dr. George William Walster, the head of the Sun Russian projects with whom I worked very productively on Sun compilers in the 1990s;

Dr. Shahrokh Mortazavi, my colleague and great friend for many years since the 1990s when he worked with me as Sun compiler back-end manager; later, since 2003, as Microsoft Phoenix manager; and now as my partner as Microsoft High-Performance Computing team manager;

Dr. John Lefor, my colleague and great friend since 2003 when I got acquainted to him as the Microsoft Research Phoenix manager, and received from him the first Phoenix CD for a non-Microsoft person; my partner on Phoenix research projects;

Dr. Robert Coleman, my great friend since our joint work with Sun in the 1990s; my partner in our international joint projects; one of the founders of the just-in-time (JIT) compilation approach, as shown in the book below.

Thanks to many other compiler experts worldwide not mentioned above with whom I have been lucky to work with.

Special thanks for the teaching and support to the two great experts and people whom I consider my teachers, with a warm feeling of gratitude, although I haven't passed their university courses: *Dr. Alfred A. Aho*, Professor of Columbia University, a classicist of compilers and the author of the greatest book in this area—*the Dragon Book*, a pattern for other compiler teachers—and *Dr. Lawrence Bernstein*, Professor of Stevens Institute of Technology and the scientific editor of the Wiley Trustworthy Computing Series.

Thanks a lot to all the people who have been members of my compiler teams since 1977 when I started doing compilers, especially to my doctoral students working with me on compilers and tools projects—Daniel Vassilyev, the implementer of Phoenix-FETE; Olesya Mikhaleva, the implementer of a toolkit for editing and visualizing .NET assemblies based on Microsoft Phoenix; and Sophia Chilingarova, the developer of optimizing JIT compiler version academic version of .NET—SSCLI/Rotor.

Thanks to all the users of our compilers since the 1970s up to now, from many countries and organizations, especially to the users of our Pascal compilers for the "Elbrus" system, and to the customers of the Sun Pascal compiler from Siemens, Fannie Mae, and a number of other companies and universities from all over the world.

Thanks to all my compiler students who has attended my lectures and seminars on compilers and got very enthusiastic by this old but rapidly evolving and prospective area. I hope that, due to this book, the number of my compiler students will be increased worldwide.

VLADIMIR O. SAFONOV

St. Petersburg University

Chapter *1*

Introduction

This chapter is an introductory one. It introduces the basic concept of a *trustworthy compiler* used throughout the book. Also, it covers the basics of compilers and compilation from a modern viewpoint—different kinds of compilers and the phases of compilation—and summarizes compilers history and compiler development technologies.

In traditional meaning, a *compiler* is a program that translates the *source code* written in some *high-level language* (Pascal, C, C++, Java, C#, etc.) to *object* code—native machine code executable on some hardware platform (e.g., ×86, ×64, or Scalable Processor ARChitecture [SPARC]). In this sense, compilers seem to be an old and well-studied topic. However, right now, the concept of a compiler is much wider. Also, there are many reasons stimulating further growth of compilers and progress in compiling techniques, in particular:

- the development and wide spread of novel hardware architectures, like *multi-core*, *Very Long Instruction Word* (*VLIW*), *Explicit Parallelism Instruction Computers* (*EPIC*), and others, that require much more "intelligence" from the compiler than before, in particular, require from the compiler to perform *static parallelizing* of program execution and *scheduling* parts of hardware working in parallel;
- the progress and wide popularity of two novel software development platforms, Java and .NET, whose computing and compilation model

Trustworthy Compilers, by Vladimir O. Safonov
Copyright © 2010 John Wiley & Sons, Inc.

stimulated research in new approaches to compilation, *just-in-time* (*JIT*) and *ahead-of-time* (*AOT*), that make runtime performance of programs on those platforms more optimal;

- the support of *multi-language programming* on .NET platform. On that new platform, different modules of a large application can be developed in any languages implemented for .NET, for example, C#, Visual Basic.NET, Managed C++.NET, and others. For that reason, now we are witnessing a real *compiler development boom* for .NET platform (exceeding the previous compiler boom of the 1970s when a lot of new programming languages were invented): more than 30 languages are already implemented for .NET, and the number of implemented languages continues to grow. We are also witnessing a related *boom of compiler development tools* (ANother Tool for Language Recognition [ANTLR], SableCC, CoCo/R, and hundreds of others);

- the popularity of *Web programming* that stimulated the evolution of Web programming languages with extensive *dynamic typing* features (Perl, Python, Ruby, JavaScript/ECMAScript). In this relation, the task of their efficient implementation is very important;

- the popularity of *trustworthy computing* (TWC) and, therefore, the challenge to make compilers more trustworthy, verifying, and verified, as described below in this chapter and in Chapter 2;

- the rapid development of *mobile devices*, and the related progress in developing compilers for mobile platforms.

1.1 THE CONCEPT OF A TRUSTWORTHY COMPILER

Keeping in mind the TWC [1] paradigm that inspired this book as well as our previous book [1], one of the major issues in compiler development should be *how to make a compiler trustworthy* and *what is a trustworthy compiler*. Here is our vision of trustworthy compiling and of the concept of a trustworthy compiler, based on our own compiler experience, and on related heuristics and pragmatics.

A *trustworthy compiler* is a compiler that satisfies the following conditions (or, practically speaking, at least some of the conditions) listed below:

1 *A compiler that generates a trustworthy object code.* The users will trust the compiler, at first, if the object code generated by the compiler (any kind of native code, or virtual code) is trustworthy, since code generation is the primary task of any compiler.

2 *A compiler that demonstrates a trustworthy behavior.* The user will trust the compiler, which should do all jobs, from lexical analysis to code generation, with no surprises for the users—no hangs, unexpected stops, or other faults. For example, the user will not trust the compiler after

the first use, if the compiler suddenly issues an unclear message and stops compilation. This requirement looks evident, but the practice shows that such nontrustworthy issues are sometimes demonstrated even by industrial compilers.

3 *A compiler that uses trustworthy data* (sources, tables, intermediate code, libraries, etc.) and *protects them from occasional or intended corruption.* In other words, the *privacy* of all compiler input and intermediate data at any moment should be guaranteed; otherwise, the results of compilation can be falsified at some stage.

4 *A compiler whose design and implementation (source code) is trustworthy*, that is, satisfies the principles of TWC (see Section 2.1 for more details). The most radical and formal and probably the most difficult approach to making the code of the compiler trustworthy is to enable that the compiler is *verified*, following Leroy [6], that is, the compiler code meets its formal specifications. We'll consider Leroy's approach to verified compilers and other related approaches below in Sections 2.2 and 2.3. A simpler, more practical approach to make the compiler code trustworthy is to use *assertions* or *design-by-contract* when designing and developing the compiler code.

5 *A compiler that trustworthily performs error diagnostics and recovery* during all analytical phases of compilation—lexical analysis, parsing, and semantic analysis. As a counter-example, in our compiler practice, when testing some early version of a C compiler in mid-1990s, that compiler, in case of syntax errors like a missing bracket, issued a mysterious message of the kind: "*Syntax error before or at symbol: {*" ; then, after 20–30 lines of code, complained to be unable to compile any more and aborted the compilation. Compiler developers should keep in mind that such nontrustworthy compiler behavior jeopardizes the trust of users to compilers at all. The main principle in this respect, as shown in Chapters 3–5, is as follows: Even if the source code to be compiled contains any kind and any number of lexical, syntax, or semantic errors, the compiler should *issue reasonably clear and brief error diagnostics messages and continue the compilation until the end of the source code*, for the purpose of catching as many errors as possible.

6 *A compiler that works* as a *verifying compiler*, following Hoare's terms [7], that is, the compiler verifies the trustworthiness (including *semantic* correctness) of the source code it compiles, and does not allow nontrustworthy and nonverified source code to pass through. In an ideal case, the compiler should give to the user recommendations how to change the source code to make it trustworthy, rather than just complain of some error. Please see Section 2.2 for more details.

Actually, we don't know any compiler yet (at least in the industry) that would fully satisfy the above definition of compiler trustworthiness. Though, as we show in the book below, there exist trustworthy compiling techniques implemented in real compilers.

1.2 KINDS OF COMPILERS

The variety of kinds of compilers being used now is amazing. It would be naive to think that there are only compilers to native or virtual machine code. Here are the most widely used kinds of compilers:

- *Traditional* (*classical*) *compilers* are those that compile a source code written in some high-level language (e.g., Pascal, C, or C++) to native machine code. The source language is usually strongly typed (see Chapter 5 for more details). This kind of compilers is covered by classical compiler books such as Dragon Book [5]. From a novel viewpoint, this scheme of compilation can be referred to as *native* compilation. As proved by our experience of research and development work, even in the area of classical native compilers, it is quite possible to make a lot of innovations.

- *Interpreters* [8] are yet another way to implement programming languages. Instead of translating the source code to some machine code, the interpreter *emulates* (*models*) the program execution in terms of the source code, or of some high-level intermediate code to which the program is compiled before its interpretation. An interpreter approach is known to slow down runtime performance of a program, in average, in 100–1000 times, as compared with an equivalent program compiled to native code. However, there are languages that intensively use dynamic types, dynamic data structures, and program extension features: for example, the old symbolic information processing languages LISP and SNOBOL, and a newer language FORTH widely spread in the 1980s and based on the ideas of using postfix notation as a programming language, and an extensible set of *commands*—primitive language constructs. The nature of such dynamic languages makes their interpretation much simpler and adequate than compilation. It's worth mentioning in this relation that Java 1.0 was also implemented in 1995 as a pure interpreter of Java bytecode. JIT compiler was added to Java implementation later, since Java 1.1.

- *Cross-compilers* are compilers that work on one (typically more powerful and comfortable, like ×86 or ×64) hardware platform and generate code for another target hardware platform (typically, an embedded microprocessor with limited resources).

- *Incremental compilers* [9], very popular in the 1970s, are compilers that allow the users to split the source code of a program to *steps*. A step can be a definition, a declaration, a procedure or function header, a statement, or a group of statements. The source program can be entered into an incremental compilation system step-by-step. The selected steps can be edited and recompiled. The resulting program can be tried and tested for execution, even if not all its steps are already developed. Such approach is comfortable for incremental program development and debugging, but the efficiency of the object program is poor, since such programming system has to use an *interpreter (driver) of steps* at runtime.

- *Converters* are compilers from one high-level language source code to another. They are used for *reengineering*, to port programs from older languages (e.g., COBOL) to newer ones (e.g., Java or C#). Another typical reason of using this approach is a research targeting to extend a programming language with some advanced (e.g., *knowledge management*) features: In this case, the extensions can be implemented by conversion to the basic language constructs and specific API calls. We use this approach in our Knowledge.NET [10] knowledge management toolkit for .NET based on C# extension by knowledge representation constructs.

- *JIT compilers* are compilers that work at runtime and compile each first called method from the intermediate code to the native code of the target platform. JIT compilers are inherent parts of Java and .NET technologies. They are covered in Chapters 6–8.

- *AOT compilers* (or *precompilers*) are also used in Java and .NET to avoid JIT compilation and to improve runtime performance: Those compilers translate platform-independent intermediate code to native code prior to program execution and work similarly to traditional compilers for more conventional languages like C or Pascal.

- *Binary compilers* are compilers directly from binary code of one platform to binary code of another one, without using the source code. Binary compilation is used as a method to port applications from older hardware platforms to newer ones.

- *Graph compilers* are compilers that compile some graph-like representation of a program (rather than its source code) to other graphs, of to native or virtual code; this novel kind of compilers is covered in Chapter 9.

1.3 EVOLUTION OF JAVA COMPILERS

Requirements of modern programming—the need to make an object code platform independent and the need to support rapidly dynamically changing program structure—lead to more complicated scheme of implementing modern languages like Java than traditional native compilation.

The first version of Java implementation (Java 1.0) that was made available to software developers in 1995, included the *compiler from source Java code to bytecode*—intermediate code of the *Java Virtual Machine* (*JVM*) based on postfix notation, and the *JVM* implemented as a pure *interpreter* of Java bytecode. It was kind of a surprise to experienced software developers who had used highly optimizing compilers for decades before Java appeared. The runtime performance of programs in Java 1.0 based on pure interpretation model was poor.

So, the second version of Java, Java 1.1, shipped in 1996, for the purpose of improvement of runtime performance, included the first Java JIT compiler as part of JVM, alongside with the bytecode interpreter.

The next major version of Java, Java 1.2, which appeared in 1998, made further steps toward making runtime performance of Java applications more optimal and comparable to that of natively compiled applications. Java 1.2 included *HotSpot performance engine*—an enhancement to JVM based on a *profiler* to determine "hot spots" in Java applications—the most often called and resource-consuming methods. Those "hot" methods were JIT compiled, whereas the rest of the methods remained in bytecode representation. The average runtime performance increase due to using HotSpot appeared to be two times, as compared with their performance in the previous version of Java.

It should also be mentioned that, although Sun's Java implementation doesn't contain Java native compilers, many integrated development environments targeted to Java software development (e.g., Borland JBuilder) support native compilation of Java programs as an option. So, native compilation (or AOT compilation) is now used as an alternative way of Java implementation.

1.4 COMPILATION FOR .NET

.NET is a multi-language software development platform. Several dozen languages are already implemented for .NET, and their number continues to increase. The most popular languages used in .NET environment are C#, Visual Basic.NET, and Managed C++.NET, implemented by Microsoft.

The implementation of a language for .NET is based on a similar principle as Java implementation. The compiler translates the source code to *Common Intermediate Language (CIL)* code, also known as *Microsoft Intermediate Language (MSIL)*. The architecture of CIL is similar to Java bytecode and based on postfix notation. Alongside with CIL code, the compiler generates *metadata*—information on the types defined and used in the compilation unit. Then, at runtime, each first called method is JIT compiled to native code. The important distinction of .NET approach from Java is the open nature of .NET—its principles stimulate compiler developers to implement more and more languages, whereas Java technology prescribes using the Java language only; the only alternative of using other languages with Java technology is to use *native methods* that should be implemented in C or C++.

Microsoft's implementation of .NET provides the *ngen* (native generator) utility to precompile the code to avoid JIT compilation.

The .NET's *Common Language Runtime (CLR)* supports *managed execution* mode, with full runtime type-checking, security checking, memory management, and garbage collection.

A common principle of developing compilers for .NET is to leave all or most of the optimizations to the JIT compiler.

One of the most important results in .NET area, from the viewpoint of trustworthy compiling, was the development by Microsoft Research of a novel programming system *Spec#* [11], an extension of the C# language by formal specifications in *design-by-contract* [12] style, with a built-in verifier to prove correctness of programs in Spec#. Actually, Spec# can be considered the first worldwide known trustworthy compiler.

1.5   PHASES OF COMPILATION

After the above short introduction to modern compilers and tools, let's summarize the *phases* (*steps*) of compilation.

The formal model of the process of compilation can be represented as the five main successive phases: *lexical analysis*, *parsing* (or *syntax analysis*), *semantic* (or *context-dependent* or *type-dependent*) *analysis*, *code optimization* (as an optional phase), and *code generation*. Each phase takes, as the input, the result of the previous phase and passes its output to the next phase.

Actually, this model is formal, simplified, and nonoptimal, and the architecture of real compilers can differ from it.

The purpose of the *lexical analysis* phase is to translate the *source code* (the program code written in a high-level language and represented as a text file or a logically related group of text files) to *stream of tokens*. A *token* is a primitive unit of a programming language—*identifier* (*name*), *keyword*, *number*, *character literal*, *string literal*, *operator symbol*, or *delimiter* (e.g., left and right parentheses). Lexical analyzer ignores *white space characters* and *comments* in the program source code, and processes *pragmas*—special instructions inserted in the source code to control the compiler behavior and switch on or off its options. Also, during lexical analysis, some (relatively minor) *error diagnostics and recovery* can happen, for example, in case a number has too many digits. Although, from a formal compilation model viewpoint, lexical analysis is a separate compilation phase, in most of the compilers, to save compilation time, lexical analysis is implemented as a *subroutine*, *method*, or *function* to be called by the parser each time it needs the next token from the source code.

The goal of the next phase, *parsing*, is to translate the sequence of tokens, the output of lexical analysis, to a *parse* (or *derivation*) *tree* representing the syntax structure of the program to be compiled. Usually, parsing is based on representing the model of the program syntax by *context-free grammars*. Traditional parsing techniques and algorithms are covered in classical compiler books [5]. Another important goal of parsing is *syntax error diagnostics and recovery*, since program developers often make mistakes like missing bracket, or semicolon, or keyword. The task of the parser in such situations is to keep a trustworthy behavior, provide clear diagnostics, and parse the erroneous program code up to its end, for the purpose of catching as many more syntax errors as possible.

The next phase, *semantic analysis*, is intended to translate the parse tree to *intermediate representation* (*IR*), more comfortable for the code generator, for example, to *postfix notation*. During this phase, all compile-time checks are performed that couldn't be made at the previous, parsing phase. For the first turn, the semantic analyzer performs *lookup*—for each *applied occurrence* of an identifier, it finds the appropriate *definition* of that identifier, if any. The next major subtask of semantic analysis is *type-checking*—it checks that, in each operation, the types of the operands are appropriate. Finally, the semantic analyzer translates the program code to IR. Surely during this phase, a lot of bugs can be found, so an important task of the semantic analyzer, similar to that of the parser, is to provide *semantic error diagnostics and recovery*, which is an inherent part of a trustworthy compiler.

The next, optional, phase of the compiler is *code optimization*. This phase is usually turned off by default but is very important to enable better runtime performance of the resulting object code. The optimization phase usually works as follows: It takes the IR of the program and generates the optimized IR. Optimization includes solving a number of interested and complicated mathematical problems described in the excellent book by Muchnick [13].

The final phase of the compiler is *code generation*. It takes the IR of the program and generates its *object code*—either *native code* of the target platform (e.g., ×64 or SPARC), or *virtual code* of some *virtual machine* that performs runtime support of the program on the target platform (e.g., Java bytecode or .NET CIL code).

1.6   OVERVIEW OF COMPILER DEVELOPMENT PRINCIPLES AND TECHNOLOGIES

As we've already seen, the architecture of a compiler is complicated and consists a lot of phases. So, compiler developers need to apply specific design principles and technologies to make the development easier and more systematic.

Front-end and back-end. The first compiler design principle used in practically all compilers is the separation of the compiler to two major parts— *front-end* and *back-end* (recall the allegoric picture on the front cover and its explanation in the Preface). Of the five compiler phases explained in Section 1.5 above, the *front-end* of the compiler consists of the three first, source language-dependent phases—*lexical analysis*, *parsing*, and *semantic analysis*. The *back-end* of the compiler is the collection of the two remaining phases, the *optimizer* and the *code generator*. The front-end of the compiler can be otherwise referred to as the *source language-dependent* part, and the back-end as the *target platform-dependent* part. Why is it so convenient to represent the compiler in such a way? Because, typically, for any hardware platform, a whole *family of compilers* needs to be developed—say, from M source languages—C, C++, Pascal, FORTRAN, and so on. Due to the separation of compilers to front-ends and back-ends, we can develop M front-ends to use the same common IR, and only *one back-end*, common for the whole family of compilers, that takes the IR and generates a native code for the target platform. If we have N target platforms and need to develop the compilers from all M source languages for all of them, using this approach, we should develop M *front-ends* and N *back-ends* only, that is, $M + N$ major compiler components, instead of $M * N$ components in case we use a straightforward approach and develop each of the front-ends and back-ends from scratch, without any kind of code reusability among them. A good example of such family of compilers developed according to such principles is *Sun Studio* [14], compilers from three languages C, C++, and FORTRAN, working on two target platforms, *Solaris* (on SPARC and ×86/×64 machines) and *Linux* (on ×86/×64 machines). To our knowledge, the best example of a toolkit for developing optimizing compiler back-ends for an extendable set of target platforms is Microsoft Phoenix [3] covered in Chapter 10.

One-pass versus multi-pass compilers. To make the work of developing a compiler more modular, and to parallelize it between several developers, it is quite common to implement the compiler as *multi-pass*. With this scheme, each phase of the compiler (except for lexical analysis) is implemented as a separate *pass*, that is, as a module that analyzes the whole source program (represented by the source code or any kind of intermediate code) and converts it to some output IR suitable for the next pass. As we'll see later on, for most source languages, it is not possible to make the compiler one-pass because of the specifics of the language, typically because of using identifiers or labels defined later in the source code. A legend on an old PL/1 compiler says that the number of its passes was equal to the number of employees in the appropriate department of the compiler developer company.

As an alternative to multi-pass approach, for some simpler languages (e.g., for Pascal), compilers are developed as *one-pass*, for the purpose to make the compiler faster. For one-pass compilers, to resolve the situations like forward references mentioned above, the technique of *applied occurrences lists* can be used (more details in Chapter 5). With the one-pass compiling scheme, the compiler source code combines fragments of different phases in a procedure or method that compiles some source language construct (e.g., *if* statement)—lexical analysis, parsing, semantic analysis, and code generation for the construct are intermixed in one compiler module. Typical compiling technique used in one-pass compilation is *recursive descent* (see Chapter 4). It should be noted, however, that such compiler architecture may be dangerous, since it can lead to design flaws of *temporal cohesion*, speaking in terms by Myers [15]: If in a compiler module's source code the boundaries are not clear between the statements implementing fragments of one phase and those implementing the other phase, the risk of making a bug of omitting some of the statements is high.

Bootstrapping. Another popular technique of compiler development is referred to as *bootstrapping*, which, as applicable to compilers, means that the source language is used as a tool for developing a compiler from the same language, so *the compiler is used to compile itself*. More exactly, the developer of the compiler uses, as a development tool, the version of the compiler for the subset of the language to be implemented, or uses some other, maybe less efficient, version of the compiler for the same language to compile the source of the "good" compiler written in the same source language.

The first method of bootstrapping is as follows. Let L be the source language to be implemented on the target platform T (let's also denote T as the assembly language of the target platform). To make the task easier, we choose some subset of L referred to as L_0, and develop the compiler from L_0 to T in T. So now we have a tool for further development, more comfortable than the assembly language T. Next, we develop a compiler from some larger subset L_1 of the language L in L_0, and so on. Finally, for some n, we develop the compiler from $L_n = L$ in L_{n-1}, and our job is done. As compared with the straightforward solution—writing a compiler from L to T in low-level language T—due to the use of the bootstrapping technique, we only use low-level language at the first step, when writing the compiler from L_0 to T in T.

The second variant of bootstrapping is used to gradually improve the quality of the compiler. Using the above notation, our first step will be to develop a "good" compiler from L to T written in L. Let's denote that compiler as C_0. Due to the use of high-level language as a tool, it will be easier for us to enable C_0 to generate efficient object code, perform various optimizations, and so on. But C_0 cannot work yet, since we didn't provide a way to translate it into T. To do that, we perform the second step—develop a "poor" compiler C_1 from L to T written in T (with no optimizations and object code quality improvements, just a compiler with straightforward code generation). Next, we perform the first bootstrapping—compile C_0 by C_1. The resulting compiler (let's denote it as C_2) should be as good as C_0 from the viewpoint of the code quality it generates, but this version of the compiler is probably not so fast (since its source was compiled by the poor compiler C_1). To improve the compiler's efficiency, we perform the second bootstrapping—compile C_0 by C_2 and so on. I know Pascal compiler developers who were as patient and persistent as to make 10 bootstraps to improve their compiler written in Pascal. They claimed that the quality of the compiler became better with each bootstrap.

The bootstrapping techniques described above were especially important for older hardware platforms that were lacking high-level languages
already implemented on those platforms, ready to be used as tools for
compiler development. Nowadays, the situation is quite different: There
are enough high-level languages implemented on any platform appropriate for use as compiler writing tools. In practice of modern research and
commercial compiler projects, most of the compilers are written in C of
C++. Also, to make a compiler or a compiler development tool portable,
it has become a common practice to write it in Java.

Compiler compilers. Due to the need of developing more and more compilers, in the late 1960s, the idea of a *compiler compiler* was coined by
compiler experts. A compiler compiler is a tool that takes a formal definition of syntax and semantics of a programming language and generates
a ready-to-use compiler from that language. Theoretical model of compiler compiler is based on *attributed grammars* [16], a formalism invented
by Knuth to combine formal definitions of programming language syntax
(by a *context-free grammar*) and semantics (by *semantic actions* attached
to each syntax rule to evaluate *semantic attributes* of the grammar
symbols participating in the syntax rule). Attributed grammars are
described in detail in Chapter 5. In the 1970s, attribute-based compiler
compiler projects became very popular. Among them, there were
DELTA [17] developed in France, and the Soviet system SUPER [18]
developed in the Computing Centre of the Russian Academy of Sciences.
The most widely known compiler compiler is *YACC* [19] by Johnson,
still used in many industrial compilers, for example, in Sun Studio, and
stimulating development of a lot of similar compiler compilers, like *bison*
[20] and newer compiler development tools—*JavaCC* [21], ANTLR [22],
CoCo/R [23], and SableCC [24] covered in Chapter 4. In short, the
approach of tools like YACC is different from the approach of tools like
DELTA, since YACC is more practical. The goal of tools like DELTA
was to formalize the syntax and the semantics of the source language
completely, which is a more complicated task than implement part of
the compiler "by hand." Instead, YACC offers a combination of formalized syntax (for automated parser generator) with informal semantic
actions, to be written in the compiler implementation language like C,
attached to each syntax rule. So YACC's approach provides more flexibility, in particular, in using any other compiler development tools, any
algorithms of semantic analysis and code generation. Actually, one of
modern approaches to compiler development is to automatically generate lexical analyzer and parser, based on tools like YACC or ANTLR,
and develop the semantic analyzer by hand, using its API calls in semantic actions of the grammar. As for code generator and optimizer, there
are modern tools like Phoenix that enable automation of developing
those phases also.

Technological instrumental package (TIP) technology [1,2,25]. In our own
practice in the 1970s and 1980s, for the compiler development for
"Elbrus" [2] computers, and later in the 1990s, for the compiler development for Sun, we used our own compiler development technology
referred to as *TIP technology*, an enhancement of modular programming
and abstract data types. From a modern viewpoint, TIP technology can
be characterized as modularization of the compiler, enhanced by using
predefined design and implementation schemes for compiler architecture. With TIP technology, a compiler is designed and implemented as
a hierarchy of *TIPs*, each of them implementing a set of operations on
some data structure used or generated by the compiler—identifier table,
table of type definitions, IR to be generated by the front-end, and so on.
Each TIP is designed according to the following predefined scheme of
abstraction layers and vertical cuts (groups of operations). The *abstraction layers* of a TIP are as follows:

- *representation layer*—a set of operations on the data structure in terms
  of elements of its concrete representation;
- *definition layer*—a set of operations on the data structure in terms of
  intermediate concepts;
- *conceptual layer*—a set of operations on the data structure in more
  adequate and abstract terms, convenient for the user (other compiler
  developer) who wants to work with the data structure in terms suitable
  for the task being solved.

The *vertical cuts* (groups of operations) of the TIP are:

- *generation interface*—operations that generate elements of the data
  structure;
- *access interface*—operations that access elements of the data
  structure;
- *update interface*—operations that update elements of the data
  structure;
- *output interface*—operations that output elements of the data structure
  in symbolic form, or, speaking more generally, convert elements of data
  structure to some other output format, for example, object code.

The lower layer of the TIP is its *concrete representation* implemented
by a group of definitions and declarations.

Each operation of the TIP is implemented by a method, function,
procedure (subroutine), or macro definition. Only the conceptual layer
of the TIP is directly accessible for the user; other layers are encapsulated
in the TIP definition. The TIP is implemented bottom-up, from the representation layer to the definition layer, and then to the conceptual layer.
Each layer n uses operations of the layer $n - 1$ only.

For example, let's consider the *Types* TIP representing a table of type denotations (see Chapter 5 for more details). Its representation layer and generation interface can include the operation *TGetMem* (*size*) that returns a pointer to the memory area (table element) of the given size. The definition layer can include the operation *TGenField* (*id*) that generates the element representing a record field with a given identifier. The access interface, at the conceptual layer, can include an operation like *TGetField* (*rec, id*) that seeks in a record type a field with the given identifier, and returns a pointer to the field found (if any), or *nil* if not found.

The readers should take into account that the TIP technology was invented in mid-1980s and applied for an implementation language of C level. Our experience with TIP technology has shown that it helped to increase the productivity of the developers and to improve the readability and reliability of the compiler's source code. Due to the application of the TIP technology, we developed a whole family of compilers for "Elbrus" computers—from Pascal, CLU, Modula-2, BASIC, ALGOL (incremental compiler), SNOBOL, FORTH, and REFAL (interpreters) in a few years, with a small group of less than 10 people. Our experience was so successful that we also applied the TIP technology to refurbish the Sun Pascal compiler later in the 1990s [25].

We do think that TIP technology is still quite applicable when developing compilers in C or C-like languages. It is important for compiler development, since it helps to make the design and the source code of the compiler more clear, systematic, more easily maintainable, and therefore more trustworthy.

1.7 HISTORY OF COMPILER DEVELOPMENT IN THE U.S.S.R. AND IN RUSSIA

The history of compiler development is described in classical compiler books [5]. It is well known that the first compilers of the 1950s were written in low-level assembly languages. Later, in the 1960s and 1970s, high-level languages like FORTRAN and C started to be used for compiler development. Among worldwide classicists of theory and methods of compiler development, the first to be mentioned are Alfred Aho, John Hopcroft and Jeffrey Ullman [5], and David Gries [26].

However, the history of compiler development in U.S.S.R. and Russia may appear to be less known to the readers, so in this section, we'll summarize it.

The first widely known Soviet compiler from ALGOL-60 for Soviet computers M-20, M-220, and M-222 was developed in 1962 and named TA-1M (for *Translator from Algol, version 1, Modernized*) [27]. The scientific advisor of this project was my teacher, Dr. Svyatoslav S. Lavrov. This compiler (in terms used in the 1960s—*translator*), as well as the ALGOL-60 language itself, played an outstanding part in university teaching and scientific computing in the U.S.S.R. When I was a student in mid-1970s, I wrote my educational programs in ALGOL and used TA-1M to compile them (the program source code was input into the computer from a deck of punched cards), as many thousand of Soviet students did. It appeared that, during several years of the TA-1M compiler use, we haven't experienced any compiler bug or issue. This is a good example of compiler implementation quality, even for modern software development companies (recall that TA-1M was an academic project). Due to the wide popularity of ALGOL compilers in the U.S.S.R. and the enthusiastic activity by Dr. Lavrov, ALGOL-60 became, for many years, the most popular programming language for university teaching, and the first programming language for most Soviet students to learn in the 1960s–1970s. Please note that the situation in our country differed from that in the U.S.A., Canada, and Western Europe, where, for many years, FORTRAN, COBOL, and BASIC had been used for university teaching.

Another interesting Soviet compiler systems of the 1960s and 1970s were ALPHA [28] and BETA [29], developed in Novosibirsk, Academgorodok, as the result of the projects supervised by Dr. Andrey Ershov who later became the first Soviet academician in IT. One of the leaders of those projects was also Dr. Igor Pottosin. ALPHA was a compiler from the extension of ALGOL and performed a lot of code optimizations. BETA was an attributed compiler compiler (see Section 1.6); in addition, it used a universal internal representation of source programs, common for all compilers generated by BETA. The latter decision allowed the authors of BETA to use a common back-end within the BETA toolkit.

We already mentioned in Section 1.6 the SUPER-attributed compiler compiler developed in the 1970s in the Computing Center of Russian Academy of Sciences, Moscow. The project was supervised by Dr. Vladimir M. Kurochkin.

A really amazing compiler project in the 1970s was developed at our St. Petersburg University—implementation of ALGOL-68 for Soviet clones of IBM 360 [30]. The project was lead by Dr. Gregory S. Tseytin who gathered a team of about 20 best compiler experts from our university. Due to the enthusiasm of the developers, the compiler and the ALGOL-68 language were used for about 10 years for university teaching at our university, and for large commercial and scientific software projects performed by our university specialists.

As one of the most famous compiler projects in the U.S.S.R., we should also mention our own projects on developing a family of compilers and interpreters for Soviet "Elbrus" computers [2]. We developed in a few years, by a small team of less than 10 young software engineers, the following translators: compilers from Pascal, CLU (that was the first CLU implementation in the U.S.S.R. completed in 1985), Modula-2, and BASIC; interpreters of LISP, SNOBOL-4, FORTH-83, and REFAL [31]; and a translator from system programming language ABC [32] designed by Dr. Lavrov. This project started with the supervision of Dr. Lavrov and continued under my supervision. It made our team well known in the country. Our compilers for "Elbrus," especially Pascal, were used in major industrial and academic organizations of the U.S.S.R., including the Spaceship Control Center near Moscow. Other compiler groups for "Elbrus" who worked in Moscow, Novosibirsk, and Rostov developed the compiler from EL-76 [33], the high-level language used by "Elbrus" system programmers; compilers from SIMULA-67, C, FORTRAN, COBOL, Ada, and PL/1; and an interpreter of PROLOG. Most of the worldwide known languages, a total of about 30, were implemented for "Elbrus." That phenomenon can only be compared with the current work on implementing a variety of languages for .NET. The "Elbrus" compiler experience and the TIP technology we applied in those compiler projects became a good basis for our subsequent work with Sun on compilers for the SPARC platform. Our original methods we used in our "Elbrus" compilers constitute an important part of this book.

EXERCISES TO CHAPTER 1

1.1 What is a trustworthy compiler, and what do you think is especially important to enable to make a compiler trustworthy?

1.2 In what respects and why Java 1.2 and Java 1.1 compilation schemes differ from those of Java 1.0, and what is the effect on changing Java compilation schemes on runtime performance?

1.3 Please try to classify the compilers you have ever used on the basis of our classification of compilers in Section 1.2.

1.4 What are the main characteristics of the .NET approach to compilers and language implementation, and why do you think .NET is so attractive for compiler developers?

1.5 What are the compiler front-end and the compiler back-end? Please determine and explain how to name, use, and control the front-end and the back-end of the compiler you are using in your programming practice.

1.6 Please list the phases of compilation; give each of them a short characteristic, and summarize the most important (in your opinion) features and mechanisms in each phase to make a compiler trustworthy.

1.7 Why doesn't a one-pass scheme of compilation work for most programming languages to be implemented?

1.8 What is the idea and purpose of bootstrapping technique for compiler development?

1.9 How does a compiler compiler work? What is its input and output? What is the theoretical basis of a compiler compiler?

1.10 Please list and explain the meaning of the abstraction layers and vertical cuts in TIP technology.

Chapter *2*

Theoretical Foundations and Principles of Trustworthy Compilers

This chapter is nontraditional in a compiler book: It goes right after the introduction, instead of the chapter on lexical analysis (covered in Chapter 3).

However, this chapter is a keystone to the book. It explains in more detail the concept of a trustworthy compiler and summarizes known approaches to trustworthy compiling.

2.1 THE TRUSTWORTHY COMPUTING (TWC) INITIATIVE

The *TWC initiative* [34] was initiated by Microsoft in 2002 and became one of the moving forces for this book and for my previous book [1], as well as for many other new books in this area. Principles of TWC are explained and analyzed in detail in my previous book [1]. In this section, we briefly summarize them.

The four key principles (*pillars*) of TWC, as formulated by Microsoft in [34], are as follows:

> *Security—The customer can expect that systems are resilient to attack and that the confidentiality, integrity, and availability of the system and its data are protected.*
>
> *Privacy—The customer is able to control data about themselves, and those using such data adhere to fair information principles.*

Reliability—The customer can depend on the product to fulfill its functions when required to do so.

Business integrity—The vendor of a product behaves in a responsive and responsible manner.

To speak in simpler terms, the *security* of a program means that the program protects its data and functionality from external attacks. *Privacy* means that the program does not use private (or confidential) information, or uses it only in limited ways, explicitly approved and controlled by the user. *Reliability*, in practice, means that the program works without any faults or failures (or with low rate of those), and its behavior is always predictable, according to the accompanying documentation. *Business integrity* is twofold: First, it means that the product maintenance team should be responsive to the users and fix bugs quickly; second, it means that the developer company runs its business correctly. Please find a more detailed analysis of the TWC initiative's principles in my previous book [1, chapter 2].

2.2 TWC AND TRUSTWORTHY COMPILERS

We already formulated the definition of a trustworthy compiler in Section 1.1. Let's discuss in more detail what the above stated TWC principles mean, as applicable to compilers, what are the relationships of our concept of trustworthy compilers to TWC principles, and, based on that, what should be the theoretical and methodological foundations of trustworthy compilers.

Our definition of a trustworthy compiler is more precise and more specific than general TWC recommendations for any kind of programs (including compilers). The maximal requirement included into our definition (even now, almost 60 years after the first compilers were developed, yet looking too "ideal"), is that the compiler should be both *verifying* [7], that is, should verify the programs that it compiles, and *verified* [6], that is, its code should meet its formal specifications. The concepts of verified and verifying compilers are good patterns for compiler researchers to follow, but they don't seem practical for compiler industry up to now, since their implementation would make the process of compiler development much more complicated and time- and human resource-consuming. So, our definition of a trustworthy compiler can be regarded as a *trustworthy compiler development checklist*, a set of recommendations for compiler developers. Of special practical importance, from our viewpoint, are our recommendations to make the behavior of the compiler itself trustworthy, and its phases (like parsing or semantic analysis). Unfortunately, industrial compiler developers sometimes neglect such recommendations because of lack of time and human resources. The result is poor quality of the compiler and dissatisfaction of the users.

The concept of a *verifying compiler* (as "grand challenge for computing research") was formulated by Hoare [7]. According to Hoare, "verifying compiler uses mathematical and logical reasoning to check the program that it compiles" [7]. It is of major importance in this definition that a verifying compiler should check the *semantic correctness* of the program—this principle assumes that the program should be formally specified (or annotated) in some way, and the compiler should have a built-in formal verifier to check that the implementation of the program meets its specifications. Up to now, there are no (at least open use) verifying compilers as industrial products, neither are there widely known verifying compilers as research products.

Actually, the idea of a verifying compiler is much older. Hoare [7] referred to early computing papers of the 1940s–1950s by Turing and McCarthy as laying foundations of that concept. To our knowledge, verifying compiler principles were actively developed and implemented in a major research product in the 1970s, in relation to the concept of abstract data types [1]. The ALPHARD language [35] designed and implemented at Carnegie-Mellon University in mid-1970s was intended as the language of developing correct (verified) algorithms based on abstract data types. Each abstract data type (referred to as *form* in APLHARD) should have its formal specification, alongside with the implementation. The formal specification in ALPHARD consists of *preconditions* and *postconditions* for each abstract operation of the form. In addition, each form should also have its *abstract invariant* and *concrete invariant*—the conditions to hold on abstract and concrete elements of a form's object. The invariants should be formally checked to hold on performing each abstract operation on an object controlled by the form. ALPHARD didn't become an industrial programming language but served as an advanced prototype to stimulate further research in the area of verifying compilers.

A novel approach to verifying compiler that (please let me suppose so) was inspired by ideas of ALPHARD, is implemented in the *Spec#* project [11] by Microsoft Research. Spec# is an extension of C# by formal specifications in design-by-contract style. Spec# is covered in Section 2.4.

Another verifying compiler project by Microsoft Research, actually developed by the same team as Spec#, is *verifying C compiler* (*vcc*) [36]. The compiler takes annotated C programs, generates formal verification conditions, and formally verifies the C program code against the generated set of verification conditions.

Yet another academic research and educational project on verifying compilers to be mentioned is *Pi verifying compiler* (*piVC*) [37] by Stanford University. *Pi* is a simplified programming language designed at Stanford and used in teaching students for verified program development.

So, the challenge of the verifying compiler that was stated by Hoare is accepted and is being actively researched by many compiler professionals. It became popular to such an extent that compiler development community established a special Web site [38] devoted to research on verifying compilers.

What should be the theoretical and methodological foundations of verifying and, speaking more general, trustworthy compilers? Let's consider our definition of a trustworthy compiler (see Section 1.1) and analyze what kind of methods and formal models should be developed and used in trustworthy compiler development to meet each of our recommendations given in the definition.

> *Trustworthy object code generation.* This requirement actually comprises several requirements: The object code should be *error-free*; *efficient*, according to some criteria, most typical, to execute minimal time possible; *multi-threaded (MT) safe*—safe for execution in an MT environment so that the same code could be safely executed by several threads in parallel; and *resilient to attacks*, that is, preserve its integrity and consistency, and those of its data. *Error-free object code* means that the compiler should not use *wrong code generation models* and shouldn't generate buggy codes. An example of a code generation model bug from our compiler practice is as follows: The common compiler back-end, based on the common intermediate representation for all implemented languages, can generate and optimize a code using a wrong model of one-level nesting of functions or methods. That model is suitable for C and early versions of FORTRAN; however, for ALGOL- and PASCAL-like languages, with *block structure* and possible *uplevel addressing* of local variables of the outer function from the inner one, the "flat" one-level nesting model is not suitable and can be the source of code generation and optimization errors. More details are found later in Chapters 6 and 7. The *efficiency* of the object code can be achieved due to code *optimizations* (see Chapter 7). *MT safety* of the object code could be implemented as a compiler option. An MT-safe version of the object code should, for example, include implicit actions injected by the compiler to create synchronization objects (semaphores, monitors, mutexes, or locks) for static entity definitions in the code, and put into "synchronization brackets" (like *wait/signal* operations on a semaphore) each update operation of a static entity that can be potentially used by parallel threads. *Resilience* of the object code *to attacks* can be achieved by implicit *code integrity checks* on its runtime load into the execution system, and checks of *security permissions* prior to doing any risky action (e.g., opening a file) in the object code. Both kinds of checks are implemented in .NET, in its *Common Language Runtime (CLR)*, and also in Java runtime. For language implementations on other platforms, such code consistency and security checking techniques should be implemented. So, to solve the task of object code trustworthiness, adequate formal models of dynamic behavior of programs written in the source language, code execution and the execution engine, code security, and control flow and data flow (the latter two—for code optimizations) should be built and used.

> *Trustworthy behavior of the compiler.* To avoid surprises for users in compiler behavior, it looks sufficient, at the design stage, to build a kind of *UML* (Unified Modeling Language) *activity diagrams* as a formal model

depicting possible kinds of actions by the user, and the corresponding expected trustworthy reactions by the compiler, and later at the implementation stage, enable this functionality to be performed by the compiler. The formula of the compiler's trustworthy behavior can be stated as follows: *No unexpected stops; no hangs; perform all steps of compilation, or at least maximum steps possible and reasonable to do (in case of bugs in the source code); process all the source code (no matter it can be buggy), without unexpected interrupts of the compilation process; provide clear and nonredundant error diagnostics to the user.* More details in the subsequent Chapters 3–7 are devoted to the phases of compilation.

Trustworthiness of the compiler data and preserving their privacy and integrity. It may seem that, for compilers, unlike databases or networking systems, the requirement of data trustworthiness (integrity and consistency) is not so important. However, a compiler, as a complicated toolkit whose functioning is a sequence of several steps resulting, in turn, in several successive intermediate representations of the program generated by the appropriate compiler phase, can be subject to attacks targeted to the compiler's data corruption. Such attacks can intercept into the compilation process and convert the intermediate representation of the program in some malicious way (e.g., inject some malicious code, or delete some critical code). For example, this is possible with the typical scheme of compiler architecture in UNIX, Solaris, or Linux (in particular, with Sun Studio compilers). This scheme is based on using the *compiler driver*—a control program that processes compiler options, calls the phases of the compiler as separate processes, and passes to them the appropriate intermediate representations stored in temporary files. An attack to the compiler could be as follows: In parallel to the compiler driver, find in the working directory an appropriate file of intermediate code, delete important security checks from the code, and store the truncated intermediate code into the same temporary file that the compiler driver passes to the code generator. It is quite possible to do if the developer of the malicious software knows the architecture of the internal representation used in the compiler (e.g., if the compiler is an open source, like a GNU compiler). How can we protect a compiler from such attack? A possible way is to use an encryption of intermediate representation when writing it to a temporary file by the front-end, and its decryption by the code generator when reading it. Another simpler data protecting solution is to use a kind of hash code or checksum to check the consistency of the input intermediate representation file when the appropriate phase starts. We don't know yet any compiler that can do that, but in the current era of cyber crimes, compilers should be designed and implemented to take into account the need in such protection measures.

Trustworthiness of the implementation code of the compiler; as an ideal— having the compiler source code verified. Practically speaking, the source of a real compiler can have a size of 10,000–100,000 lines of code; so at first glance, it doesn't seem realistic to formally specify and verify such a large and complicated software product. Besides that, formal specification and verification themselves are likely to have bugs, even more likely because specifying and verifying can be much more complicated than developing the compiler source code itself. However, there appeared the pioneers of formal verification of compilers like Leroy [6]. See the next, Section 2.3, for more details of his approach to verified compilers. If it looks impractical to have the compiler source formally verified, the source code of the compiler should be designed and implemented according to the principles of TWC considered in Section 2.1. In particular, the compiler code implementers should use *assertions* to check critical conditions to be true in different parts of a compiler; should use principles of reliable program and data structuring (modular programming and abstract data types); should design compiler internal interfaces, which are expected to be complicated, in some systematic way (very helpful in this respect is our technological instrumental package [TIP] technology—see Section 1.1). Another implementation trustworthiness recipe is to use *code patterns* for typical modules of the compiler.

Trustworthy error diagnostics and error recovery performed by the compiler. Numerous silly error messages issued by a compiler are one of the most critical factors to jeopardize the users' trust to it. This principle seems so evident that it's surprising why compilers still demonstrate nontrustworthiness in this respect. We think the reason is as follows: It is much easier to develop compiler code that doesn't attempt to do any kind of error recovery—just "works until the first bug in the source program"—than to build into the compiler any kind of error recovery techniques that make the process of compilation much more complicated. Let's recall, for example, the first version of the Turbo Pascal compiler in mid-1980s. Its attractive feature was an integrated development environment that allowed the user, on detecting a bug in the source program by the compiler, to jump into the text editor to the point in the source code where the bug was detected. But the deficiency of that first version was that *the compiler stopped after detecting that first bug.* It means if there were, say, 100 bugs in the source due to the user's typos (which is quite common), the user had to compile the source 100 times to detect and fix all those bugs, instead of compiling just once to catch all the bugs in one compiler call, and to be able to jump in the text editor from one bug to another. Later versions of Borland's compilers provided such desirable functionality, which is now quite common in industrial compilers and integrated development environments. Please see Chapters 3–5 for a more detailed description of error recovery techniques in compilers and related theoretical models.

Checking the correctness of the program compiled (verifying compiler functionality). As already stated above, the most general approach to verifying functionality of the compiler should be based on annotations or formal specifications of the source code to be compiled, and automated verification that the implementation of the source program meets its formal specifications (or annotations). But, as well known, formal methods are still not so widely used in software engineering [1] because of inadequacy of their mathematical models to the dynamic nature of programs.

Let's consider the classical mathematical models of program semantics: *Floyd's and Hoare's program calculus* (*Hoare's triples*) [39]; *operational semantics* [40]; *denotational semantics* [41]; and *algebraic semantics* [42], from the viewpoint of their applicability to trustworthy compilers.

Hoare's semantics approach is based on the ideas of constructing a *logical calculus* to prove the properties of programs. The *axiom schemes* and *inference rules* in this calculus are of the kind: $P \{S\} Q$ (referred to as *Hoare's triples*) where P is the *precondition*; Q is the *postcondition* (both considered to be predicates defined on the tuple of free, or global, variables of the program); and S is a program code. The interpretation of this formula is as follows: If P holds prior to S execution, then S executes normally, and Q holds after its execution. This technique was used for many years, primarily for research purposes. Later research showed that it was incomplete, since procedures with procedural parameters and recursive procedures are poorly specified using that model, and it's necessary to use higher-order calculi to keep the adequacy of the model to real complexity of programs. But, in our opinion, the main issue of this model, as well as of any other kind of logic-based program semantic models, is that it relies on the *mathematical concept of a variable* (as a denotation for an entity whose value is constant within some reasoning block), rather than on the quite different *concept of a variable in programming*—as a named cell whose value is changeable by special executable statements, which follows the ideas of von Neumann's computer architecture model of the 1940s. So, any assignment statement or any other, more complicated kind of update of a variable or of an element of some collection should be specified by a logic inference rule relying on the static concept of mathematical variable, which is not appropriate. For that reason, this technique is not used in the industry, although it's widely taught at the universities. The other practical reason is that, usually, software engineers are not great experts in mathematics or mathematical logic, or just forget, after a few years of their industrial programming practice, all mathematics and logics they were taught at the universities. In particular, it doesn't look realistic to use this approach to formally specify and verify an industrial compiler of several dozen thousand lines of code, or to have the developers of programs in the language implemented by a compiler to annotate each major statement in their programs by any logical formulas.

Operational semantics looks like a more practical approach, much closer to everyday activity of software engineers, and understandable not only by pure theorists of computer science. This approach defines program semantics in terms of some *abstract machine*, or a related *collection of abstract machines* (or *automata*). One of the recent formal models of this kind is *Abstract State Machine* (*ASM*) by Gurevich et al. [43]. Practical applicability of operational semantics is proved by Leroy [6] who applied it for formal specification and verification of a C compiler used in the industry. However, operational semantics, which seems an adequate way of thinking for highly skilled computer scientists and system programmers as compiler writers, doesn't seem to be appropriate for most of application software developers who are thinking of their tasks in terms of the programming languages they use, or in terms of the mathematical models they implement in their programs, rather than in terms of any formally specified abstract machines of complicated architecture, far from their everyday tasks. So, this approach looks suitable for *verified* compilers but doesn't seem applicable for *verifying* compilers.

Denotational semantics approach is based on nontrivial mathematical ideas and foundation principles. This approach considers a program to be a *predicate transformer*—a kind of *higher-order function*, or *functional*, speaking in mathematical terms. The classicists of denotational semantics are Scott, Strachey, and Donahue. Its main idea is as follows: At any point of execution, the state of the program can be specified by the *predicate* $P(x_1, \ldots x_n)$ where x_i is the global variable of the program. Since the program changes the state of its execution, it can be considered as a *predicate transformer*, that is, a higher-order function. Denotational approach was popular among computer scientists in the 1970s–1980s, due to its generality. But, in our opinion, its shortcoming is an overcomplicated mathematical model based on the use of higher-order functions. So, we don't think it is practical in the industry, and it will hardly be used for trustworthy compilers—either verifying or verified.

Algebraic semantics approach originated in the 1970s, due to popularity of the concept of abstract data types, and due the need to build an adequate formal model for them. From an algebraic viewpoint, a data type (abstract) is a *multi-sorted algebra*, a well-studied, though complicated, formal algebraic structure. The multi-sorted algebra consists of the *carrier S*—a finite number of *sorts* $S_1, \ldots S_n$—sets to be used as domains and ranges of the algebra's *operations*; the *signature F*—a finite number of *operations* (or *functions*) $F_1, \ldots, F_m$ such that each F_i is a function from a Cartesian product of zero or more sorts S_j to some sort S_k from the carrier. A function with zero arguments is a *constant*. The third component of the algebra is the finite set E of algebraic *equates* of the kind: $t_1 = t_2$ where each t_i is an algebraic *term* comprised of compositions of calls of the operations F_j with *domain variables* and *constants* as arguments. The set of equates E is the "heart" of the algebra, from a formal semantics model viewpoint, since it defines the *semantics* of functions F_j in terms of their algebraic dependencies from each other. For example, we can define the type *List* with traditional LISP-like operations: *Cons* (x, l)—construct a list from the first element x and another list l; *Car* (l)—take the "head" element of the list l; *Cdr* (l)—take the "tail" from the list l, the list l without its first element. In these terms, we can define the formula

$$Cons(Car(l), Cdr(l)) = l \tag{2.1}$$

that clearly specifies the semantics of and the relationships between *Cons*, *Car*, and *Cdr* (the relation "=" should be interpreted as element-by-element equality of lists). The above example shows the advantage of this approach: Algebraic equates are one of the simplest mathematical methods to explain any dependencies of program semantics, understandable even by a software engineer who almost forgot mathematics. On the other hand, the above formula 2.1 shows some issues of the algebraic approach: It is not quite convenient to specify *exceptions* and *exceptional conditions*. If the list *l* is empty, the above formula does not make sense, so it should be augmented by specific "boundary conditions," and, moreover, by some "boundary values." We have to add the domain constant *nil*—an empty list, and also the abnormal *error* value to indicate an exceptional condition when the arguments are improper. So, we add to 2.1 the following formulas

$$Car(nil) = error$$

$$Cdr(nil) = error$$

and also have to formally specify what is a *non-empty list*, and that *l* in the above formula 2.1 should be a non-empty list. To make the example closer to software engineering practice, we have to make the concept of *error* more specific and introduce different error values for different situations, similar to different kinds of exceptions in programming languages. It's easy to see that it may lead to combinatorial explosion of the number of the formulas in our formal semantic models (since we have to specify the results for each combination of normal and error arguments). So, we doubt the algebraic approach will be practically applicable either for domain-specific application developers, or for compiler writers, to make the compilers more trustworthy, although this approach is undoubtedly very helpful from a theoretical viewpoint, since it specifies the dependencies of operations as shown above.

So, we have analyzed a lot of principles and approaches to trustworthy compilers and came to the conclusion that the most applicable of them are *operational semantics* (as formal model), *principles of TWC*, and our *trustworthy compilers checklist*.

With this vision in mind, let's now consider two theoretically consistent and practically important approaches to trustworthy compilers—*Leroy's verified compilers* [6] and *Spec#* [11]. They are summarized in the two subsequent sections.

2.3 VERIFIED COMPILERS

Leroy's papers [6] are pioneering in such a complicated theoretical research as formal proof of correctness of a real compiler from the language equivalent to those recommended to be used for critical software systems in avionics. The compiler Leroy that managed to formally verify is referred to as *CompCert*. It compiles sources in *Clight* language, a subset of C, to PowerPC assembly code. What is especially important is that Leroy managed to formally verify even the most complex, optimization phase of the compiler. For verification purposes, Leroy used the *Coq* proof assistant toolkit based on reasonable combination of higher-order logic and functional specification style close to ML [44] functional language. *Coq implements the calculus of inductive and coinductive constructions, a powerful constrictive, higher-order logic, which supports equally well three familiar styles of writing specifications: by functions and pattern-matching, by inductive or coinductive predicates representing inference rules, and by ordinary predicates in first-order logic* [6]. As the author noted, Coq is the result of many years of research by experts in mathematical logic and computer science, prior to Leroy's work.

The style of writing specifications using functions is very close to operational semantics, so it allows us not only to specify application algorithms, but is also suitable to formally specify typical implementation mechanisms such as *stack*, *activation record in a stack*, *allocating and addressing local variables*, *jumping into the entry point of a function*, *using registers*, and so on. We prefer to avoid citing formulas from Leroy's papers: They may seem too complex to the beginners and practitioners. However, this is not so: In spite of the necessary mathematical consistency, formal specifications in Coq specification language comprise very practical and understandable elements like *eval_op*—function to evaluate the value of an operation, *stacksize*—the size of a stack frame, and so on. Our goal here is for the readers to feel the "system programming spirit" of these specifications, unlike those using pure logical calculi.

The verified part of the CompCert compiler was developed using the following technique. First, the compiler was formally specified in a purely functional subset of the Coq specification language. Second, this formal specification of the compiler was translated into source code in Caml [45] functional language. The resulting Caml code was used as the source code of the compiler. The CompCert compiler consists of 14 passes and uses 8 intermediate languages. The semantics of the source language, Clight, and that of each intermediate language, are formally defined in operational style. The size of the formal specification and the proof of the compiler performed in interactive style supported by Coq, is 42,000 lines. It took the author 3 years to formally specify and prove the compiler. So the work performed by Leroy, its scientific level, and its novelty are unique. His research on verifying compilers should be considered as an outstanding step toward practical application of formal methods in software engineering industry. We do think Leroy's experience should be learned, and his ideas and models should be applied to formal verification of compilers from modern languages—Java and C#, for the first turn.

In our opinion, there is, however, one difficulty in making this approach widely learned and used. Most of the compiler writers are pure software engineers that don't have such strong mathematical background as Leroy and his scientific school. Functional languages—ML, Caml, Objective Caml [46], and F# [47] are quite popular among the elite of computer scientists with strong academic and university background. This is the reason of the success of Leroy's research based on his unique personality and knowledge. However, for the vast majority of system programmers, including compiler developers, a more traditional way of thinking and working in terms of C, C++, Pascal, Java, or C# is practiced. What kind of formal methods should be adapted to be usable by this community for verified and verifying compiler development? This is still a serious intellectual challenge to be solved.

2.4   SPEC#: MICROSOFT'S APPROACH TO VERIFYING COMPILERS

Spec# [7] is an extension of C# by formal specifications in design-by-contract [12] style. This is yet another approach to verified compilers, which we think is practical for software engineers. The idea of design-by-contract by Meyer is to use formal specifications to specify *contracts* between the developer of a module (class or method) and the rest of the application. The purpose of the module developer is to *require* some preconditions on the module's arguments and other data to hold prior to calling the module. For example, the method *GCD* to calculate the greatest common divisor of two integral numbers m and n can require that $m > 0$ and $n > 0$. This is one part of the contract. The other part is the contract is for the module (developer) to *ensure* some postcondition (on its output data) to be true on finishing the module execution. To continue our *GCD* example, the *GCD* method should ensure that the result be the greatest common divisor of the two arguments. Also, to enable the consistency of the module's data, the *object invariant* should be specified—the condition on the module's data (fields) to be preserved by each operation on the object. For example, the *Stack* class should declare the object invariant saying that the stack pointer should always be a nonnegative integral number (provided the stack is implemented by an array with the integral stack pointer). Those *require* and *ensure* conditions, together with the module *invariant*, form the foundation of the design-by-contract approach, now widely used in developing object-oriented software.

Spec# is implemented as an add-in to Visual Studio 2008 and Visual Studio 2005. That means the user can develop Spec# programs in a comfortable development environment provided by Visual Studio. There are special kinds of projects—*Spec# projects*—that the user can choose when creating a new project in Visual Studio. The extension of a source code file in Spec# is *.ssc*.

The Spec# programming system includes the following components:

- *The Spec# programming language*—an extension of C# by formal speci- fications and some extra kinds of concepts and constructs: *non-null types* (like *String! s*, to enable that the value of the argument *s* is not *null*);

checked exceptions and appropriate throw clauses (to compensate the lack of checked exceptions present in Java but absent in C#); *method contracts* (*requires* and *ensures* specification clauses for each method, as explained above); and *object invariants* (as explained below).

- *The Spec# compiler*—a compiler from Spec# source code to .NET assembly—postfix style *Common Intermediate Language* (*CIL*) binary code and *metadata* recording the types defined and used in the compilation unit. The specific roles of the compiler, to enable trustworthiness of the object code, are as follows: First, the compiler statically checks (where possible) that the actual arguments declared to be of non-null types are not *null* (or injects the object code to check that at runtime, on calling the method). Second, the compiler generates and injects a code to check the object invariants and method contracts at runtime. So, the user pays the overhead of extra execution time (to make the above checks) for the trustworthiness of the code. This approach is characteristic of modern software development platforms—Java and .NET. Also, the Spec# compiler records the contracts and invariants as part of metadata (represented by so-called *custom attributes*) stored in the same file as the binary code and available to all the utilities that "understand" them, but not preventing from the normal work of other utilities. That is another important principle of .NET (we use the same principle in our Aspect.NET toolkit [1]).

- *The Spec# static program verifier* (code-named *Boogie*)—a component that analyzes the Spec# source code, including formal specifications, and generates *verification conditions* used by the built-in *theorem prover* to check the formal conditions to hold on the Spec# program, or produce a list of *verification error messages* if any of the conditions are violated. The communication with the verifier is performed by the user in *interactive mode*. If necessary, the user can modify either the specification part or the implementation part of the Spec# source code, to meet the verification conditions.

We pay a lot of attention to Spec# and do consider this programming system as *the first commercial trustworthy compiler*. Though Spec# is the result of a Microsoft Research project, it is plugged into the Visual Studio environment used by a lot of software engineers all over the world. So, using Spec# is a good way for programmers to learn in practice what is trustworthy programming and trustworthy compilers.

Here is an example of code in Spec#—a method that swaps the values of the elements of the given array with the given indexes (as arguments):

```
static void Swap(int[]! a, int i, int j)
 requires 0 <= i && i < a.Length;
 requires 0 <= j && j < a.Length;
 modifies a[i], a[j];
```

```
ensures a[i] == old(a[j]);
ensures a[j] == old(a[i]);
{
    int temp;
    temp = a[i];
    a[i] = a[j];
    a[j] = temp;
}
```

The static method *Swap* has three arguments—an array *a* (the "!" symbol after the array type means that *a* is of *non-null type*, that is, the actual argument cannot be null, which is checked at compile-time or at runtime by specially injected code) and integers *i* and *j*—the indexes of the *a*'s elements whose values are to be swapped. Please note the *requires, ensures,* and *modifies* specifications (assertions) built into the code. The *requires* assertions specify the preconditions to hold on the indexes *i* and *j* of the array *a*. Those preconditions are checked at runtime when the method is called. The *ensures* assertions specify the postconditions to hold on returning from the method. The *old* keyword denotes the *initial* values of the elements when calling the method, as opposed to their resulting values on returning from the methods. The *modifies* specification declares what entities the method is allowed to be modified (this condition is checked by the verifier).

As can be seen from the example, specifications written in the style supported by Spec# are easy for software engineers to develop (unlike, say, algebraic specifications, or those using denotational, operational, or any other kinds of formal semantics)—just as simple or difficult as the source code implementation itself. This allows us to hope this style will get more and more popular.

2.5 PERSPECTIVES OF VERIFIED AND VERIFYING COMPILATION

Please note that Spec# code provided as an example to Section 2.4 is not taken from any research paper: This is an example of practically acceptable, simple, and convenient to use style of verified programming in a Microsoft-implemented extension of one of the most worldwide spread language—C#, supported by widely used and comfortable integrated development environment—Visual Studio. We hope, due to all of that, Spec# will be broadly taught and learned and will become a common use language; the style of verified programming will, in the nearest perspective, dominate in the practice of program development; and the positive trustworthy compiling initiative by Spec# developers will be supported by other compiler writers, in particular, by the developers of Java technology.

We foresee that in a few years, all widely used languages (Java, C, C++, FORTRAN, Perl, Python, JavaScript, etc.) will adopt the style of verified programming pioneered by Meyer and his design-by-contract programming language Eiffel [12] in mid-1980s, continued and enhanced in Spec# nowadays. The next step to that is the *vcc* verifying compiler project we already mentioned above. So we think that, following the success of Spec# and *vcc*, verifying compilers for many languages will be developed in the near future, since the need in formally verified software is growing because of its complexity. Surely this will require a lot of advanced research on adopting formal specifications and developing formal verifiers for all common use languages. Another research challenge will be to try to convert a bulk of legacy code to the new style of verified programming: Industrial tools for automated deduction of specifications from the source code will be needed.

As for verified compilers, we prefer to be more cautious in our forecasts. Right now, there is only one well-known research project in this direction— *CompCert* verified compiler (covered in Section 2.3) developed in a very specific way and in a very specific language. So this great achievement can hardly become a pattern for a lot of compiler developers, since most of them write their compilers in C or C++. We think that, no matter how important verified compiler development is as a new field, new innovative ideas and methods should be invented—how to make verified compilers as ubiquitous as ordinary compilers, without having every compiler developer to become an expert in higher-order logic and functional languages, in algebraic specifications, or in other kinds of subtle mathematical formalisms. New, simpler to use and to understand forms of software specifications have to be developed— this is a challenge not only for the area of trustworthy compilers.

EXERCISES TO CHAPTER 2

2.1 Define each of the four "pillars" of TWC initiative by Microsoft— *security*, *reliability*, *privacy*, and *business integrity*—and explain their role and importance using practical examples from your own software development and software usage practice.

2.2 What is verifying compiler as defined by Hoare? What verifying compilers do you know?

2.3 What is verified compiler as defined by Leroy? What verified compilers do you know?

2.4 List the principles of trustworthy code generated by a compiler and explain why, as you think, they are so important to follow.

2.5 What is, in your opinion (based on your own practice), trustworthy and nontrustworthy behavior of the compiler and why? Describe examples of both kinds of compiler behavior from your practice of using compilers.

2.6 Why is it important for a compiler to protect its data (internal representations of the source program stored in files, for the first turn) from attacks? How can an attack to a compiler be organized? What kind of countermeasures can be used by the compiler?

2.7   Why is error recovery so important to make a compiler trustworthy? Explain why it is inconvenient for the user when the compiler stops compilation after it found and reported the first bug in the source code. Provide examples from your experience when the compiler you use didn't behave in a trustworthy way, with regard to error diagnostics and recovery.

2.8   What is the idea of Hoare's approach to semantics? Why do you think it isn't widely used in the industry now (in particular, in compiler development)?

2.9   What is denotational semantics, and why is it not so comfortable for compiler developers?

2.10   What is operational semantics, and why can it be more attractive for compiler developers than the other kinds of formal semantics considered in the chapter?

2.11   What is algebraic semantics, and what are its advantages and shortcomings, with regard to its possible use in compiler development?

2.12   Please outline Leroy's approach to verified compilers. What is the source language of his verified compiler CompCert?

2.13   Please download Spec# from http://research.microsoft.com/specsharp, install it as an add-in to Visual Studio, compile, verify, and run the samples bundled with the Spec# distribution.

2.14   Please implement in Spec# a sample project containing the method to compute the greatest common divisor of two integral positive numbers using Euclid's algorithm. Provide the *requires* and *ensures* specification for that method. Compile, verify, and run your Spec# project.

Chapter *3*

Lexical Analysis and Its Trustworthiness Principles

After the introduction to trustworthy compilers in Chapters 1 and 2, let's now proceed with the detailed consideration of the first phase of compilation—*lexical analysis*—and the principles and methods to make it trustworthy.

From a theoretical viewpoint, lexical analysis is the phase of compilation that transforms the *input stream* of the program's *source code* into the *output stream* of *tokens* (*lexemes*)—elementary units of the source programming language.

The source code of the program to be compiled can be physically represented by a text file with the appropriate name extension, for example, *.c*—for C code, *.pas*—for Pascal code, *.java*—for Java code, *.cs*—for C# code, and *.scc*—for Spec# code. For large software projects, the source code is represented by a logically related set of text files. The lexical analyzer considers the source code as a single input stream of symbols.

3.1 TOKEN CLASSES

Each token is characterized by its *lexical class*. The main functionality of the lexical analyzer (if implemented as a function or method) is to recognize a token in the input stream and deliver its token class. Here is the set of typical token classes common to most of the programming languages (following the tradition of *yacc* [19] parser generator, we denote them by constant identifiers started with *YY*):

Trustworthy Compilers, by Vladimir O. Safonov
Copyright © 2010 John Wiley & Sons, Inc.

- *YYID*—*identifier*; typically consists of letters and digits starting with a letter. In some languages, identifiers may start with an underscore or a dollar symbol. Used to denote variables, constants, and other named entities of the source programming language. For example, *ArrayIndexOutOfBoundsException*—a very long (30 characters) pre-defined identifier in Java used to denote an exception thrown when an attempt detected to index an array by a value out of its bounds. Surely this is an extreme example; most of the identifiers used are 1–10 characters long.

- *YYNUMBER*—denotation of a *number, integer, or float*, for example, 12345 or 3.14. In some compilers, instead of one token class *YYNUMBER*, two separate token classes, *YYINT* and *YYFLOAT*, are used to distinguish between integer and float number denotations at the lexical level.

- *YYCHAR*—denotation of a *symbol*, usually taken into apostrophes, for example, *'a'*. Please note that it appears to be more practically convenient and more trustworthy to use different lexical classes for denotations of a symbol and of a string, although in some languages (e.g., in Pascal), both of them are taken into apostrophes. The reason of the different token classes is *different typing*: The type of a symbol denotation is usually *char*, whereas the type of a string denotation is *string* or some special kind of character array (in Pascal—*packed array [1..n] of char* where *n* is the length of the string).

- *YYSTRING*—denotation of a string, for example, *"abcdef"*. In some languages (like Pascal), strings are taken into apostrophes, as well as symbol denotations. In other languages (like C, C++, Java, and C#), strings are taken into double quotes, which makes it easier for a lexical analyzer to distinguish tokens between characters and strings by the first symbol.

- *YYBEGIN, YYEND, YYIF*, and so on—a separate lexical class for each *keyword* of the source language. A *keyword* is a special reserved identifier (word) to denote structured brackets of the source program, kinds of its executable statements, declarations, definitions, operators, and so on. In all modern languages, a keyword is graphically undistinguishable from an identifier, in the sense that there are no special symbols (dots, quotes, apostrophes, etc.) used to indicate the start and (or) the end of a keyword. However, in the implemented dialects of earlier languages (e.g., ALGOL-60), there were different spellings of the same keyword, for example, *.BEGIN* or *'BEGIN'*. Pascal and C seem to be the first languages to stop the tradition of highlighting keywords by any special characters. But Pascal-like approach to keywords caused another problem: Let a sequence of letters and digits has been detected by the lexical analyzer; how can this be detected efficiently whether it is an identifier or a keyword? We'll return to our solution of this problem later in this chapter. Another compiler implementation issue related to keywords is as follows: Is it more convenient to denote each keyword by a separate lexical class, or to use some kinds of "grouping" lexical classes, like *delimiter*, *operator*, and so on? Most compiler development practitioners choose the former option.

- *YYDOT*, *YYLPAR*, and so on—a separate lexical class for each of the operator symbols and delimiters. In our example, the token class *YYDOT* denotes the "." (dot) symbol used in most languages to denote the operator that extracts a field from a record, structure, or object, by using a construct like *p.X*. The token class *YYLPAR* denotes the "(" symbol, *left parenthesis*, used alongside with the *right parenthesis* ")" for grouping parts of compound expressions;

- *YYEOF*—a special token class for the *end-of-file* symbol, returned by the lexical analyzer when the source code is finished. This specific token class is of special importance during the next phase of compilation, *parsing* (see Chapter 4).

3.2   THE OUTPUT OF THE LEXICAL ANALYZER

As we've already noted above, in compiler practice, lexical analyzer is not implemented as a separate pass; that would be too inefficient. Instead, lexical analyzer is implemented as a *function* (*method*) that extracts the current token from the source, shifts the current pointer to the source code, and returns *the lexical class* of the current token, one of those considered above. Following the tradition of *yacc*, let's denote the lexical analyzer function *yylex ()*. So we can write:

yylex ( ) -> current token class

This result is informative enough for tokens like *YYBEGIN* or *YYDOT*. For identifiers, numbers, characters, and strings, some extra result values are returned by the lexical analyzer. They are usually passed to the parser via *global interface variables* of the lexical analyzer, since an alternative solution— aggregating all the output of the lexical analyzer to a structure or object— worsens the efficiency, which is critical for the lexical analyzer. Here are the global interface (output) variables of the lexical analyzer:

- for *identifiers*—a *pointer* (or *index*) in the *identifier table* where the lexical analyzer stores the identifier. Let's refer to the identifier table as *id_tab*, and to the output variable as *id_ptr*;

- for *integral numbers*—the *value* of the number; let's denote the corresponding output variable *ival* (for *i*nteger *val*ue);

- for *float numbers*—the *value* of the number; let's denote the output variable *fval* (for *f*loat *val*ue). Please note that *ival* and *fval* have to be different variables because of different typing of integral and float numbers;

- for *characters*—the *value* (*code*) of the character; let's denote the output variable *cval*;
- for *strings*—the *pointer* (*index*) of the string in the *string table* where the lexical analyzer stores each string found—*str_ptr*.

Also, lexical analyzer outputs *error and warning messages*, if any (details later).

Auxiliary functionality of a lexical analyzer. Besides extracting (*scanning*) the current token, its main functionality, a lexical analyzer performs some *auxiliary actions*:

- skips the *white space symbols* between the tokens—*spaces* and *tabs*, and *comments*; white spaces and comments are regarded as *token separators*;
- processes *pragmas*—compiler control *directives* (*commands*), special sequences used to switch on or off *compiler options*. Pragmas can be represented similar to language constructs but starting with some specific symbol, most typically "#." For example, *#pragma inline* in C or C++ source code means that the current function being compiled should be implemented by *inlining* (substituting the code of its body to the point of the function call). More details about inlining are found later in Chapter 6. Also, compiler control directives can be provided in the source code as special kinds of *comments*, referred to as *control comments*. For example, in many implementations of Pascal, the control comment *{$l+}* is used to switch on the option of printing the source code onto the standard output.

Delegating such "mundane" actions to a lexical analyzer simplifies the subsequent phase of the compiler—*parsing* (see Chapter 4), since, from the parser's viewpoint, the source program is just a sequence (or stream) of tokens, no matter if there were comments or pragmas in the original source code or not—they are considered to have been already processed by the lexical analyzer.

3.3 PROCESSING WHITE SPACES, COMMENTS, AND NEW LINES

Now it looks evident that in all source languages, symbols and sequences such as white spaces, comments, pragmas, and the symbols *new line, line feed*, and *carriage return* are considered to be token separators. This is quite natural, since the user of the compiler would hardly intend to break a token (e.g., identifier) with a new line symbol and to place its end in the next line. However, in our practice of using some earlier compilers, new line symbols are not always treated correctly. For example, the ALGOL compiler for the Polish mini-computer Odra 1204 we used in mid-1970s, when compiling the following code:

```
x  :=  n
M  :=  1  ,
```

issued the diagnostic message: "*nM undeclared.*" Surely the code is incorrect: The semicolon symbol is missing at the end of the first line. But the lexical analyzer just ignored the new line symbol (instead of considering it a token separator), and mistakenly merged two identifiers, *n* and *M*, into one nonexistent identifier *nM*, which, at later compilation phases, the semantic analyzer surely considered to be undeclared. This absurd situation occurred because of "misunderstanding" new line symbols by the lexical analyzer.

3.4 THEORETICAL MODELS OF LEXICAL ANALYSIS

Most of compiler books start the chapter on lexical analysis from detailed considerations of its theoretical models. Our approach is more pragmatic: Lexical analysis, for most languages, is quite a simple compilation phase, so there is no need to go into details of theory, which is well studied. But, surely, the theory of lexical analysis is necessary to study for developers of *lexical analyzer generators* like *lex* considered later in this chapter. Our primary goal is to explain the design and efficient implementation recipes of lexical analysis, to investigate trustworthy issues of lexical analysis, and advise how to solve them. So we prefer to briefly summarize the theoretical models of lexical analysis and consider examples of their use for realistic programming languages.

There are three theoretical models of lexical structure of a programming language and lexical analysis well known from many classical papers—*automata grammars*, *finite-state automata*, and *regular expressions*.

An *automata* (*or right-linear*) *grammar* is a context-free grammar:

$$G = <V_N, V_T, P, S>$$

where V_N is the finite set (alphabet) of *nonterminal symbols*, V_T is the finite set of *terminal symbols*, P is the finite set of grammar *derivation rules*, and S is a *starting nonterminal symbol* from V_N. For automata grammars, each rule should be of the kind:

$$A \rightarrow a$$

or

$$A \rightarrow aB$$

where A and B are nonterminal symbols and a is a terminal symbol. Please note that, in general, for arbitrary context-free grammar, the right part of a rule can be any chain of terminal and (or) nonterminal symbols, including the empty chain.

The *language* $L(G)$ of the grammar G is the set of all possible chains of terminal symbols that can be, directly or indirectly, derived from the starting symbol S.

Example. The grammar with the following set of rules:

$$\{ \; S \rightarrow + \; , \; S \rightarrow - \; , \; S \rightarrow * \; , \; S \rightarrow / \; , \; S \rightarrow = \; , \; S \rightarrow = E \; , \; E \rightarrow = \; \}$$

defines the lexical structure of operator symbols of a programming language—four arithmetic operators (+, –, *, and /), equality (==), and assignment (=). We cannot avoid the nonterminal symbol E (denoting "=") in this definition, since we are limited by the properties of the grammar. So the grammar looks a little bit awkward. So, even this simple example shows an issue of lexical analysis: When a symbol "=" is found on the input stream, the next one (*lookahead*) should be analyzed to determine the kind of the token—equality or assignment. Such issues are characteristic for many programming languages, C in particular.

Regular expressions are a more convenient and more practical formalism to define the same class of languages. Given the finite alphabet of terminal symbols A (in the above notation of grammars, $A = V_T$), a regular expression is defined as a *set of chains in alphabet A*, generated by the following rules:

1   The singleton set $\{ \varepsilon \}$ of the empty chain ε is a regular expression.
2   The singleton set $\{ a \}$ of any symbol a from A is a regular expression; usually, in regular expression languages, it is denoted by the symbol itself—a.
3   If R and S are regular expressions, then the following are also regular expressions:
   - $R\,S$—*concatenation* of R and S; the set of concatenations $\{ r\,s \}$ where r and s are any elements of R and S, respectively;
   - $R \mid S$—*alternation* of R and S; union of the sets R and S, denotes the set of all chains either from R or from S;
   - $R*$—*iteration* of R zero or more times; denotes the set of all sequences of symbols from R repeated zero or more times;
   - $R+$—similar operation: *iteration* of R *one* or more times.

Any regular expression defines the lexical structure of some token or set of tokens. For example, let:

$$D = 0 \mid 1 \mid 2 \mid 3 \mid 4 \mid 5 \mid 6 \mid 7 \mid 8 \mid 9$$

be a singleton set of a digit from 0 to 9. Please note that the digits in the above definition actually denote singleton sets consisting of themselves, as accustomed in regular expressions. Next, the regular expression $D+$ denotes any non-empty sequence of digits, or, in other words, an unsigned integral number.

Formulas as the above definition of D are referred to as *regular definitions*. Instead of explicitly listing all symbols from some continuous range, in regular expressions, the following abbreviation is used: 0–9 (taken into brackets if necessary to avoid confusion).

The lexical structure of an identifier in most programming languages can be easily defined by a simple regular expression $L (L | D) *$ where L denotes any letter and D denotes any digit. Such notation is self-explanatory and convenient (much more than automata grammars). For this reason, regular definitions form the basis of many utilities related to text analysis and compiler development—*lex* (lexical analysis generator), *yacc*—parser generator, *grep*—text search utility, and so on.

The third formal model of a lexical analyzer is a *deterministic finite-state automaton*, formally defined as a 5-tuple of the kind:

$$T = <A, S, S_0, g, F>$$

where A is an input *alphabet*, S is a finite set of states, S_0 is the initial state of the automaton (belonging to S), g is the *transition function* $g: A \times S \rightarrow S$ evaluating the next state as a function $g(a, s)$ where a is a symbol from A and s is the current state from S; F is a subset of S, the set of *accepting states*. The task of the automaton is to analyze the input text consisting of symbols from A. The automaton works as a sequence of steps. Before each step, the automaton is in some *current state s*. At each step, it reads the current input symbol a, moves the pointer to the next input symbol, and switches to the new state $g(a, s)$. The automaton stops when its input text is over. If the final state belongs to F, the automaton *accepts* the input text. Otherwise, it *rejects* the input text.

The classical Kleene's theorem states that all three of the above formalisms are equivalent. More exactly, any formal language generated by an automata grammar is recognizable by some deterministic finite-state automaton and can be described by some regular expression, and vice versa. Intuitively, right-linear grammars are very close to finite-state automatons. For example, the rule $A \rightarrow aB$ can be interpreted as follows: If the automaton is in the state A and reads the current symbol a, it switches to the new state B.

Of all the above formalisms, regular expressions are the most practical kinds of description of lexical structure of a programming language. A classical lexical analyzer generation utility *lex*, part of classical UNIX tools, is based on regular expressions. It will be considered in more detail below.

In practice, a lexical analyzer is most often implemented as a routine that scans and delivers the next token from the source. Such architecture of lexical analyzer is much more practical and efficient than implementing it as a separate pass of the source code.

In this relation, in some compilers there is a distinction between a *lexical analyzer* and a *scanner*. A *lexical analyzer* fills out a buffer of current tokens of some constant length, as needed by the specifics of the source language. A *scanner* is a routine that retrieves the current token from the source code stream. Such architecture of a lexical analyzer is helpful to implement looka-head by one or more tokens if needed.

3.5 LEXICAL ERRORS, ERROR DIAGNOSTICS, AND RECOVERY

A lexical analyzer looks like a simple routine. Nevertheless, there are some kinds of lexical errors that need error diagnostics and recovery. Example of such error is to exceed the allowed amount of digits in a mantissa of a number. The actual maximal amount is determined by the target hardware platform. For integral numbers, such situation should be regarded as a severe error because it is not possible to ignore the extra digits without corrupting the value of the number. For float numbers, it can be considered a recoverable error, and the relevant recovery action is truncation of the extra trailing digits of the mantissa. In the former case, the compiler should issue an error message and recover the bug by replacing the integer value by some reasonable one, for example, *maximal integer*. In the latter case, the compiler can issue a warning message saying that the "extra" trailing digits of the mantissa are ignored.

3.6 PROCESSING IDENTIFIERS AND KEYWORDS

For *processing identifiers* during lexical analysis, we offer our own efficient method, which is important not only for lexical analysis but also for subse-quent parsing and semantic analysis (see Fig. 3.1).

Each identifier is stored into a hashed identifier table referred to as *id_tab*. A *unique copy* of each identifier is stored in the *id_tab*, unlike some other

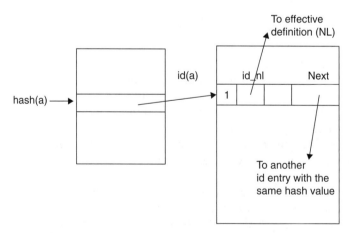

Figure 3.1. *The structure of the table of identifiers id_tab.*

compilers we know that allow the copying of the external representation (symbols) of an identifier between various tables. The first advantage of our decision is that we can use the pointer to the *id_tab* entry for a given identifier (its *id_ptr*, as denoted in Fig. 3.1) as its unique representative, or "anchor" of the identifier at each of the subsequent phases of compilation. The second advantage is the principle of *current effective definition* (CED) supported by our method. The *id_tab* entry for an identifier contains not only the length of the identifier, its characters, and the pointer to the next entry with the same hash value, but also the pointer to the *current definition* of the identifier, if any. So, due to this method, it is very simple and fast to find out whether the identifier is defined, and, if so, what is its current definition (or declaration) within the current scope. The details of our CED method are discussed later in Chapter 5 on semantic analysis.

The table of identifiers *id_tab* is a hashed table. That means, there is another table referred to as *hash_hdr* (see Fig. 3.1) that contains, for each *h* from 0 to the maximal possible value *H* of the hash function used, a pointer to the *list* of *id_tab entries* of identifiers whose hash values are all the same (equal to *h*).

The idea of a hash function is well-known and widely used in information management and system programming. For each identifier (*id*), an integer-valued function *hash(id)*, referred to as the *hash function*, is evaluated, whose value is between 0 and some *H*. The hash function should be chosen in such a way that it depends on all the characters of the identifier the same way ("symmetrically"). Examples of good and bad hash functions are as follows:

1. Let $id = a_1 \ldots a_n$. We define $hash(id) = [ord(a_1) + \ldots + ord(a_n)] \, mod \, P$, where *P* is, typically, a prime number; *ord* (*a*) is the code of the symbol *a*. This hash function depends on all the symbols of the identifier symmetrically, so it is a good hash function.

2. In older compilers, to optimize memory usage, the length of an identifier was usually limited by some *w*, where *w* is the number of characters in a machine word (4 or 8), or two machine words. If such a limitation is taken, each identifier *id* is actually truncated to *id_w*—the identifier truncated to *w* characters and padded by spaces up to the boundary of the nearest machine word if necessary. For example, if *w* = 8, but the length of the identifier is one symbol, it will be padded by seven spaces. Then, we can define:

$$hash(id) = mid \, (id\_w * id\_w)$$

where *mid* returns *k* bits from the middle of a word. Here, *id_w* is considered as an integral number. Surely this hash function is good, but the principle of limiting the length of identifier by a very small integer is poor: With that principle, for example, the identifiers *identifier1* and *identifier2* would be considered the same identifier. So in modern compilers, such strict limitation is not used. Please recall a real example of a 30-character predefined identifier from Java (see Section 3.1).

3 Taking the code of the first (or the last) symbol as a hash function would be bad: For example, the identifiers like *a*, *ab*, *abc*, and so on would be on the same hash list.

Much more examples of hash functions and related hashing techniques are covered in Reference 26.

If a hash function is chosen well enough, the total number of operations to perform the search of a new identifier in *id_tab* is *hashed* (which means *cut*, or *reduced*), in average, in *H* times.

Separating identifiers from keywords. During lexical analysis, each identifier retrieved from the source code is stored in some *buffer*—an array of bytes, or characters, and then its hash function is evaluated, and a hash-based search in the *id_tab* is performed. Please note that, due to the nature of the hash function, the lexical analyzer has to scan only a small list of already processed identifiers with the same hash value. If the new identifier is found in the table, the pointer to the corresponding *id_tab* entry is returned. If not, the new identifier is recorded in the *id_tab* and on the corresponding hash list, preferably at the *beginning* of the hash list. The underlying heuristic principle suggesting where in the hash list to place the new identifier is as follows: If the program is correct, the first occurrence of any identifier is expected to be its *definition*, so this identifier is very likely to be often used afterward and should be therefore put into the *beginning* of the hash list, to find it faster.

But there is one problem: keywords of programming languages are graphically nondistinguished from identifiers (look like identifiers). Please note that in older programming languages it was *not* so: For example, in ALGOL-68, one can define a variable of the *int* type, and the name of the variable could also be *int*, due to the fact that, according to the standard of ALGOL-68, all keywords are prefixed by a dot symbol (e.g., *.int*). Later (more exactly, since Pascal invention in 1970), all keywords became nondistinguishable from identifiers and were not prefixed or followed by any specific delimiters.

So, when the lexical analyzer processes an identifier, it should at first check whether this is actually a keyword or not. How is it done efficiently? The problem is simplified by the fact that the set of the keywords for the source language is a priori known. So, anyway, the lexical analyzer at first should use some method of checking if the sequence of characters in its buffer is a keyword or not (the simplest but nonefficient decision is just to make a linear search in an array of all the keywords of the language). If the search succeeds, this is a keyword. If it fails, this is an identifier.

We offer and have used in a number of our compilers the following more efficient method to distinguish between identifiers and keywords.

Let's choose the hash function in such a way that it is *one-to-one* (*injective*) for the keywords of the language. So, for each two different keywords w_1 and w_2, their hash values should be different: *hash* (w_1) *!* = *hash*(w_2). How to find such a hash function programmatically? One of the possible methods is to seek the hash function in the form $[ord(a_1) + ...+ ord(a_n)] \bmod P$, where P is a prime number, by selecting minimal possible prime P that enables one-to-one property of the hash function for the language keywords. Implementing a program to seek such a hash function is a simple exercise (see Exercise 3.2).

The idea of the method is as follows: Since there can be at most one keyword with the given hash value, it is enough to perform at most one string comparison of the token in the buffer to the keyword whose hash value is the same, if any, instead of doing a linear search in a constant table of all keywords, with $n/2$ comparisons in average, where n is the number of keywords (usually n varies from 50 to 120 in real programming languages).

Here is the scheme of our algorithm to separate identifiers from keywords:

```
Algorithm K. Separate identifiers from keywords

K1. (buf = identifier or keyword) : h = hash(buf);
K2. if string_compare(keywords[h], buf) // This is
    a keyword
      exit (token class = token_classes[h]);
    Assertion at this step: hash is one-to-one for
    all keywords
K3. (This is an identifier -> hashed search in id_tab):
    Search of the identifier stored in buf
    in the appropriate hash list in id_tab,
    starting from hash_hdr[h]
K4. if found (i) {
      id_ptr = i;
      exit (token class = YYID)
  }
K5. (Not found in id_tab):
    Create a new id_tab entry;
    new_i = pointer to the new id_tab entry;
    Add new_i entry to the h hash list as first element;
    id_ptr = new_i;
    exit (token class = YYID)
```

The idea of the algorithm is as follows.

The lexical analyzer uses the buffer *buf* to store the current identifier or keyword, a constant table *keywords*, and a "parallel" constant table *token_classes* whose indexes h are hash values.

First, the hash value *h* is evaluated. If *keywords[h]* is not empty, compare its value (string) to *buf*. If the comparison succeeds, the token is a keyword, and the entry *token_classes[h]* with the same index *h* contains the token class of the keyword.

Otherwise, this is an identifier, and the lexical analyzer performs a hashed search in the *id_tab* we already considered before.

In the above scheme of the *K* algorithm, we used the following denotations:

- *buf*—the byte buffer by the lexical analyzer to store the current token suspected to be an identifier or keyword;
- *id_ptr*—the output interface variable of the lexical analyzer to store the pointer to *id_tab* for the current identifier;
- *string_compare*—a library function to compare two strings symbol-by-symbol;
- *keywords*—the hashed table of the keywords; *keywords [h]* is the keyword whose hash value is *h*, if any; otherwise *null*; please note that this table is sparse: most of its elements are *null*'s;
- *token_classes*—the table "parallel" to the *keywords* table; contains token classes of the corresponding tokens.

3.7   THE ARCHITECTURE OF A LEXICAL ANALYZER AND THE PRINCIPLES OF ITS IMPLEMENTATION

Here is a code template in a C-like language how to implement a lexical analyzer as a routine to return the next token:

```
int yylex()
{ ...
  new_symbol:
   switch (c = getchar()) {
     case 'a': … case 'Z':  return identifierOrKeyword();
     case '0': … case '9':  return number();
     case '(': … case ')':  return specSymbol();
     case '\'': return characterOrString();
     case EOF: return YYEOF;
     default:
      error(INVALID_TOKEN);
      goto new_symbol;
   }
```

The body of the lexical analyzer should be organized as a big *switch* statement that chooses one of the alternatives of processing one of the token classes.

Generally speaking, it is the first nonwhite space symbol that determines which of the alternatives shown in the template to choose.

Depending on that, the lexical analyzer processes either identifier or keyword using the algorithm explained before, or one of the special symbols (delimiter, operator, etc.), a number, a character literal, a string literal, or end of file.

If there appears some other (unexpected) symbol in the source code, the lexical analyzer should issue an appropriate error message and, as a reasonable error recovery mechanism, skip this invalid symbol and make a shift over the source code to proceed with its next symbol, as shown in the code template above.

That's why there is a loop implemented by a label and a *goto* statement, which works in case an invalid symbol detected only, and forces the lexical analyzer to scan the next source symbol.

Principles of a trustworthy and efficient implementation of a lexical analyzer. Besides the general scheme of lexical analysis, there are some important principles for its implementation.

First, please keep in mind that a lexical analyzer is the most performance critical part of the compiler. Just imagine that, during the analysis of the source code, the lexical analyzer is called, so to say, to analyze each symbol. It means that the lexical analyzer should be implemented *very* efficiently by the most experienced software engineer of the compiler development team. In our "Elbrus" compiler team, for example, I personally developed "by hand" lexical analyzers for most of the compilers we implemented, without using any lexical analyzer generation tools.

As for efficiency, linear search or big sequences of "if" statements to seek an appropriate alternative of processing a token should be avoided as much as possible. For example, for processing identifiers, a hashed table is necessary, rather than a blind linear search of each identifier in a giant table of all the identifiers already found.

Similarly, very efficiently organized tables should be used in a lexical analyzer, hashed or indexed appropriately, to avoid long loops or chains of checks for an appropriate alternative.

Also, it is very important, for efficiency reasons, that built-in lexical analysis libraries (like regular expression analysis APIs for Java and C#), if possible, should *not* be used in lexical analyzers, or used with caution, since those APIs may not be implemented efficiently enough. For example, they can be based on multiple passes of the source code. The only predefined routines we recommend to use in lexical analyzers are those to convert denotations of integral or float numbers into its traditional binary form. In C libraries, in particular, those routine's names are *atoi* and *atof*. However, as a self-test in lexical analysis, it may be a helpful exercise to implement such a routine "from scratch."

It should also not be forgotten that a lexical analyzer should provide good error diagnostics and reasonable error recovery, for example, if the maximal number of digits in an integer is exceeded, a reasonable reaction could be to issue an appropriate error message and replace the wrong number by the maximal integer value.

Please also keep in mind that the lexical analyzer should not be over-complicated: In particular, if a two-level architecture "scanner/lexical analyzer" is not necessary (and it is really not necessary for most of the programming languages), then just implement a routine *yylex*, following the code template above, that delivers the lexical class of the next token in the source code.

Ambiguity issues and the need in lookahead in lexical analysis. There are issues arising in lexical analysis, even for such simple languages like Pascal, which violate the quiet process of deterministic finite automata-based analysis. For example, if, in Pascal, the lexical analyzer has already scanned the sequence "1." (*one, dot*), it cannot be sure if it has scanned the real number 1.0. If the next symbol appears to be "." (*dot*) again, the lexical analyzer will scan *two tokens* in turn: the *integer number* 1, and the *subrange delimiter* ".." (*double dot*). If the next symbol is a digit (e.g., 5), the lexical analyzer should scan a single token—a float number 1.5.

So, to correctly process this ambiguous situation, the lexical analyzer should have an internal *lookahead token buffer*, at least for one extra token already scanned. In the "1.." example above, the second token after the integer number 1 should be "double dot." So, as the result of the *next* call, the lexical analyzer should return this buffered "double dot" as the currently scanned token.

In a variety of programming languages, there is only one, uniquely complicated language—ALGOL-68, from the viewpoint of lexical analysis and parsing. The result of its lexical analysis may even depend partially on the result of its *semantic analysis*, since new keywords (like, for example, *.myplus* or *.myint*) may be defined in the source code by a special kind of definitions. Fortunately, it is only ALGOL-68 that has such functionality.

Another complication of lexical analysis takes place in FORTRAN. Since its first version designed by Backus in 1957, a FORTRAN programmer can use identifiers with any number of intermediate spaces: For example, *IDENT* means the same as *I D E N T* (with space between each pair of the symbols), and the lexical analyzer therefore must recognize such situations and process both the above occurrences as the same identifier. Moreover, such property makes the process much more complicated not only in lexical analysis, but also in parsing and even in semantic analysis. A classical example is the sequence like:

```
DO I = 1,3
```

This is a typical beginning of a loop (*do*) statement in FORTRAN. "DO" is the starting keyword of the loop; "I" is the loop variable; and "1,3" are the lower (1) and the upper (3) bounds of the loop's iterations. Next, imagine, that, because of a typo, the program developer used "." (dot) instead of "," (comma). The sequence now looks like:

```
DO I = 1.3
```

Because of the only typo, this slightly different sequence will be understood by the FORTRAN compiler in a completely different way: "DOI" (taken without spaces) will be interpreted as the identifier of a new variable (which, according to another nontrustworthy FORTRAN rule, is considered to be *implicitly defined* as a float variable by its first occurrence); "=" is treated as an assignment statement; and "1.3" is interpreted as a float number. So, the only typo (at the lexical layer) in a FORTRAN source code can completely corrupt the FORTRAN program. This example is well known in the history of programming.

3.8   THE LEXICAL ANALYZER GENERATOR *LEX*

Although, for efficiency reasons, we do recommended to implement lexical analyzers "by hand," using only a minimal set of predefined routines, in practice, to speed up compiler development, many software engineers use lexical analyzer generation tools, rather than implement lexical analyzers "from scratch." It is quite understandable, but compiler developers should keep in mind that automatically generated lexical analyzer is likely to work not as fast as expected, and its source code is likely to be much larger than expected.

In this chapter, we'll consider two lexical analyzer generation tools: *lex* (as a classical tool) and *ANother Tool for Language Recognition* [*ANTLR*] [22] (a modern and widely used lexical analyzer and parser generation tool).

There is a classical tool for generating lexical analyzers—*lex*. It is an inherent part of UNIX tools, as well as *yacc* and *make*.

The *lex* utility is based on representing the syntax of tokens by *regular expressions*. It takes as input a text file containing the description of a lexical structure of a language by regular expressions, and *semantic actions* to be performed for each kind of tokens detected. The output of *lex* is the source code of the lexical analyzer written to the file named *lex.yy.c*.

The generated lexical analyzer in C has the following prototype:

```
int yylex();
```

Lex can be considered to be a *rule*-based system. The structure of *lex* rules is as follows:

Pattern Action

where *Pattern* is a regular expression, and *Action* is a sequence of C statements implementing a semantic action to be performed when a token complying to this pattern is detected on the standard input.

This principle confirms our observation that rule-based systems are the driving force of most UNIX tools (including *yacc* and *make*).

The structure of an input file for *lex* (the file name usually has the *.l* extension) is as follows.

There are four parts in the *lex* input file, separated by some specific lines:

```
%{
C pre-processor include and define directives
%}
regular definitions
%%
rules
%%
user-defined routines in C
```

Preprocessor directives are needed to refer to other routines used and to make some useful denotations.

Regular definitions are *lex*-specific denotations: A regular expression is denoted by an identifier, to be used in the *lex* rules below.

User-defined routines define a working environment for *yylex*, including the *main* routine.

An example of an input file for *lex* is the specification of a sample lexical analyzer that recognizes integer numbers, *begin* and *end* keywords, identifiers, and the "+" operator:

```
%{
#include <math.h>
#include <stdio.h>
#include <mylex.h> /* all token defines and lex var
                       externs are here */
%}
DIGIT [0-9]
ID          [a-z][a-z0-9]*
%%
{DIGIT}+       {yyival = atoi(yytext);  return(YYINT);}
begin          {return(YYBEGIN);}
end            {return(YYEND);}
{ID}           {yyidptr = identifier(yytext);
                return(YYID);}
```

```
"+"             {return(YYPLUS);}
.               {printf("Invalid token: %s", yytext); }
%%
char * identifier(char * newid) { ... }
  // implementation of the routine to process an identifier
```

In the preprocessor definitions part of the file, we refer to the header file *mylex.h*.

We imply that this file should contain all *define* directives for the denotations used in the rules part: the names of token classes (**YYBEGIN, YYID,** etc.) and the *extern* declarations for the output variables of *yylex()*, like *yyidtpr*—a pointer to the *id_tab* entry for an identifier.

Please note the following specifics of rules and semantic actions.

Since each semantic action becomes part of the *yylex()* routine in the final generated code, they should contain exactly the actions to be performed for each token class, including the return from *yylex()* if necessary (no default *return* provided).

If the explicit return is forgotten, *yylex()* will proceed with the next token, and so on.

During each call of *yylex()*, the standard input will be checked against the patterns in the textual order of the rules. If the input does not comply any of the patterns, the last rule activates.

The specific regular expression "." (dot) used in the last rule means "any other input not complying to the above patterns."

In this case, an invalid symbol of the input will be matched to the "." pattern and printed as part of the error message, according to the semantic action, and the set of patterns will be tried again, starting with the next input symbol.

The *user routines* part of the file should contain full definition of the *identifier* routine called by the lexical analyzer to process identifiers.

As you can notice from this example, there is a tradition related to *lex* use, that all publicly visible identifiers belonging to *lex* and to the generated lexical analyzer generated by *lex* are prefixed by **YY** (double Y).

There are some useful global variables and routines provided by the *lex* library—*libl.a*.

The token character buffer of *lex* (array of characters) is available as *yytext*, and *yyleng* is the variable to store the actual length of the current token.

To append the next token to *yytext*, one can use the *yymore ()* routine.

The *yyless (n)* routine truncates the current token to *n* characters.

The current symbol *c* from the input can be extracted by the *input()* routine and returned back to the input by the *unput (c)* routine. It is a built-in feature of *lex* to support *lookahead* functionality—the need in lookahead in lexical analyzers is already discussed above.

There is even the default *main* routine provided by the *lex* library. But it is not suitable for compilers, since it calls *yylex()* once only, for the whole input text, rather than for each of its tokens. So when using *lex* utility for compiler development, one has to redefine the *main* routine.

The correct way of compiling the generated lexical analyzer that uses the *lex* library is as follows:

```
cc -ll lex.yy.c
```

Please note that static linkage with *libl* (denoted by the –ll option) is necessary.

Now let's compare the *lex* approach to our algorithms proposed in this chapter. We should note that the above lexical analyzer from the example will not process keywords and separate them from identifiers efficiently enough: According to the above *lex* rules, the lexical analyzer will, first, try to recognize *begin* on the input stream; if it fails, it will try to recognize *end*, and so on. If it were a lexical analyzer for Pascal whose standard contains 57 keywords, using the same approach would be too inefficient. So, as we can summarize, the advantage of using *lex* is simple and self-evident specification of tokens; its shortcoming (if used in a "straightforward" way) is possible inefficiency of the lexical analyzer generated. So we think *lex* is good for rapid prototyping of lexical analyzers.

On the modern software development platform of .NET, software engineers often use predefined Microsoft.NET Framework's regular expressions engine available from the *System.Text.RegularExpressions* namespace. So .NET users can apply this built-in tool to develop lexical analyzers and even for implementing simple languages with regular syntax. But, to be honest, this engine doesn't work efficiently enough. Again, the compiler developers have a choice of simplicity (when using a built-in tool) versus efficiency (when spending much more time; but they can develop a more efficient lexical analyzer "from scratch," according to the principles explained in this chapter).

3.9 LEXICAL ANALYZER GENERATION IN ANTLR

ANTLR [22] is a modern compiler development toolkit that contains lexical and parser generators. Currently, it supports code generation in Java, C#, ActionScript, and JavaScript languages. We'll cover the corresponding features of ANTLR (for lexical analyzer generation, parser generation, abstract syntax tree support, etc.) in this and the next chapters.

Since ANTLR is an object-oriented toolkit, any compiler component it generates should be specified in object-oriented style, and any ANTLR-generated code is also in an object-oriented manner.

The input grammar file for ANTLR is a text file with the name extension *.g* (for *grammar*). The grammar file specifies both the lexical analyzer and the parser.

Here is the general form of the lexical analyzer (or *lexer*, in ANTLR terms) specification in the input *.g* file:

```
class MyLexer extends Lexer;
options {
  some options
}
{
  lexer class members
}
lexical rules
```

For example, here is a simple lexer that pulls out from an arbitrary HTML file all the <p> and <br> tags:

```
class T extends Lexer;
options {
    k=2;
    filter=true;
}
P :  "<p>"  ;
BR:  "<br>"  ;
```

Here, *k* is the *lookahead length* of the ANTLR-generated lexer—the size of its lookahead buffer (the buffer elements are available via the method *LA*(i) where *i* is the number of the lookahead symbol); *filter* is the option that switches the lexer into the filter mode (to filter out the tokens of the given classes). So, in filter mode, the lexer works similar to classical *awk* tool in UNIX: it "sees" only the tokens of the classes defined in its specification.

For the readers to better feel the object-oriented flavor of the ANTLR-generated lexers in Java (as opposed to those generated by *lex* in C), here are some details at the source code level.

To deliver the next token, the *nextToken* method is provided, as part of the predefined *TokenStream* interface:

```
public interface TokenStream {
    public Token nextToken() throws TokenStreamException;
}
```

Here, *Token* is the enumeration type to specify the token classes. As many other modern object-oriented parsers and lexers, ANTLR-generated lexers and parsers signal of lexical and syntax errors by throwing exceptions. So, the *TokenStreamException* is the class of possible exceptions the *nextToken* method can throw. Although such measure as throwing an exception for each bug appears "too strong" and causes possible inefficiency, it guarantees better reliability and, therefore, better trustworthiness of the lexer and the parser that calls *nextToken*: According to Java semantics, the caller *must* process possible checked exceptions thrown by the method, and cannot "forget" them, otherwise the Java compiler will issue an error message.

Another example of ANTLR-generated Java code is as follows. Let the following lexer rules are defined:

```
INT : ('0'..'9')+;
WS : ' ' | '\t' | '\r' | '\n';
```

to specify integer numbers and white spaces, accordingly (please note the similarity of the *INT* definition to *lex* style). Then, the lexer generated by ANTLR will contain the *nextToken* method with the following code:

```
public Token nextToken() throws TokenStreamException {
    ...
    for (;;) {
        Token _token = null;
        int _ttype = Token.INVALID_TYPE;
        resetText();
        ...
        switch (LA(1)) {
          case '0': case '1': case '2': case '3':
         case '4': case '5': case '6': case '7':
          case '8': case '9':
            mINT(); break;
          case '\t': case '\n': case '\r': case ' ':
          mWS(); break;
          default: // error
        }
        ...
    }
}
```

In the above Java code, *mINT* and *mWS* are the methods to process integer numbers or white spaces in the source stream.

In general, ANTLR is based on *LL(k) predictive parsing* [5]. It can resolve lexical and parsing conflicts that may arise when using *LL* analysis, since the structure of real programming languages doesn't always obey the strict *LL* limitations, as we'll see later in Chapter 4.

Similar to *lex*, ANTLR provides a lot of predefined tools to examine the current token buffer, and so on, but formulated in modern object-oriented style.

ANTLR is now widely used both in research and in industry. In particular, Sun uses ANTLR in its worldwide spread open source NetBeans development environment.

EXERCISES TO CHAPTER 3

3.1 Implement a lexical analyzer for Pascal as a method in C#, including the algorithm to process identifiers and keywords.

3.2 Implement a method to seek a "good" hash function one-to-one for the keywords of the source programming language (e.g., Pascal).

3.3 Implement a lexical analyzer for Pascal using C# API for processing regular expressions, and the *HashTable* class to implement the hashed table of identifiers.

3.4 Implement a method or function to analyze a denotation of an integral number (without using any predefined routines).

3.5 Implement a method or function to analyze a denotation of a float number (without using any predefined routines).

3.6 Implement a lexical analyzer for Pascal using ANTLR.

Chapter *4*

Parsing and Trustworthy Methods of Syntax Error Recovery

This chapter covers *parsing* (or *syntax analysis*)—the next phase of compilation after lexical analysis described in Chapter 3.

We consider the most practical and widely used parsing techniques—*recursive descent* and *LR parsing*.

Also, in this chapter, we pay attention to trustworthy *syntax error recovery* techniques, which are of special importance for stable behavior of the compiler in case of syntax errors in the source code, and, therefore, for stable trust to the compiler by its users.

The purpose of parsing is to convert a *stream of tokens* received from the previous phase, lexical analysis, into the *parse (derivation) tree*—a tree-like representation of the program specifying its syntax structure, more compact and comfortable for the subsequent phases than the source code.

In practice of modern compilers, the parser constructs an *abstract syntax tree (AST)*—more abstract version of the parse tree, with the nodes for the brackets and other delimiters (like *begin* and *end* keywords) omitted. The AST form allows the compiler developers to avoid analyzing redundant layers of detail, avoid constructing and analyzing extra tree nodes, and to tie the semantic attributes and actions to really meaningful syntax constructs of the source language. AST for the expression $A * (B + C)$ is depicted in Figure 4.1. If it was a traditional parse tree, there would be redundant nodes for each of the brackets and for the whole bracketed subexpression $(B + C)$.

Another goal of parsing is to enable trustworthy *syntax error diagnostics and recovery*.

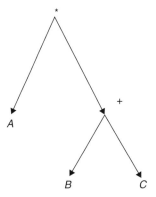

Figure 4.1. *Abstract syntax tree for the expression A * (B + C).*

4.1 BASIC CONCEPTS AND PRINCIPLES OF PARSING

For each of the programming languages, except for already mentioned ALGOL-68, the syntax can be formally defined by *context-free* (CF) *grammars* whose general format of rules is as follows:

$$A \to \eta$$

where A is a nonterminal symbol, and η is a chain of terminal and nonterminal symbols (that can be empty).

As a more practically convenient alternative, syntax of programming languages can be defined by *Extended Backus–Naur Forms* (*EBNF*), functionally equivalent to CF grammars, as known from the theory of formal languages. EBNF rules make the syntax specifications more intuitive and clear. They will be used later in this chapter. In EBNF, instead of using one symbol (letter) to denote a syntax construct, its clear and understandable name is used. To specify the right parts of the rules, EBNF uses regular expressions. For example, a simplified EBNF starting rule to define the syntax of a program in a programming language could look like this:

$$Program = \{Statement \; "\;;" \} \; *.$$

Here, *Program* is the starting symbol (like S in the theory of grammars); *Statement* is the syntax notion to specify the syntax of statement in a program; and the brackets *{ , }*, the asterisk (*), and the dot (.) are self-evident *meta-symbols* used, in their turn, to group syntax constructs, to denote the *iteration* operator, and to terminate the right part of a syntax rule.

The compilation phase of parsing depends on the previous phase of lexical analysis the following way: *Tokens* retrieved from the source code by the lexical analyzer are considered to be *terminal symbols* of the grammar or

EBNF that specifies the syntax of the source language. This implicit convention will be used elsewhere in this chapter.

The left part of any syntax rule is the name of syntax construct of the source language. From a theoretical viewpoint, it is just one *nonterminal symbol*.

The right part of the rule provides the syntax of the construct.

In ALGOL-68, both syntax and semantics are defined by a special kind of *two-level grammars* invented by Van Vijngaarden et al. [48]. Their consideration is beyond the framework of this book.

Once we assume that the syntax of the source language is defined by CF or EBNF grammar, we can conclude from the theory of formal languages that the parser should be some form of *stack-based automaton* (which can be *deterministic* or *nondeterministic*).

In general, the theory of parsing formal languages [49] investigates several kinds of parsers—global analyzers, nondeterministic analyzers, and so on.

But, for practical reasons, and due to relative simplicity of syntax for most of the programming languages, in practice of compiler development, only *left-to-right* and *deterministic* parsers are used. They analyze the source program from left to right and don't make any rollbacks to redo parsing for those parts of the source code that had been already analyzed. However, novel approach to parsing has been recently developed—*generalized parsing* [50], covered later in this chapter, which takes into account and parses different alternatives of syntax in parallel, and behaves as nondeterministic parser.

In addition, compiler parser should use trustworthy *error recovery* mechanism, to analyze the whole input source code (even in case it contains syntax errors), for the purpose of diagnosing as many syntax errors as possible. To stop compilation, when detecting the first syntax error, is not an appropriate strategy for a trustworthy compiler. On the other hand, error recovery should not lead to a bunch of error messages misguiding the user. Of such messages, usually only one or two first error messages really make sense, the others can be induced by the first bug detected and often can be ignored without any loss of useful information. Error recovery and avoiding a bunch of absurd error messages are of special importance for compiler trustworthiness.

For a real compiler, just *to reject* the source code because of incorrect syntax (as stack-based automata that analyze CF syntax do in theory of parsing) is not suitable. The user should be able to get reasonable error messages for all or most of the bugs, and pointers to them in the source.

The primary goal of the parser is to construct the *parse (derivation) tree* specifying the syntax structure of the program, or its more abstract version—*AST*. In that tree, nonterminal nodes will represent syntax constructs, and terminal nodes (leaves) will correspond to *terminal symbols* (*tokens*) of the source code. In this respect, all parsers can be subdivided into two classes—*top-down* and *bottom-up*. Intuitively, these terms reflect the sequence of steps of constructing the parse tree: top-down—from root to leaves of the parse tree (following the arrows in Fig. 4.1)—and bottom-up—in the opposite direction. More formally speaking, a top-down analyzer emulates in some way the derivation of the source code from the starting symbol of the grammar—from left parts of the rules (syntax constructs) to right parts (their syntax provided by the rule). On the contrary, a bottom-up parser emulates the process of derivation from right-hand parts of the rules to their left parts, and collects in its stack, symbol by symbol, right parts of rules (referred to as *handles* [5]), and, when the right part is fully collected on the stack, replaces it by the left part symbol (the latter action is referred to as *reduction* [5]). The final goal of the bottom-up parser is to reduce the source code to the starting symbol.

For the reasons explained above, the following parsing techniques are mostly used in compilers:

- *recursive descent*—left-to-right, top-down, deterministic parsing technique that requires the grammar of the language to be LL(1);
- *LL(1)* [5], table-based, left-to-right, top-down, deterministic parser that requires from the grammar the same properties (limitations) as a recursive descent parser. LL parsing is the basis of modern parser generator ANother Tool for Language Recognition (ANTLR) whose parsing features are covered in this chapter;
- *LR(1)* [5], table-based, left-to-right, bottom-up, deterministic parser— much more complicated than all the above but accepts a wider class of languages, and more suitable for *phrase-level recovery* (localizing the detected error in up to minimal possible syntax construct);
- *LALR(1)* [5], table-based, left-to-right, bottom-up, deterministic parser— a kind of LR(1) parser, with more compact structure of the parsing table, and much smaller number of states. This technique is used by the classical *yacc* parser generator utility, and by many of its clones overviewed later in the chapter.

LL parsing is fully covered in References 5 and 49, so it will not be considered in this book.

4.2 RECURSIVE DESCENT AND SIMPLE LOOKAHEAD MECHANISM

Recursive descent is the simplest kind of parsing techniques.

Its great advantage is its self-evidence: Each, even nonexperienced, IT student or software engineer, after reading this section, will be able to write a recursive descent parser. Moreover, each of the steps of a recursive descent parser, unlike many other parsing techniques, is quite understandable for a compiler developer, easily modifiable, and debuggable.

Recursive descent is widely used by many computer scientists and software engineers all over the world, for a variety of languages—from Pascal to C#.

Recursive descent seems to be the favorite parsing method by Wirth, the inventor of Pascal, Modula, and Oberon, and for his scientific school at ETH Zürich.

In the material of our book related to recursive descent parsing, we'll use some definitions and denotations from Wirth's book on compilers [51].

The idea of recursive descent is very simple.

Let's consider a grammar of the source programming language in EBNF form.

Each rule of the grammar has the following general format:

$$A = X_1 \ldots X_n$$

It defines the syntax of some construct A. Based on the structure of the syntax rule, let's develop the *parsing procedure Pr(A)* for the construct A.

When the syntax of the construct A is defined as a sequence of its *subconstructs* $X_1, \ldots, X_n$, in this simplest case, $Pr(A)$ is just a *sequence of calls*: $Pr(X_1)$; $\ldots Pr(X_n)$.

Please note that, from a more general viewpoint of knowledge management, the above principle is just an application of more general *heuristic* of reducing a task to subtasks: *If you don't know how to solve a task, please try to transform it to a sequence of subtasks and try to solve each of them in turn.*

In case the right-part symbol is a *terminal* symbol x (in other words, *token*— we already know that these terms are synonyms, from the viewpoint of the parser), its parsing procedure $Pr(x)$ is just "eating" (passing) this "mandatory" token and shifting the source code pointer to the next token.

So, to analyze a mandatory token t, the parser should check if the input token is t; if so, shift the input to the next token; if not, issue an error message that the token t is missed.

Pascal-like pseudocode to implement the *eat(x)* routine is as follows:

```
procedure eat(t: tokenClass)
   begin
     if token = t
     then token := yylex()
     else error(MISSINGSYMBOL, t)
   end { eat }
```

Please note that, from an error recovery viewpoint, this code is quite trustworthy: Reporting on a missed token can be regarded as *inserting* this token. So, the parser assumes that x is inserted, notifies the user about it, and continues parsing. Surely actual insertion of the missing token into the source code isn't performed by the parser, since this is not the task of the compiler; such actions as source code modifications are left for the source program developer to do using text editor of the integrated development environment.

Now let's formulate more general principles of constructing $Pr(A)$ for all possible kinds of the right part of a rule, as shown in Table 4.1.

In EBNF, the right part of each rule is a *regular expression* (see Chapter 3). So, here are the principles of constructing $Pr(A)$ for all kinds of regular expressions, the right parts of syntax rules.

TABLE 4.1. Recursive Descent Parsing Procedures for All Kinds of Syntax Constructs

A	Comment	Pr(A)
sym	Token, or terminal	*eat(sym)*
B C	Concatenation	*Pr(B); Pr(C)*
B | C	Alternation	*if token in First(B) then Pr(B) else Pr(C)*
B*	Iteration	*while token in First(B) do Pr(B)*
B+	Iteration	*Pr(B); Pr(B*)*

If the right part is a terminal symbol x, as we saw above, $Pr(A)$ should be just *eat(x)*.

If the right part is a *concatenation* of two or more constructs, $Pr(A)$ is a succession of calls of the *Pr* procedures for all its components.

If the right part is an *alternation*, $Pr(A)$ is an *if* statement trying to call *Pr* for the first suitable alternative B such that the current token can be the first terminal symbol of a sentential form derived from it, that is, the value of *token* belongs to *First(B)* [5,49]. If *token* does not belong to *First(B)*, the parser calls $Pr(C)$, the parsing procedure for another alternative of the syntax of A.

Sure we assume here that the sets of *First* tokens for the alternatives in one rule (B and C) don't intersect; otherwise, such rule could produce undesirable nondeterminism.

Similarly, if the right part is an *iteration*, that is, a sequence of zero or more occurrences of a syntax subconstruct B, the implementation of the parsing procedure $Pr(A)$ should be a *while* loop processing as many B's as possible while the current input token allows it, that is, while *token* belongs to *First(B)*.

Let's formulate more clearly what we are assuming here about the grammar, when proposing the above principles of parsing procedures implementation. Here are the assumptions we made:

1   *First(B) ∩ First(C)* = Ø (assumption for the rule using alternation);
2   *First(B) ∩ Follow(A)* = Ø (assumption for the rule using iteration).

Speaking informally, when implementing $Pr(A)$ for the rule using iteration, we assume that the parser cannot mix up two alternatives: the one that corresponds to *absence of A* in the source code, and the other one that corresponds to starting an occurrence of B. Otherwise, the loop condition *token in First(B)* doesn't work. So, for our approach to be usable, *Follow(A)* and *First(B)* should not intersect.

Summarizing all of our assertions about the grammar, we see that they are equivalent to those specified as a definition of *LL(1) grammar* [5]. Informally speaking, an LL(1) grammar is a CF grammar that enables the construction of a top-down parser to be built according to the structure of the grammar (either a recursive descent parser, or an LL(1) table-based parser [5]) that can parse the source code left-to-right deterministically, and each time if the parser has to make a choice between the syntax alternatives of a construct, this choice is fully determined by the current token only.

The above principles can be used either when writing a recursive descent parser "from scratch" or when developing a tool that can generate such a parser automatically, given an LL(1) grammar of the language.

When developing a recursive descent parser, please remember the following conventions to be followed for *Pr(A)* for any *A*:

- *before* calling *Pr(A)*, the first token of *A* should be already scanned by the lexical analyzer and stored in its global interface variable, referred to as *token* (see Chapter 3);
- *after* calling *Pr(A)*, the last token of *A* should be "eaten," that is, actually, the first token following *A* should be scanned and be assigned to the *token* variable.

By the way, forgetting to call the routine to "eat" a token is one of the most common bugs in recursive descent parsers, so please do your best to avoid such bugs. Using assertion mechanism in the implementation language may help in such situations: If the assertion on the current token fails, an internal error message is issued, or the compiler will terminate by an exception (depending on the implementation).

Another danger of recursive descent scheme of compilation, from a trustworthy compiling viewpoint, is as follows. Actually, when using such a scheme, the compiler developer has to mix up in the source code of the same procedure *Pr(A)* various fragments of code logically related to quite different phases of the compiler: calling lexical analyzer, syntax checks, semantic analysis, optimization, code generation, and error diagnostics and error recovery for different phases of the compiler—all in one piece of the source code implementing *Pr(A)*. Usually, each of those fragments is just one or two statements. This may cause a lot of bugs like "forgetting" any such statement, swapping the neighbor statements, corrupting the code by insertion of any such statement into the wrong point of the source code (as a result of improper bug fixing), and so on.

Two kinds of technologies are helpful in this respect, to make the implementation more trustworthy. Both are intended to improve the intermodule coupling, speaking in classical software engineering terms by Myers [15]. The first technology we recommend is our *technological instrumental package (TIP) technology* [2] covered in Section 1.1: It helps to properly design the parts of the compiler and give proper mnemonic names to their corresponding functions, so that the compiler developer can work in high-level terms of those functions, rather than in direct terms of the implementation language statements. The second useful approach is aspect-oriented programming [1]: Each part of the compiler can be implemented as an *aspect*, and the automated insertion of the proper compiler function's call into the proper point of the compiler source code will be guaranteed by the aspect-oriented programming (AOP) technology. Please see Reference 1 for more details.

Non-LL(1) issues and a simple lookahead method. After the consideration of the basics of recursive descent, we now formulate the main issue with the recursive descent: *all real programming languages* (Pascal, C, Java, etc.) *are non-LL(1)*.

The most typical case of non-LL(1) set of rules is the set of rules to define the syntax of statement. Below is a simplified syntax of the *statement* construct in Pascal:

```
statement = id := expr ';' |  /* assignment */
            id ';' |          /* call with no
            arguments */
            id (args) ';' .   /* call with
            arguments list */
```

As we can see, each of the syntax alternatives starts with *id* (identifier), so the current token class (*YYID*) is not enough for the recursive descent parser to choose one of the alternatives for further parsing, that is, the above condition 1 violates.

But it does not mean that the technique of recursive descent is useless: It is flexible enough to be adapted to cover LL(1) conflicts of the language.

Informally, each statement can start with an identifier. But such starting symbol as identifier does not fully determine the subsequent flow of parsing, since the next symbol after the identifier can be either an *assignment symbol* (in that case, the construct is an assignment statement) or a *left parenthesis* (in that case, the construct is a *call statement*).

So, as the example shows, in real programming languages many typical syntax rules require at least *two first tokens* of the right part to be known to choose an appropriate alternative of syntax.

This issue can be resolved using the following method.

Let's add to our recursive descent parser a simple functionality to *look ahead* by one token and, accordingly, to *step back* when the parser, using the lookahead token, has determined the right alternative for further parsing.

At the design level, the idea is to add two routines: *lookAhead()* and *stepBack()*.

Please note that we introduce only the functionality to look ahead or step back by *one* token, rather than by *several tokens*. In the latter case, we would have to implement a *token buffer* of appropriate length (like in ANTLR). But our goal is to implement lookahead as simple and as efficient as possible.

First, let's consider which variables should we add and how to implement the *lookAhead* routine.

We should have two flags: a *lookAheadFlag* to indicate that the lookahead has taken place and a *stepBackFlag* to indicate that lookahead and step back have been performed, so the two current successive tokens are scanned.

To store these neighbor tokens, we introduce two variables: *curToken*—to store the current token before lookahead—and *nextToken*—to store the next token before step back.

Keeping all of this in mind, the implementation of *lookAhead* becomes evident. The two things to be mentioned are first, we explicitly check that there has been no attempt to perform lookahead by more that one token; second, if we perform the lookahead for the first time, we should store the next (lookahead) token in the *nextToken* variable. In any case, *curToken* is the current token.

Pascal-like pseudocode of the implementation of *lookAhead* is given below:

```
procedure lookAhead();
  begin
    if lookAheadFlag then InternalError()
    else if stepBackFlag then /* lookahead 2nd
    time */
    begin
       lookAheadFlag:= true;
       token:= nextToken;
    end
    else /* lookahead 1st time */
    begin
       looAheadFlag:= true;
       curToken:= token;
       token:= nextToken:= yylex();
   end
end /* lookahead */
```

The implementation of *stepBack* is also very simple.

Two things should be kept in mind: first, we should check for an internal error in case we mistakenly try to step back without prior lookahead; second, we should keep in mind that the lookahead/step back pair of actions may be performed more than once (please see the above example of the syntax of statement).

Please note that *stepBackFlag* is not cleared either by *lookAhead* or by *stepBack* routines. It should be cleared by the *lexical analyzer* when it moves on from the scanned pair of tokens to the next token.

Here is the Pascal-like pseudocode for *stepBack* implementation:

```
procedure stepBack();
begin
  if (not lookAheadFlag) then InternalError()
  else
  begin
     lookAheadFlag:= false;
     if stepBackFlag then /* stepback for the 2nd
     time */
     begin
        token:= curToken;
     end
     else /* stepback for the 1st time */
     begin
        stepBack:= true;
        token:= curToken;
     end
  end
end /* stepBack */
```

The changes to be made in the lexical analyzer to support the above lookahead/step back mechanism are as follows.

First, when the lexical analyzer detects that the *lookAheadFlag* is not cleared, it means an internal error in the compiler because we don't allow trying to look ahead by more than one token.

Second, when the lexical analyzer detects that the *stepBackFlag* is set, it means that the next token should be taken from the "internal storage" (more exactly, from *nextToken*), and the *stepBackFlag* should be cleared.

In all other cases, lexical analysis proceeds as usual. Fragment of pseudocode of the updated lexical analyzer is given below:

```
function yylex (): tokenClass;
begin
  if lookAheadFlag then InternalError()
  else if stepBackFlag
  then
  begin
     stepBackFlag:= false;
     token:= nextToken;
  end
  else …
    /* continue lexical analysis as usual:
      take the next token from the source */
end /* yylex */
```

4.3 OVERVIEW OF ERROR RECOVERY IN PARSING: ERROR RECOVERY FOR RECURSIVE DESCENT

As we've already noted before, good error recovery mechanisms are especially important for parsing.

In our practice, we've used a commercial compiler that, in case a syntax error occurs in the source code, issued mysterious messages like:

Syntax error before or at: <symbol name>,

next, kept silence for 20–30 lines of code, and, finally, complained that it was unable to continue parsing because of severe errors, and stopped compilation at all.

Such behavior is not suitable for a good compiler product: Users will not like such poor quality of error diagnostics and recovery, and will switch to another product.

There are several techniques of error recovery in parsing [5]. In this section, we'll offer our own error recovery techniques, in addition to explaining the classical ones.

The simplest one is referred to as *panic mode*—skipping the source until some *synchronizing* token is found that can be the start of a new major construct—definition or statement. So, a synchronizing token is a token "not-to-be-missed." Panic mode is used by recursive descent parsers and LL(1) parsers. For example, if the following erroneous Pascal code is parsed:

```
type t = *integer;
var v: t;
```

the parser detects the wrong symbol "*." Such bug can be made by a programmer who switched from C to Pascal: The "*" symbol denotes the pointer type in C; in Pascal, on the contrary, the "^" symbol is used to denote pointer types. A top-down LL or recursive descent parser whose error recovery mechanism is based on panic mode will issue an error message on invalid syntax of the type in the type definition, and skip the input tokens until the *var* keyword (that starts the variable definition part). The *var* keyword should be included into the set of synchronizing tokens. The above will be an acceptable error recovery measure for such kind of syntax errors but is not suitable for all kinds of those, as we'll see below.

A more subtle technique is *phrase-level recovery*. Its purpose is to recover up to the end of the nearest syntax *phrase*—expression, statement, definition, or declaration. For this purpose, one of the following recovery actions can be undertaken—*insertion*, *deletion*, or *changing* a token or several neighbor tokens.

An example, taken from our practice of using Sun Pascal compiler, is given below:

```
i: integer; j: real;    /* the starting VAR keyword
missing */
```

The error recovery mechanism of this compiler, invented and implemented by Joy, is as smart as to insert the missing *var* keyword at the beginning of a Pascal variable declaration. This mechanism will be covered below in this chapter.

Phrase-level recovery approach is typical for bottom-up parsers, for example, for LR(1) parsers, and will be considered later in this chapter. The *reduce* actions of bottom-up parsers are quite suitable for embedding phrase-level recovery mechanisms.

A systematic approach to error recovery, taken by the authors of parser generators like *yacc*, is referred to as *error productions*. Error production is a syntax rule of a grammar that contains the specific *error* nonterminal symbol. It can be one of the alternatives (typically the last one) of syntax of some construct, like statement, or some of the alternatives can contain this *error* nonterminal. The recovery action related to *error* nonterminal is as follows: skipping the source up to a token from *Follow(A)* where *A* is the left part of the syntax rule, and then reduce to *A*.

Error productions are helpful to explicitly include typical cases of syntax errors into syntax rules, and to associate proper semantic actions to them—issuing appropriate error messages and so on.

Here is an example of error production written in *yacc* syntax:

```
statement:
 id YYASSIGN expr | id YYLPAR param | id error .
```

Error recovery in recursive descent. The simplest way to do *error recovery* in recursive descent is the *panic mode*.

If the parser finds an error in the source code (a nonexpected token as input), it skips the source code until some "reasonable" token that could be a start of some major construct—a definition, a compound statement, and so on. Such token is referred to as *synchronizing token*.

For each syntax context (e.g., the beginning or the end of a definition or of a statement), a reasonable set of synchronizing tokens should be proposed.

An appropriate set of synchronizing tokens for Pascal, for any syntax context, is given below:

```
begin  end   if   case   for  while  repeat
const  type  var  procedure  function  EOF
```

The implementation of the panic mode routine *skipUntil* is simple: in a loop, we scan the current token and check whether it already belongs to the given set of synchronizing tokens. If so, we return; if not, the loop continues. Here is a Pascal-like implementation pseudocode for *skipUntil*:

```
type SetOfTokens = set of TokenType;
procedure skipUntil(s: SetOfTokens);
begin
 while not (token in s)
 do
   token:= lex();
end; /* skipUntil */
```

Surely we assert above that the set of tokens *s* contains *EOF*.

Issues of syntax error recovery. There is a traditional kind of choice to be made by the error recovery mechanism—if an unexpected token found on the input, whether to skip it or to close all the open blocks and scopes at this point.

In this relation, all compiler developers can be subdivided into "skippers" and "closers."

Both kinds of decisions may appear to be right or wrong, depending on the syntax context.

The two examples given below demonstrate both situations.

In the first example written in Pascal, the "=" symbol is missed in the *t1* type definition:

```
type t1 1..10; t2 = 2..5; var v1: t1; v2: t2;
```

Typical reaction of the compiler whose syntax error recovery mechanism is based on panic mode only is as follows:

Error: '=' missed in t1 definition;

Recovery by skipping until var (causes the t2 definition to be ignored);

Error: t2 undefined

The latter is surely an absurd error message.

If the recovery action to be chosen is to skip until a synchronizing token, the parser will skip the source until the *var* symbol, that is, until a new (variable) definition.

The improper consequence of such decision is as follows: Because of Pascal unified syntax, it is really not possible for a top-down parser to skip the source until the beginning of another type definition *t2* because that type definition is not marked by any special "anchor" keyword. So, the *t2* type definition will just be ignored. Hence, in the *var* definition section, the compiler will issue a dumb message "*t2* undefined," even if *t2 was* actually defined.

The second example is written in C:

```
{
   int i, j, k; #i = 1; j = 2; k = 3;
   …i … j … k … /* A bunch of silly error
   messages here */
}
```

In this example, the unexpected symbol "#" occurs in a variable definition section (e.g., as the result of a typo). Imagine that the parser, as opposed to the previous example, makes a decision, in case an unexpected symbol occurs, not to skip it but, on the contrary, to close all the open blocks and scopes at this point as a recovery action.

The result of such action is as poor as the result of an opposite decision in the previous example: Several definitions of local variables (i, j, and k) will be ignored because, if the current block is "closed," all of them automatically become undefined. So such decision may produce a bunch of silly error messages.

So we came to the idea that, for better error recovery, the syntax context should be taken into account: A recovery action should not be "global" (context-independent).

"Intelligent" panic mode. For recursive descent parsers, we offer a modified version of the panic mode we refer to as *intelligent panic*. We've successfully used this technique in a number of our compilers based on recursive descent [2].

The idea is to take into account *paired tokens—opening* and *closing* tokens of a compound syntax construct, like left and right parentheses, *begin* and *end*, and so on.

If the parser started to analyze a construct beginning with some *opening* token—"(," "[," *begin*, *if*, and so on, it should remember that a paired *closing* token is now expected—accordingly, ")," "]," *end*, and *then*.

When the construct ends, the parser should mark in its internal state that it does not wait for the paired closing token any more.

Please keep in mind that such constructs may be nested. So the parser should keep counters *how many times* it is currently waiting for each token class.

To implement this idea, we introduce an array named *count* whose indexes are token classes and whose elements are integers—the counters of waiting for each token class.

If the parser starts processing a construct with an "opening" token, like "(," it should add one to the *counter* of the corresponding "closing" token ")." When that closing token is really found at the end of the construct, its *count* should be decreased by one. Let's denote the above two actions as follows: *expect (token)* and *nonExpect (token)*.

When the compilation of a source code starts, the parser should initialize to one the *counts* of all tokens "always-not-to-be-missed," like *begin* or *var*.

So, if a recursive descent parser needs to skip until a synchronizing token, with intelligent panic, it skips the source until the first token whose *count* is >0. To introduce this "intelligent" (context-dependent) check for a synchronizing token, it is enough to replace in the above *skipUntil* procedure the loop condition:

```
(token in s)
```

to:

```
(token in s) and (count [token] > 0) .
```

Example where intelligent panic helps. Now let's consider an example when intelligent panic helps:

```
var i: integer; a: array[1..10] of integer;
 begin
    for i:= 0 to 9 do
      begin writeln(a[i+1 end;
    writeln("finish")
 end
```

In this Pascal source, in line 4, there are two syntax errors: Both right parentheses in the index expression and the right square bracket in the indexed variable are missing.

Due to intelligent panic mode, when skipping the source, the parser stops at the *end* token after the erroneous indexed variable, since *count* [*end*] = 2.

Then, the parsing procedure for the index variables checks that the right square bracket is missing, and issues the corresponding error message (so to say, "inserts" the missing square bracket).

After that, similar actions are performed by the parsing procedure for the procedure call: It checks for a closing right parenthesis, issues an error message that it is missing, "inserts" it, and the parsing continues, with no "garbage" error messages.

Error recovery by skipping until a pair of synchronizing tokens. As our experience shows, when using recursive descent, in some contexts, a helpful error recovery mechanism is to skip until a *pair* of synchronizing tokens (rather than until one synchronizing token). In particular, in Pascal-like *constant* and *type* definitions, the error recovery mechanism of skipping until the pair of tokens:

identifier "="

works well. It can help to localize a syntax error up to *the nearest defini-tion*, rather than up to the next definition part—until *type, var, proce-dure,* or *function* keyword. The latter option would inevitably cause a bunch of induced error messages on undefined identifiers, since part of the definitions are skipped. For example:

```
const a; b = 1;
type t1 = integer  t2 = array [a..b] of real;
var v: t2;
```

This Pascal code contains two quite common syntax errors:

* in the constant definition part, the definition of the constant *a* is incom-plete—the "=" symbol and the value of the constant are forgotten;
* in the type definition part, the semicolon (";") is omitted after the *t1* type definition.

Please note that "straightforward" panic mode and even intelligent panic mode don't help here. With panic mode, to recover from the error in constant definition part, the source will be skipped until the *type* keyword, so the definition of the constant *b* will be ignored. To recover from the error in the type definition part, the source will be skipped until the *var* keyword. As a result, absurd error messages on undefined *b* and *t2* will be issued by the semantic analyzer. With the error recovery tech-nique of skipping until the *id "="* pair of tokens, the definitions of *b* and *t2* will be processed, and no silly error messages will be issued.

We used this technique in many of our compilers [2], in combination with the intelligent panic method considered before.

4.4 LR(1) AND LALR(1) PARSING

Among *bottom-up* parsers, the most widely used in compiler practice are several kinds of *LR* parsers. The material of this section devoted to LR parsing is based on the book [5], which we consider the classics of LR parsing theory.

LR parsers were invented by Knuth in early 1970s. His classical paper [53] written in 1965 is also one of the best sources for reading about LR parsers.

To better understand the specifics of LR parsers, let us first recall the basics of bottom-up parsers.

Top-down and bottom-up parsers. The general idea of top-down parsers, like recursive descent or LL(1) parsers, is to emulate *leftmost inference* of the source program code to be parsed, that is, each step of top-down parsing corresponds to a step of derivation of the source program based on the CF grammar of the language, with each rule applied to the *leftmost occurrence* of a nonterminal symbol in the current *sentential form*: $xAy => x\lambda y$, where A is the leftmost occurrence of a nonterminal into the sentential form xAy.

Speaking informally, an LL(1) bottom-up parser tries to construct a parse tree of the source program depth-first, from the root to its leaves, moving from each node to its left child, then to its descendants, next to the second sibling, and so on.

As opposed to top-down parsing, the general idea of *bottom-up* parsers is to emulate *rightmost inference in reverse order*, that is, $xBy <= x\lambda y$ where B is the rightmost occurrence of a nonterminal into the sentential form xBy.

A bottom-up parser tries to reduce the source code of the program to the root of its parse tree—the starting symbol S of the grammar. Each step of a bottom-up parser corresponds to *reversed* step of derivation of the source program based on the CF grammar, with each rule applied (*in reverse order*—reducing the right part to the left part) to the *rightmost occurrence* of a nonterminal symbol in the current *sentential form* [5]—a chain of terminal and nonterminal symbols derivable from the starting symbol.

A step by bottom-up parser to replace the right part of a syntax rule by its left part is referred to as *reduce* action. The right part and its position in the sentential form are referred to as *handle*.

A bottom-up parser collects in its stack a *viable prefix* of a sentential form, including the possible handle that is always on top of the stack, due to rightmost nature of the inference emulated.

The actions of a bottom-up parser are *shift* (push the current token onto the stack and get the next token) and *reduce* (pop the handle from the stack and push the left part nonterminal onto the stack). So bottom-up parsers are also called *shift–reduce parsers*. LR parser is one of those.

The relationship of the LL(k) and LR(k) classes of languages. Let's briefly overview the theoretical issues related to the LL and LR classes of formal languages [5,49].

All the programming languages (except for ALGOL-68 as you hopefully remember) belong to these classes.

Let $LL(k)$ be the class of all languages whose syntax can be defined by an LL(k) grammar for some $k >= 1$. Then, the problem to check if $LL(k) = LL(1)$ for some k is undecidable.

Practically, it means that, if there is an LL(k) grammar for some $k > 1$ that defines the syntax of some formal language, then there is no algorithm to check if this grammar can be transformed to LL(1) grammar, probably having more syntax rules, that generates the same formal language.

Let $LR(k)$ be the class of all languages whose syntax can be defined by an LR(k) grammar for some $k >= 1$.

The *LL* class of languages is strictly narrower than the *LR* class, and the *LR* class of languages is wider than *LL*. There are a lot of examples [5] to demonstrate a syntax, which belongs to the LR class but does not belong to the LL class.

All currently known programming languages, except for ALGOL-68, fall into the LR class.

The general issue of a grammar to prevent its language from being an LL language is *left recursion*: When parsing a syntax defined as E -> E '+' T, *LL* parser falls into an infinite loop. The same happens with a recursive descent parser: in its *Pr(E)* procedure, the parser has to call *Pr(E)* again and so on. The recipe how to transform a grammar to an LL grammar generating the same language is as follows: replace left recursion by right recursion.

LR parsers don't have such infinite recursion issue.

The general architecture of the bottom-up shift–reduce parser is as follows.

The parser takes an input of n symbols (or tokens) $a_1 \ldots a_n$. The nth symbol is *EOF*, which indicates the end of the source text.

The parser has a finite number of states: *States = {S_1 , ... S_k}*.

The stack of the parser can contain nonterminal as well as terminal symbols, that is, any symbols from $V = (V_t + V_n)$ paired with the corresponding states the parser takes on "passing" the symbol.

The current state is always on top of the stack. So, the stack always looks like as follows: *(S_0 X_1 S_1 ... X_m S_m)*, where S_m is the *current state*.

Speaking informally, a terminal symbol x is pushed onto the parser's stack when x is *shifted* from the input; a nonterminal symbol X is pushed onto the parser's stack as the result of the *reduce* action related to some grammar rule whose left part is X.

To control the functioning of the parser at each step, there are two tables—*action* and *goto*.

The *action* table is a two-dimensional array whose first index is a grammar symbol X or *EOF*, and the second index is the current state S.

The action may be:

- *shift* the current input symbol x to the stack and switch to some other state *S1*;
- *reduce* to some grammar rule: replace its right part accumulated on top of stack by the left part nonterminal symbol of the rule; the new state is determined from the *goto* table;
- *accept* the whole input (happens when X is *EOF* and the parser is in the final state);
- *error*—happens in all other cases.

Here is the rule to formalize the content of the action table:

$action[X,S] = $ **shift S1 | reduce A->α | accept | error**

where X belongs to $(V + \{EOF\})$, and S belongs to *States*.

The *goto* table is used to determine the new state of the parser after the *reduce* action. Accordingly, it is a two-dimensional array whose first index is a *nonterminal* symbol Y (the left part of the rule), and the second index is the current state previous to the *reduce* action:

$goto[Y,S_{cur}] = S_{next}$—the next state after reduce by a rule of
the kind $Y \to \beta$

where Y belongs to V_n.

The parser stops when an accept action is performed (*success*), or when an error action occurs (*failure*).

Example. Now, following Reference 5, let's analyze the issues of general shift–reduce parsing scheme explained above.

Here is a simple grammar that may cause issues in shift–reduce style parsing:

$$\{T \to T * T \mid T \to id\}$$

The grammar defines a simplified syntax of a *term* (denoted by a nonterminal T) in a programming language. The terminal symbol *id* denotes an identifier. Please note that we don't define the structure of an identifier here, since, from the viewpoint of the parser, all identifiers are specified by the symbol (token class) *id*. According to this grammar, a term is an identifier (*id*), or any sequence of the kind: $id * \dots * id$.

Let's consider the chain $id * id * id$, its rightmost inference, and possible behavior of a shift–reduce parser, based on the above grammar, when parsing this chain.

The rightmost inference of the above chain is as follows:

$$T \Rightarrow T * T \Rightarrow T * T * T \Rightarrow T * T * id \Rightarrow T * id * id \Rightarrow id * id * id$$

Here is a possible behavior of a shift–reduce parser. At each step, except for steps 2 and 4, the parser chooses the only possible action to do.

Initially: stack = ( ) input = $id * id * id$ EOF

1 *shift:* stack = (id) input = $*$ id $*$id EOF
2 *shift or reduce?* We get a *shift–reduce conflict*: the parser can either reduce (*T->id*) or *shift* further. In practice, such conflicts often resolve in favor of *shift*. After following this recommendation, we get:

stack = (*id* $*$) input = $id*id$ EOF

3 *shift:* stack = (*id* $*$ *id*) input = $*$ *id* EOF

4   We have a *shift–reduce conflict* again; resolving it in favor of *shift*, we get:

$$\text{stack} = (id * id *) \text{ input} = id \ EOF$$

5   *shift*: stack = (*id* * *id* * *id*) input = *EOF*
6   *reduce*: stack = (*id* * *id* * *T*) input = *EOF*

At step 6, the parser fails, since in such state it cannot perform any more actions.

The reasons of the failure, evidently, are the bad grammar and the bad action table.

The example suggests us that an arbitrary choice between *shift* and *reduce* is not recommended, in case some *conflicts*, several alternatives of the parser's actions equally applicable, can take place. In compiler development practice, it happens very often.

So, "blind" CF application of the heuristic to resolve a shift–reduce conflict in favor of shift fails. We'll see below how to struggle with such situations, and how to take into account the context of parsing in the current state.

Shift–reduce and reduce–reduce conflicts and how to resolve them. In general, shift–reduce parsers can have two kinds of conflicts—*shift–reduce* (either a shift action or a reduce action is possible for the given input and current state) or *reduce–reduce* (the parser can perform a *reduce* action by two different rules for the given input and current state).

Shift–reduce conflicts are quite common in compiler practice. For example, the grammar of Sun Pascal language used by *yacc* in the Sun Pascal compiler we were doing for 5 years, had 27 shift–reduce conflicts.

In practice, compiler developers use one or more heuristics to resolve them. The simplest one would be to always resolve a shift–reduce conflict in favor of *shift*, but as the above example shows, it can lead to the failure of the parser.

Usually, shift–reduce conflicts happen in parsing expressions because the priorities of the operators used in the expression are not fully determined by the grammar and from the context.

So, the right approach to resolve shift–reduce conflicts is to explicitly indicate *operator precedences* in the grammar, in the rules where ambiguity is possible. Such method is implemented in *yacc*.

Reduce–reduce conflicts are also quite common, since most grammars of real programming languages contain a lot of "redenotation" rules, especially for identifiers, as shown in the example below:

type_id -> id

var_id -> id

If two such rules are used, the parser has no way to make a reasonable choice of the rule to make a *reduce* action, without "consulting" the semantic analysis phase (see Chapter 5).

More exactly, the parser should take a look at a semantic table of all definitions trying to determine what kind of an identifier it is and which of the alternative rules is therefore suitable to make a *reduce* action.

The principles of LR parsing: LR(0) items. Now we are in a good position to discuss the principles of an LR parser.

For each construct of the source language, there can be several alternatives of its syntax.

So the idea is to let the parser remember all these alternatives by considering all applicable rules at each moment, and the status of the right part of each rule to be considered.

The parser should know the current *position* in each rule it is taking into account, that is, which part of the construct whose syntax is defined by the rule has already been parsed and which is not yet. Let's denote the current position in the rule by dot (.).

Information on the current position should be part of the *state* of the parser.

For example:

$X \to .y$—the parser is starting to parse the construct X;
$X \to z.t$—the parser is parsing the construct X somewhere inside;
$X \to w.$—the parser has already parsed X; so it can potentially do
        reduce $(X \to w)$.

Let *LR(0) item* be a rule $X \to y$ with *position before, inside, or after* the right part y, marked by a dot (.)

Each *state* of the LR parser will be defined as a *set of LR(0) items.*

An *LR(0) item* is the syntax rule with a dot standing somewhere in its right part—either before its first symbol (in case a construct is only started to be parsed), or somewhere inside (in case the parser has already analyzed some part of the construct only), or after the last symbol (in case the parser has finished analyzing the construct and as the next step a *reduce* action according to this rule is possible).

Each state of LR parser will be defined as a *set of LR(0) items* fully describing all the constructs being regarded by the parser at a moment.

LR parser: The augmented grammar. Let $G = <V_t, V_n, P, S>$ be a CF grammar.

As usual, V_t, is a set of terminal symbols (in other words, tokens), V_n is a set of nonterminal symbols (syntax constructs of the language), P is a set of rules, and S from V_n is a starting symbol.

For the purpose of LR parsing, to guarantee that the starting symbol does not occur to the right parts of the rules, we define an *augmented* grammar G' whose language is evidently the same as that of the grammar G.

We add a new starting symbol S' and the only new rule $S' \to S$.

From now on, the specific "starting" LR(0) item $S' \to .S$ will correspond to the *initial state* of the parser, and the specific "final" LR(0) item $S' \to S.$ will correspond to the final state of the parser.

The closure function for LR(0) items. Now let's define the *closure* function—one of the basics of an LR parser.

Recall that any parser state will be represented as a *set of LR(0) items*.

So the *closure* function is defined on any I, a set of LR(0) items, and its result *closure(I)* will also be a (wider) set of LR(0) items.

The goal of the *closure* function is the following: to take into account all possible subconstructs (and sub-subconstructs, etc.) whose parsing is started in the current state of the parser.

The basic idea is as follows: If I contains a rule whose right part starts with a nonterminal B, then we add to *closure(I)* all the LR(0) items based on the syntax rules for B, with the dot standing before the first symbols of their right parts. Then we should apply this mechanism recursively because the new LR(0) items may also start with nonterminals, and so on.

The scheme of the algorithm for constructing the *closure* function [5] is given below:

```
Algorithm closure:
Let I - set of LR(0) items. Construct closure(I).
1. For each x in I, add x to closure(I)
2. Repeat the following step until no more items
   can be added
   to closure(I):
   for each A -> x.By in closure(I)
   such that B in Vₙ and the rule B -> z belongs to P,
   add an LR(0) item B ->.z to closure(I)
```

Example: Let $P = \{ S' \to E , E \to E+P , E \to P , P \to (E) , P \to id \}$
Let $I = \{ S' \to .E \}$.
Then, *closure (I)* = $\{ S' \to .E , E \to .E+P , E \to .P , P \to .(E), P \to .id \}$

From the example, it is clearly seen that for an initial rule $S \to E$, the closure consists of five LR(0) items involving all five rules of this very simple grammar that defines the syntax of expressions.

So, a closure of I can be substantially larger than the initial set I.

The goto function for LR(0) items. The second basic function of LR parser is the *goto(I, X)* function. As well as for the *closure* function, I is a set of LR(0) items. The result of the *goto* function is a set of LR(0) items.

The purpose of the *goto* function is as follows.

Any action of the LR parser—*shift* or *reduce*—can be regarded as "passing" the symbol X of the grammar, that is, switching the parser to the appropriate new state after "passing" the symbol X.

The *shift* action corresponds to "passing" a terminal symbol X, that is, to scan the next token and shift X onto the parser stack, together with the new current state of the parser.

The *reduce* action corresponds to "passing" a nonterminal symbol X, that is, to replacement by X on the parser's stack the right part of a syntax rule whose left part is X.

Please note that $goto(I, X)$ can be empty for some I and X. It means that in the current state I, it is *not possible to "pass" X* in any way.

From a formal viewpoint, the *goto* function is defined very simply, as shown below [5]:

```
Algorithm goto:
Let I - set of LR(0) items, X in (Vt +Vn).
Construct goto (I, X).
 for each  A -> a.Xb  in  I,
 add  all LR(0) items  A -> aX.b  to  goto(I, X)  .
```

So we take each LR(0) item from I where the dot is standing before X, move the dot after X, and thus get a new LR(0) item for $goto(I, X)$.

Please note that this method does not depend on whether X is a terminal or a nonterminal symbol of the grammar.

Example: Let $I = \{ S' -> .E \}$, and P is defined as in the above example for the *closure* function. Then:

$$J = closure(I) = \{ S' -> .E \text{ , } E -> .E+P \text{ , } E -> .P \text{ , } P -> .(E), P -> .id \}$$
$$K = goto(J, E) = \{S' -> E. \text{ , } E -> E.+P\}$$
$$L = goto(J, +) = \emptyset \quad M = goto(K, +) = \{E -> E+.P\}$$

Please note that, for the example grammar, for the initial state J, there is no $goto(J, +)$, that is, according to this grammar, an expression cannot start with the "+" symbol.

The canonical collection of sets of LR(0) items. Now, having defined the basic $closure(I)$ and $goto(I, X)$ functions, we can proceed with generating the *set of states* for the LR parser.

Since each state is a *set of LR(0) items*, we'll be constructing the set of states of LR parser as a set of sets of LR(0) items, or, in other words, a (canonical) collection of sets of LR(0) items.

Let's denote the resulting collection C.

We'll construct C as the collection of the kind: $\{I_0, I_1, ..., I_m\}$, where each of the component sets is a *state* of the parser, that is, a set of LR(0) items.

The idea of constructing C is simple: The initial state I_0 is constructed as the *closure* of the "starting" rule of the augmented grammar, and each of the subsequent states is constructed as a *goto* from some of the previous state J, and some grammar symbol X, if the *goto(J, X)* set is not empty, and if it is a new set, not constructed already on some of the previous steps.

More exactly, we add a new state to C if it can be constructed either by shifting by some terminal symbol X or by reducing by a rule whose left part is X.

The scheme of the algorithm is as follows [5]:

```
Algorithm to construct C -
the canonical collection of sets of LR(0) items :
  1. Let I0 = closure { S' -> .S } -
     the initial state (set of LR(0) items)
  2. For each I already in C
         for each LR(0) item A -> α.xβ in I
         where x is a terminal
             add J = goto(I, x) to C
             in case J is not already in C
  3. For each I already in C
         for each LR(0) item B -> γ. in I
             add the set K = goto(I, B) to C
             in case K is not already in C
  4. Repeat steps 2 and 3 until no more sets can
     be added to C
```

SLR parser: Constructing the parsing tables. The kind of LR parser based on the above definitions of *LR(0) items*, *closure*, and *goto* functions is referred to as *SLR parser* (for *simple LR parser*). Now let's construct the parsing tables of *SLR* parser.

At first, we should construct $C = \{I_0, I_1, ..., I_m\}$—a canonical collection of sets of LR(0) items, as shown before. This will be the set of states of our parser.

Next, we are to define two tables: *action[k, x]* and *goto[k, Y]*, where k is the (*number of*) the current state, x is the current input—a terminal symbol or *EOF* (to be "passed" as the result of the *shift* action)—and Y is a nonterminal symbol to be "passed" as the result of the reduce action.

The choice of the *action* as *shift* is trivial and is based on our previous definition of the *goto* function, as shown below:

- For each (k, x) such that $goto(I_k, x) = I_j$, let *action[k, x] = shift j*.
- For each (k, x) such that an LR(0) item *A->a.* is in I_k and x is in *Follow(A)*, let *action[k, x] = reduce (A->a)*.

- If the LR(0) item $S'->S.$ is in I_k, and x is *EOF*, let *action[k, x]* = *accept*.
- For all the rest of the pairs *(k, x)*, let *action[k, x]* = *error*.
- For each *(k, Y)*, let *goto[k, Y]* = *j*, if there exists *j* such that *goto(I_k, Y) = I_j*; otherwise *goto(k, Y)* is undefined.
- If there exists a conflict in *action* or *goto* tables defined above, then, the grammar under consideration is not an SLR(0) grammar.

What is nontrivial is the choice of an appropriate input symbol for *reduce*. The problem is as follows: Which should be the input symbol *x* suitable for the *reduce* action? What should be the restriction on the input *x* in this case?

The other condition for *reduce* is obvious: The corresponding LR(0) item with the dot *after* the right part should belong to the current state.

The critical selection for the SLR parser is to perform *reduce* when *x* belongs to *Follow(A)*, where *A* is the left part of the syntax rule to be used for reduction. As we'll see later on, this selection is too restrictive and is suitable only for very simple languages, referred to as *SLR* languages.

Another notable issue is related to possible *conflicts* that could arise from such kind of constructing the parser tables.

From a formal viewpoint, if, according to the parsing table construction rules presented above, we have at least one conflict, that is, more than one alternative to fill out a cell of the *action* or *goto* table, we say *the grammar is not SLR(0)*, so we cannot construct appropriate parsing tables.

Non-SLR grammars and languages. Example. As the readers may have guessed, all the realistic programming languages are not *SLR*.

A simple example to demonstrate that is shown below:

$S -> L := R$

$L -> id$

$L -> id \char`\^$

$R -> L$

This is a simplified grammar of Pascal assignment statement whose left and right parts can be either variable identifiers, or indirect variables (the result of dereferencing a pointer).

We see from this example that an SLR parser would have a fundamental shift–reduce conflict when parsing a very simple statement like $id \char`\^ := id$: if the input is ":=," on reducing by L-> id ^, we have L on the stack and ":=" as input; so either *reduce (R->L)* or *shift(":=")* is possible. The reduce action is obviously wrong, since it leads to the failure of the parser.

The only reasonable decision that can be deduced from the example is to take into account in the parser's states the current context—the lookahead symbol.

In the above example, if we could "explain" to the parser that it should *not* make a *reduce* action when the lookahead is ":=" (the assignment token in Pascal), then the problem would be solved.

So, we come to the idea that we should add the current input to the LR(0) item, to more completely specify the states of the parser.

LR(1) items. We have just come to the idea of the *LR(1) item.* LR(1) item is actually an *LR(0) item* augmented by a *lookahead symbol x*—a terminal or *EOF*.

Formally, the LR(1) item is a pair *[A->x.y, a]*, where the rule *A -> xy* belongs to the grammar; *a* is a symbol from *(V_t + {EOF})*; the dot stands somewhere either before the right part, or inside, or after the right part.

Please note that the lookahead symbol is necessary for the *reduce* action only.

In all other cases, the second member of the LR(1) item is useless.

Namely, our parser will make a reduce only if the current state contains an LR(1) item, with the dot standing after the right part, and with the second member of *x* being exactly the same symbol as the current input (lookahead).

Later on, we'll define the analogs of *closure, goto,* and *the canonical collection* on the base of a new concept of an *LR(1) item.*

So, the main idea of this most general kind of LR parsers is to take into account all possible reductions with all possible lookaheads, and to filter out improper reductions (with the improper lookaheads).

However, we should understand what will be the overhead of transforming the states of the parser in such a way. Since, theoretically, the number of LR(1) items corresponding to one LR(0) item can be as large as the size of the terminal alphabet of the grammar, the total number of states of the LR(1) parser can be *t* times larger than for SLR parser, where *t* is the size of the terminal alphabet of the grammar.

Practically speaking, if the SLR parser has 1000 states, and the number of terminal symbols of the grammar is 30, the LR(1) parser may have 30,000 states.

The closure function for LR(1) items. At first, please let's define the *closure* function for LR(1) items. Similar to that for LR(0) items, the goal of the *closure* function is to take into consideration the start of parsing all *subconstructs* of the constructs currently being parsed.

The scheme of the algorithm to construct the closure function for LR(1) items is the following [5]:

```
Algorithm:  I - set of LR(1) items.
Construct closure(I).
```

```
1) For each x in I, add x to closure(I)
2) Repeat the following step until no more items
   can be added to closure(I):
   for each  [A -> x.By, a]  in closure(I)
   such that B in Vn and B -> z in P,
       for each b in First(ya)
       add an LR(1) item [B ->.z, b] to closure(I)
```

The algorithm looks very similar to the algorithm of constructing *closure* for LR(0) items.

But the readers should understand the fundamental difference between the algorithms at step 2, due to introducing the second member of the pair—the lookahead symbol. This is actually a more general (and more complicated) condition of reduce, as compared with the SLR parser. Namely, we add new members to *closure(I)*, taking into account all cases when the dots in the LR(1) items stand before nonterminals followed by *empty-generating* chains, and also the cases when it is not so. It is the condition:

b in First(ya)

that takes into account both kinds of these cases.

So, as you can already see even from the above considerations, in LR(1) parsers, the conditions of the reduction are context-dependent, and much more carefully tracked, as compared with SLR(0) parsers.

The goto function for LR(1) items. As the next step for constructing LR(1) parser, let's define the *goto* function, similar to the *goto* function for LR(0) items. Here is the scheme of the algorithm to evaluate the *goto* function for LR(1) items [5]:

```
Algorithm: I - set of LR(1) items, X in (Vt + Vn).
Construct goto(I,X).
for each [ A -> a.Xb, z] in I,
    add all LR(1) items from closure({[A -> aX.b, z]})
        to goto(I, X)
```

As can be seen from the above algorithm scheme, the process of constructing the *goto* function for LR(1) parser is just the same as for the SLR parser.

The only difference is the second member of each LR(1) item is the presence of the lookahead, but it does not take part in the process of constructing the *goto* function.

The canonical collection of sets of LR(1) items for LR(1) parser. Now let's construct the set of states *C* for the LR(1) parser based on LR(1) items:

$$C = \{I_0, I_1, \ldots I_m\}$$

We'll refer to the parser based on this canonical collection as a *canonical* LR parser.

Similar to SLR parser, each state is represented by a set of LR(1) items, so we'll construct the set of states C as a set (or collection) of sets of LR(1) items $I_0, I_1, \ldots I_m$.

But, unlike the SLR parser, the canonical LR parser performs a *reduce* action only if the corresponding LR(1) item, with the dot standing after the right part of the rule, belongs to the current state, and (the most important) if the current input symbol *a* is exactly the same symbol as the second member of the LR(1) item.

In other words, the canonical LR(1) parser performs reductions by a rule *A -> y* only if an LR(1) item *[A -> y., a]* belongs to the current state, where *a* is the input.

The scheme of the algorithm of constructing the set of states C [5] is just the same as for SLR parser: We take the initial state (formed as a *closure* of the "starting" LR(1) item) and then try to construct possible next states as the results of *goto* function, applied to the current state and to any symbol that has a dot standing before it in any of the LR(1) items belonging to the current state:

```
Algorithm to construct C = {I₀, I₁, … Iₘ}     -
the collection of sets of LR(1) items
for the canonical LR(1) parser:
    1. let I₀ = closure ({[S′ -> .S, EOF]})     -
       the initial state (set of LR(1) items.
    2. for each I already in C
          for each LR(1) item [A -> α.xβ, y] in I
          where x is a terminal
          and y in Vₜ + EOF,
             add J = goto(I, x) to C,
             in case J is not already in C.
    3. for each I already in C
          for each LR(1) item [B -> γ. , z] in  I
             add the set K = goto(I, B) to C,
             in case K is not already in C
    4) repeat steps 2 and 3
  until no more I-sets can be added to C.
```

The parsing tables for the canonical LR(1) parser. Let $C = \{I_0, I_1, \ldots I_m\}$—the canonical collection of sets of LR(1) items. To each of the sets, I_k corresponds to a *state* number *k* of the canonical LR(1) parser.

The *action* and *goto* tables for canonical LR parser are constructed the same way as for the SLR parser, with the only difference: The *reduce* action is stored in a cell of the *action* table only in case the current input *x* is exactly the same symbol as the second member of any LR(1) item (with the dot standing after the right part of the rule) belonging to the current state.

As usual, if there exists a conflict when constructing the LR(1) parser table, that is, if there is more than one candidate action for a cell of the *action* table, then the grammar is not LR(1).

Here is the scheme of the algorithm to construct the parsing tables for the canonical LR(1) parser [5]:

```
Algorithm: Constructing the action and the goto
parsing tables
for the canonical LR(1) parser.
1. for each (k, x) such that goto(Iₖ, x) = Iⱼ,
       let action[k, x] = shift j
2. for each (k, x) such that
    an LR(1) item [A->a.  , z] is in Iₖ,
    and x = z ,
       let action[k, x] = reduce (A->a)
3. if the LR(1) item [S'->S.  , EOF] belongs to Iₖ
       let action[k, x] = accept
4. for all the rest of the pairs (k,x)
       let action[k, x] = error
5. for each (k,Y)
       if there exists j such that goto(Iₖ, Y) = Iⱼ
       let goto[k,Y] = j
       otherwise goto(k,Y) is undefined
6. if there exists a conflict
    in action or goto tables defined above,
then the grammar under consideration is not an
LR(1) grammar.
```

From canonical LR(1) tables to LALR(1) tables. The canonical LR parser thus constructed is the most general kind of LR parsers. It covers the syntax of vast majority of the programming languages.

In our further considerations, let's call the *core* of an LR(1) item the first member of the LR(1) item pair—the rule with the dot. For any LR(1) item *[A->x.y, b]*, its *core* is the LR(0) item *A->x.y.*

The canonical LR(1) parser has one major shortcoming—its number of states is too big. The reason is clear: When we make a transition from LR(0) items to LR(1) items, we actually multiply the number of states to the size of the terminal alphabet because there appears to be many LR(1) items with the same core, but different second members—looka-heads *a, b, c,* and so on.

So, a very natural idea arises: What if we combine LR(1) items of the kind: (*core*, *a*/*b*/*c*), instead of having those almost repeated LR(1) items with the same core?

It will help us to reduce the number of states to the number of states of SLR parser, but nevertheless don't lose the precise style of the canonical LR parser.

The semantics of the "combined" LR(1) item will be as follows: The *reduce* action by the rule *core* can be performed if the current symbol is *a OR b OR c*.

This is exactly the idea of the LALR(1) parser—a modified version of the canonical LR(1) parser, with the concept of LR(1) items updated as explained before, and the states obtained from the states of the canonical LR(1) parser by *sticking the states with the same cores*.

Speaking a bit more formally, to construct the LALR(1) parser tables, let's take any $I = I_k$, set of LR(1) items, and replace all multiple items *[A -> x.y, a_1]*, ..., *[A -> x.y, a_n]* belonging to this state by *a single* LR(1) item of the kind: *[A -> x.y, a_1 | ... | a_n]*, which means that reduction is possible with any of a_1, ..., a_n as the input.

Intuitively, due to the definition of the *goto* function, it should preserve the above "sticking" transformation, so there will be no conflicts when transforming the states of the canonical LR parser to states of the LALR parser. However, some modern researchers notice that there are LR(1) grammars that are non-LALR(1).

LALR parsers are as powerful as canonical LR parsers because they take into account exactly the same parsing states and perform the corresponding actions.

This is just an overview but, as we believe, quite enough to understand the basics of LALR parsing (which is not always quite understandable by students). Further details of LALR parsing are beyond the framework of our book (see Reference 5).

LALR parsing is the basis of the classical UNIX compiler development tool named *yacc* (Yet Another Compiler Compiler) [19] and *yacc's* clones like *bison* [20].

The *yacc* tool will be considered later in this chapter.

4.5 ERROR RECOVERY IN LR PARSING

Similar to our considerations for recursive descent parsing, let's now consider the issues of *error recovery* in LR parsing.

Whereas, for recursive descent parsers, more or less intelligent *panic mode* and skipping the source until a synchronizing token are the most appropriate kinds of error recovery, for LR parsers, *phrase-level recovery* is the most suitable error recovery technique, since it is much more comfortable to perform in bottom-up parsing.

Recovery actions should be undertaken each time an LR parser detects the *error* action in its *action* table for the current state and the current input.

A typical error recovery action is as follows. When part of some handle for a certain grammar rule is already on the stack, the LR parser skips the input until a symbol in *Follow(X)* where *X* is the left part of the rule.

Then, the parser performs a *reduce* action by this rule, as if the handle were fully on the stack, and continues parsing.

Here is the scheme of phase-level recovery algorithm:

```
    Phrase-level recovery algorithm:
1.  Let for (k,y) where k is a the current state and
    y is the input, action[k,y] = error
2.  Skip the input until any z in Follow(X) + {EOF}
    where X is a nonterminal, the item X->a.b belongs
    to the current state, and part of the handle ab
    already shifted to the stack
3.  Perform the action reduce (X->ab)
4.  Continue LR parsing
```

Another kind of error recovery widely used in *yacc* and its clones is referred to as *error productions*.

Error production is a grammar rule that contains a specific nonterminal symbol *error*.

Typically, this rule is a kind of "complementary" ("error catching") rule, in addition to some "main" rule for syntax of a construct (like *statement*).

An example of such pair of "main" and the "complementary" rule for the syntax of *X* and is given below:

X -> a b

X-> a error

The recovery action is obvious: If a *reduce* action according to the main rule is not possible, but part of the handle *(a)* is already on the stack, the parser skips until *Follow(X)* and performs the *reduce* action according to the "error catching" rule.

Then, the parsing continues.

4.6 THE *YACC* PARSER GENERATOR

The most widely used compiler development utility since 1970s is *yacc* [19]. The *yacc* utility was developed by Johnson who also designed the *Portable C Compiler* (*PCC*) and the related, widely used intermediate representation of programs—*PCC trees* [54]. PCC trees will be discussed in Chapter 5.

Both *yacc* and PCC trees are classics of compiler development, still being used by commercial compiler developers for more than 30 years.

During that period of time, there appeared a lot of clones and variations of *yacc*.

That's why it is so important to learn the *yacc* principles that remain unchanged.

Yacc is essentially an *LALR(1) parser generator*. It takes an extended LR(1) grammar and generates LALR(1) parsing tables. The parser itself is part of the *yacc* library—*liby.a* (in UNIX notation).

In addition, *yacc* also generates a *semantic analyzer*, based on the *semantic actions* attached to each rule of the input LR grammar.

Both the *LR parser* and the *semantic analyzer* generated by *yacc* are major parts of the *compiler front-end*, so we can regard *yacc* as a *compiler front-end generator*.

The *input file* of *yacc* (used to have the name extension of .*y*) is a specification of LR grammar of the source language, enhanced by *syntax-directed translation schemes* for each syntax rule. It means that, for each syntax rule, there are *semantic actions* associated to that rule.

In *yacc*, semantic actions are defined in C, and the output of *yacc* is also generated in C.

The output of *yacc* is LALR(1) parser tables (stored into the file *yy.tab.c*) and the header file *yy.tab.h* with token classes and other related definitions.

As for the LALR parser itself, it is implemented in *yacc* as the *yyparse()* routine and is located in the *yacc* library (*liby.a* in UNIX version).

The following clones and enhancements of *yacc* are known:

- *bison* [20]—a GNU product, LALR parser generator, an extension of *yacc*;
- *eyacc*—*yacc* with enhanced error recovery, developed by Joy and used in the Sun Pascal compiler;
- *JavaCC* [21]—an analog of *yacc* for the Java platform (see Section 4.6);
- *CoCo/R* [23]—an enhancement of *yacc* for C++, Java, and C# languages;
- *SableCC* [24]—an enhancement of *yacc* for the Java platform with better error recovery.

It should be noted, however, that from a trustworthy compiling viewpoint, the *yacc* output—the parser and the parsing tables—is not perfect, since the parsing tables constitute several big arrays, full of numbers, with no comments, and the parser's function to choose a proper semantic action is a big *switch* statement with thousands of alternatives. Both of them are actually nonreadable and nondebuggable. But, in practice, it doesn't prevent compiler developers from worldwide use of *yacc*.

The *yacc* utility, as well as *lex*, is yet another example of a classical UNIX tool based on *productions* (*rules*). For a parser generator, that is quite natural, since the syntax is based on CF grammar rules.

The syntax of the *yacc* input (*.y*) file is similar to that of the *lex* input file:

```
{%
  defines and includes
%}
  definitions
%%
  rules
%%
user-defined routines
```

The *yacc* input file has four major parts separated by some specific lines, as shown above:

- *defines and includes*—C-specific macro definitions and references to other source files;
- *yacc-specific definitions*—token classes, operators and their precedence, and so on;
- *rules*—syntax-directed translation schemes: CF syntax *rules* and related *semantic actions*;
- *user-defined routines*—whatever routines the user likes to be part of the *yacc*-generated C source, including *yylex* (lexical analyzer), *main* (the starting point of the whole compiler application), and *yyerror*—error diagnostics routine. These three routines are the required minimum the user should provide.

As for the lexical analyzer *yylex()*, it can be either developed "by hand" or generated by *lex*, that is, *lex* and *yacc* can be used together.

Example. Now let's consider an example of using *yacc*—a parser for simplified constant expressions, expressions that consist of integer literals, "+" and "*" operators.

The parser analyzes the syntax of a given constant expression and, as the semantic part, evaluates it, and issues a message with the integer value of the constant expression:

```
{%
#include <stdio.h>
#include <ctype.h>
%}
%token '+'
%token '*'
%token INT
%%H
const_expr:  expr  {  (void) printf("The value is %d\n",
$1);  }
```

```
         ;
expr:    term /* implicit semantic rule: $$ = $1; */
       | expr '+' term { $$ = $1 + $3; }
         ;
term:  primary /* implicit semantic rule: $$ = $1; */
     | term '*' primary { $$ = $1 * $3; }
         ;
primary:  INT    { $$ = atoi($1); }
            | ( expr ) { $$ = $2; }
%%
int yylex()
{ /* lexical analyzer recognizing '+', '*' and INT */ }

int yyerror(const char * msg) /* error diagnostics
routine */
{ (void) fprintf(stderr, "%s\n", msg); }

int main (void)
{
  extern int yyparse(); /* the yacc parser */
  (void) yyparse();
  return 0;
}   /* let example.y be the source file for yacc */
```

The *include* directives used in the *yacc* input file (*example.y*) are just the same as for *lex*—references to input/output routines and to character classification routines.

The %*token* definitions in the next section are *yacc*-specific definitions of *token classes*. In *yacc*, they can be either *token class identifiers*, like *INT*, or explicit *operator symbols*, like "+" or "*."

Token definitions like *INT* are converted by *yacc* into C-specific *define* macro definitions and placed into the output file *yy.tab.h.*

Token definitions like "+" or "*" specify not only operator symbols but also their priorities, or precedence, by textual order of the definitions: The operator symbol defined later has higher priority.

Operator precedence is used for resolving shift–reduce conflicts: For example, if on the parser stack there is a handle containing the "*" operator (like *a * b*), and the input symbol is "+," the parser will choose the *reduce* action, rather than *shift*, because "*" has a higher precedence than "+."

The next section of the example contains the syntax *rules* with *semantic actions.*

The left part of a rule is separated from the right part by colon (:).

The alternatives of syntax for a construct, belonging to one rule, are separated by vertical bars (|).

Each rule is finished by a semicolon (;).

Semantic actions for a rule can be any C statements, and it is highly recommended to put them into curly brackets, even if the semantic action can be expressed by just one C statement. The implicit logic of a rule is as follows: If on the input source there is a construct whose syntax is matched to a syntax pattern, then perform the semantic action indicated for the appropriate syntax alternative.

Please note the specific denotations *$$*, *$1*, *$2*, and so on, used in semantic actions.

The implicit convention of *yacc* is the following. Each nonterminal (or a syntax construct) has its own *semantics*. The semantics of a construct is evaluated by semantic actions in parallel to parsing. Actually, it means that *yacc* has two "parallel" stacks—the *syntax stack* (for parsing) and the *semantic stack* (for semantic evaluation).

More exactly, a semantic action for a rule is executed immediately *before the reduce* action according to the rule. In my teaching and development experience, it appears to be one of the most difficult specifics of *yacc* to understand by students, and even by not very experienced compiler developers.

At the moment before a reduction, the semantics of all symbols of the right part are on the semantic stack, and it is possible to pop them from that stack and use for evaluating the semantics of the left part symbol.

The *$$* symbol denotes the semantics of the left part symbol, and the *$1*, *$2*, and so on symbols denote the semantics of the right part symbols.

By default, the type of the semantic value of a grammar symbol is *integer*.

This is exactly what is needed for our example, since the semantics of a constant expression is just its value. But in other cases, if needed, the type of the semantics can be explicitly redefined to be, for example, some structure type.

In our example, the semantic actions specify how the value of an expression depends on the values of its operands.

For the simplest case—an expression consisting just of an integer literal—the implicit *yacc's* semantic rule works: *$$* = *$1*. Such semantic rules can be omitted.

That is, if a syntax construct is redefined just to be some other construct, their semantics are the same.

The final part of the example contains the definitions of the three routines—*main* (starting point), *yylex* (lexical analyzer used by *yacc*), and *yyerror* (error diagnostics routine used by *yacc*), necessary to make the compiler application complete.

Command-line interface of yacc. The *yacc* utility has command-line user interface. The input file (*example.y* in particular) should be explicitly indicated.

By default, *yacc* generates one output file only in the current directory—*yy.tab.c*, the LALR(1) parsing tables, for example:

```
yacc example.y
```

With *–d* option, *yacc* also generates another file—*yy.tab.h*, where it puts all token definitions, for example:

```
yacc -d example.y
```

Yacc reports on the standard error output the *number of shift–reduce conflicts* and the rules unreachable from the start symbol.

The start symbol for *yacc* is the left part of the textually first rule in the input file.

Please keep in mind that, even if shift–reduce conflicts can be detected, *yacc* resolves them, based on operator precedence.

When compiling the *yacc's* output file *yy.tab.c*, the *–ly* option should be indicated to enable linking with the *yacc* library containing a lot of routines, in particular, *yyparse*—the LALR(1) parser:

```
cc y.tab.c -ly
```

If *yacc* and *lex* are used together, the *two* options *–ll* and *–ly* should be indicated to enable linking both with *lex* and *yacc* libraries:

```
cc y.tab.c lex.yy.c -ly -ll
```

4.7 THE *BISON* PARSER GENERATOR: GENERALIZED LR PARSING

Bison [20] is a yacc-compatible parser generator for C. At the moment of writing the book, the latest version of *bison* available is 2.4.1. It is a GNU product available under GNU public license.

Bison supports both LALR(1) parsing (like *yacc*) and *generalized LR parsing* [55]—the new parsing technique to support more general, *nondeterministic* LR grammars. The input file of bison is similar to that of *yacc*, with one major enhancement: *generalized parsing*.

Generalized parsers were first proposed in [56] for the analysis of natural languages related to the task of machine translation. However, recently, there is a lot of progress in development and practical application of generalized parsers and parser generators. In particular, besides *bison*, a generalized LR parser generator for Haskell [57] is implemented. The idea of generalized parsers is especially attractive, in view of the development of modern highly parallel hardware platforms (e.g., *multi-core* hardware architectures) that enable to really parallelize the activity of the parser clones, to save total compile time. In other words, modern parallel hardware architectures can enable the "dream" of parallel parsing to come true.

Generalized parsing helps to resolve shift–reduce and reduce–reduce conflicts. The generalized parser generation mode can be switched on in *bison* by the special definition:

```
%glr-parser
```

The main ideas of the GLR (generalized LR) parser are as follows. When faced with a shift–reduce or reduce–reduce conflict, GLR parser *clones* the parser to follow *both* alternatives of the conflict, thus, *splitting* the parser into two parsers. In their turn, each of the split parsers can also split in case of new conflicts occurred, and so on. So, during generalized parsing, a tree of such parser clones may exist. Next, if any of the parser clones faces with an internal parsing error (no possible actions to do), it *disappears*. If the two parser clones have reduced the input to an identical set of symbols, they *merge*. From the viewpoint of *bison*'s end users not interested in its internals, it does not make any difference whether a generalized parser is used or not. The only difference is an extra directive or two directives, as follows:

```
%glr-parser
%expect-rr 1
```

The latter directive specifies the expected number of reduce–reduce conflicts, which can be determined by prior ordinary call of *bison* without using the *glr-parser* directive. What is especially important is that no changes in the input grammar are required to apply generalized parsing.

Bison allows the user to explicitly control *precedence* of the ambiguous alternatives, and *merge* of the parser clones' *semantic actions*, if desired. For example, here is a fragment of a grammar to define the syntax of statements, expressions, and declarations:

```
stmt : expr ';' %dprec 1
     | decl %dprec 2
     ;
```

It is a possible reduce–reduce conflict, since, in some cases, the structure of expressions and declarations can be identical, that is, the grammar is essentially ambiguous (see Reference 20 for more details). From the generalized parser model, that means that the two parser clones that parse both alternatives should merge. But, in this case, the parser must take a deterministic decision which alternative to give priority after merging. The *%dprec* directive helps the parser to do that: The priority is given to the *declaration* alternative.

If, instead of resolving the conflict, the user would like to see all the parsing alternatives, the semantic actions of those should be *merged* as follows:

```
stmt : expr ';' %merge <stmtMerge>
     | decl %merge <stmtMerge>
     ;
```

where *stmtMerge* is the user-defined semantic function for both alternatives (for example, it can print out the parsing results). See Reference 20 for details.

4.8 THE *YACC++, JAVACC, SABLECC, ANTLR,* AND *COCO/R* OBJECT-ORIENTED PARSER GENERATORS

There are several parser generators, quite popular worldwide, that follow and enhance the traditions of LR(1) or LL(1) parsing, and are capable to handle parsing conflicts. This section summarizes the most common parser generators. Their common feature is that all of these parser generators are object-oriented.

> *The yacc++ parser generator* [58]. It is an analog of *yacc* for the C++ language. However, it is not just the C++ clone of *yacc*. Instead, it provides a comfortable set of object-oriented tools (in the form of the *Language Objects Library* accompanying *yacc++*) to support developing lexical analyzers, parsers, AST, and error handling.
>
> Here is a simple example of *yacc++* input grammar that combines the lexical analyzer and the parser definition:

```
class example;  // LR(1) grammar which is not
  LALR(1)
lexer
token       proc_name macro_name var_name ;
parser
sentence    : proc_name argument  "."
            | proc_name parameter  ";"
            | macro_name argument  ";"
            | macro_name parameter  "."
            ;
argument    : var_name ;
parameter   : var_name ;
```

The above grammar is LR(1) but not LALR(1) [58]. However, *yacc++* handles such grammars, unlike *yacc*.

Here is a brief overview of major features *yacc++* supports:

- *discard token* declarations, to define tokens of simple structure, like *comments*, fully analyzed by the lexer but not passed to parser (discarded);

- *public* declarations, to define the syntax notions (e.g., block, statement, expression) to be parsed, alongside with the entire compilation unit; at runtime, it is possible to construct, for example, a parser object to parse an expression only; such technique is helpful for various kinds of incremental compilers;
- *ignore* declarations, to specify the fragments of input text (like preprocessor directives) to be shifted and processed by the parser, but not stored into the parser stack and don't influence to the parser states.

The JavaCC Parser Generator [21]. JavaCC generates recursive descent parsers in Java. So, its popularity is mostly due to the popularity of the Java platform, and simplicity of recursive descent, as we've already noted above in this chapter. The input file of JavaCC contains both the lexer and the parser specifications. If the input grammar is not LL(1), JavaCC allows for resolving shift–shift conflicts by lookahead, which allows using semantic information for conflict resolution. Unlike many other parser generators, JavaCC allows us to use EBNF constructs (which is quite comfortable) in defining input grammars. Similar to *yacc++*, JavaCC supports special tokens ignored by parsing (for processing purely lexical constructs, like comments). JavaCC enables good error diagnostics. An extra advantage of JavaCC is its good debugging capabilities: The user can track down in detail both lexical analysis and parsing.

Here is a small self-evident example of an input file for JavaCC to specify the syntax of a list of identifiers (the file should have the *.jj* extension):

```
void identifier_list()  :
{}
{
  <ID> ( "," <ID> )*
}
```

The SableCC parser generator [24]. SableCC is an object-oriented lexical analyzer generator, LALR(1) parser generator, and AST framework generator. All the compiler code is generated in Java. Here is a simple example of a translator of expressions into postfix form written in SableCC. The name of the file is *postfix.grammar*:

```
Package postfix;
Tokens
number = ['0' .. '9']+;
plus = '+';
minus = '-';
mult = '*';
div = '/';
```

```
mod = '%';
l_par = '(';
r_par = ')';
blank = (' ' | 13 | 10)+;
Ignored Tokens
blank;
Productions
expr =
{factor} factor |
{plus} expr plus factor |
{minus} expr minus factor;
factor =
{term} term |
{mult} factor mult term |
{div} factor div term |
{mod} factor mod term;
term =
{number} number |
{expr} l_par expr r_par;
```

To generate the compiler, SableCC should be called the following way typical of Java applications:

```
java SableCC postfix.grammar
```

SableCC will generate Java code, with the main compiler class named *Compiler*. So, to compile the generated Java code, the user should invoke the following command:

```
javac postfix\Compiler.java  .
```

To call the compiler's Java bytecode, the following command should be used:

```
java postfix.Compiler
```

The generated Java code of the compiler is as follows:

```
package postfix;
import postfix.parser.*;
import postfix.lexer.*;
import postfix.node.*;
import java.io.*;
public class Compiler
{
```

```
public static void main(String[] arguments)
{
    try
    {
        System.out.println("Type an arithmetic
        expression:");
        // Create a Parser instance.
        Parser p =
          new Parser(
            new Lexer(
              new PushbackReader(
                new InputStreamReader(System.in),
                1024)));
        // Parse the input.
        Start tree = p.parse();
        // Apply the translation.
        tree.apply(new Translation());
    }
    catch(Exception e)
    {
        System.out.println(e.getMessage());
    }
}
}
```

The generated compiler code is given here for the readers to understand the specifics of modern object-oriented compiler construction. As
can be seen from the code, the compiler phases of lexical analysis and
parsing are represented as objects of the corresponding classes, and the
parsing itself is initiated by calling the *parse* instance method of the
Parser class.

To handle AST, SableCC provides a framework and Java code patterns for tree walkers and visitors. SableCC provides a good error recovery mechanism.

Due to its convenience and advanced features, SableCC is now therefore one of the most popular lexer and parser generators for the Java
platform.

ANTLR parser generator [22]. We already considered this lexical analyzer
and parser generator and its features to support lexical analysis in
Chapter 3. ANTLR was developed as a Java port of Purdue Compiler
Construction Tool Set (PCCTS) [59], an earlier research product aimed
to compiler generation in C++. With the new version of ANTLR, the set
of its target compiler generation platforms has been substantially
expanded. Now ANTLR can generate compiler code in Java, C, C++,
Python, C#, ActionScript, and JavaScript languages. As we should note,

that rich set of target platforms is unique among the compiler generators yet known. From the parsing features viewpoint, ANTLR supports LL(k) parsing and provides mechanism for resolving shift–shift conflicts. ANTLR also offers a variety of features for generation and further analysis of ASTs.

Here is an example that demonstrates the format of the ANTLR input file (which should have the *.g* name extension) and shows how ANTLR helps to resolve parsing conflicts using semantic information:

```
statement:
  {isTypeName(LT(1))}? ID ID ";" | // declaration
  "type varName;"
  ID "=" expr ";" ; // assignment
```

This fragment of the grammar specifies the syntax of a statement that can be either a type declaration or an assignment (such situation is quite common for many programming languages). The method to distinguish between the two alternatives is to look at the semantic table to find out whether the identifier is a type name or not. If so, the statement is recognized as a type declaration, otherwise as an assignment.

Below is the corresponding fragment of the code generated by ANTLR, with the appropriate parsing logic:

```
if( LA(1)==ID && isTypeName(LT(1)))
{
   // match the first alternative
}
else if (LA(1)==ID)
{
   // match the second alternative
}
else error;
```

In the generated code, *LA(1)* is the first lookahead token; *isTypeName (name)* is the semantic method to check if the given name is a type identifier.

Please see other ANTLR examples in Chapter 3.

The parser generator CoCo/R [23]. CoCo/R is yet another LL(k) parser generator, with the capability to resolve parsing conflicts by the *resolvers* mechanism implemented in CoCo/R. The set of target compiler code generation platforms for CoCo/R is as follows: Java, C++, Delphi, Modula-2, and Oberon. The example below shows the grammar production (with semantic attributes evaluation rules) for variable declarations in a Pascal-like language:

```
VarDeclaration<ref int adr> (. string name;
                                 TypeDesc type;  .)
= Ident<out name> (. Obj x = symTab.Enter(name);
                int n = 1;  .)
{ ',' Ident<out name> (. Obj y = symTab.
Enter(name);
                        x.next = y; x = y;
                        n++;  .)
}
':' Type<out type> (. adr += n * type.size;
                    for (int a = adr; x != null; x
                    = x.next) {
                      a -= type.size;
                      x.adr = a;
                    }  .)
';'  .
```

The core syntax production for the above specification is:

```
VarDeclaration = Ident {',' Ident } ':' Type ';'.
```

Semantic attributes will be covered in Chapter 5. In CoCo/R, there are *output* attributes (like <out name>) that specify the parameters of the symbols. There can also be *input* attributes for passing information to the grammar rule symbols.

Here is the code generated by CoCo/R for parsing according to the above production:

```
void VarDeclaration(ref int adr) {
    string name; TypeDesc type;
    Ident(out name);
    Obj x = symTab.Enter(name);
    int n = 1;
    while (la.kind == comma) {
        Get();
        Ident(out name);
        Obj y = symTab.Enter(name);
        x.next = y; x = y;
        n++;
    }
    Expect(colon);
    Type(out type);
    adr += n * type.size;
    for (int a = adr; x != null; x = x.next) {
        a -= type.size;
        x.adr = a;
```

```
    }
    Expect(semicolon);
}
```

The code generated by CoCo/R is similar to our model of recursive descent parsing considered above in this chapter. In particular, CoCo/R uses the *Expect* routine to "eat" mandatory tokens (similar to our *eat* routine). The above code is self-evident.

CoCo/R is quite popular and comfortable. We use CoCo/R in a number of our research projects.

To summarize the content of this chapter, we have considered a variety of approaches to parsing, syntax error recovery, and parsing conflict resolution, from the simplest ones as recursive descent to far more sophisticated and covering wider class of input languages—LR parsing and generalized parsing.

We also overviewed classical and modern parser generators that constitute state of the art in this area.

So, as the readers may have realized, modern compiler developers typically don't have to develop lexical analyzers and parsers "from scratch." There are several widely approved and used schemes and tools for lexical analyzer and parser generation that help to automate the process of compiler development, and to receive the resulting quite readable, understandable, and trustworthy code of the lexer and the parser, augmented by semantic actions, with built-in mechanisms of error recovery and resolving conflicts. So the progress in lexer and parser generators is evident. However, programming languages are also progressing and developing, so lexer and parser generators still remain quite a challenging research and development area for compiler experts.

In particular, in Chapter 10, we offer our own compiler generator, Phoenix-FETE [60], intended to be used together with Microsoft Phoenix [3] compiler back-end development toolkit.

EXERCISES TO CHAPTER 4

4.1 Implement a lexical analyzer for Pascal in C#, including *lookAhead* and *stepBack* routines.

4.2 Continue the work of Exercise 4.1 to develop a recursive descent parser for a subset of Pascal, at least, for its statements.

4.3 Correct the grammar in the example in Section 4.3 to allow a shift–reduce parser to work correctly.

4.4 Investigate the grammar of C# and explain why it is not SLR.

4.5 Construct the canonical collection of sets of LR(0) items for the grammar of expressions defined in the examples to this chapter.

4.6 Design and implement in Java or C# a representation of the CF grammar, construction of the *goto* and the *closure* functions, and construction of the parsing tables for SLR(0) parser and for the canonical LR(1) parser.

4.7 Implement in Java or C# the transformation of canonical LR(1) parsing tables to LALR(1) parsing tables—"sticking" the states with the same cores.

4.8 Provide practical examples where phrase-level error recovery is more helpful, as compared with panic mode.

4.9 Finish the example of using *yacc* considered in Section 4.5: Define *yylex()* and test the resulting parser against concrete examples of constant expressions.

4.10 Implement a lexical analyzer and a parser for a subset of Pascal using ANTLR, CoCo/R, yacc++, bison, JavaCC, and SableCC parser generators; compare the time and the efforts spent; and estimate the advantages and shortcomings of the approaches taken in either of the tools.

Chapter *5*

Semantic Analysis and Typing: Efficient and Trustworthy Techniques

Now let's proceed with the next phase of the compilation—*semantic analysis*.

We have already touched this topic before when discussing parser generators in Chapter 4. We have seen that a common approach to semantic analysis is *syntax-directed*, that is, tying semantic actions to syntax rules specifying the constructs of the source language.

This chapter, in addition to basic concepts and overview of known techniques, covers our own view of semantic analysis, our efficient semantic analysis algorithms we implemented for Sun Pascal compiler in the 1990s, patented by four U.S. patents [25,61–63], and our methods invented and implemented before, in the 1970s–1980s, in Pascal and CLU compilers for "Elbrus" computers [2].

Our semantic analysis algorithms described in this chapter are proven to be faster than those offered by classical compiler textbooks [5]. Detailed analysis and comparison is provided.

5.1 BASIC CONCEPTS AND PRINCIPLES OF SEMANTIC ANALYSIS

Semantic analysis (also referred to as *context-dependent analysis*, or *type-dependent* analysis) is the next compilation phase after parsing.

Actually, the phases of parsing and semantic analysis are not always implemented as separate passes of the source program, but can be fully or partially combined, as can be seen from the examples of parser generators in

Trustworthy Compilers, by Vladimir O. Safonov
Copyright © 2010 John Wiley & Sons, Inc.

Chapter 4, where the syntax definitions and the semantic actions are joined in input grammar specifications.

To speak more formally, the input of semantic analysis is the parse tree of the source program. Actually, in modern compilers, the input of semantic analysis is *abstract syntax tree* (*AST*), a more abstract form of parse tree, with the nodes for delimiters omitted (see Chapter 3).

The output of semantic analysis is an *intermediate representation* (*IR*) of the source program, in a formal more close to abstract machine code or to native object code.

The major tasks of semantic analysis are the following:

- *Lookup.* For each usage of identifier, like the use of *i* in the expression *i* + 1, the semantic analyzer should find the appropriate *definition*—for example, the definition:

```
var i: integer;
```

declaring that, within the current scope, *i* is a variable of integral type;

- *Type-checking* (also referred to as *typing*, or *type evaluation*). The semantic analyzer should check the correctness of using *types* in any expression like *i* + 1, that is, should check that, for any operator, function, or method, the types of the operands comply to the specification of that operator (function, method);
- *Other context-dependent checks*, actually related to syntax but nonexpressible in terms of context-free (CF) syntax model used by the parser;
- *Intermediate code generation.* Given the parse tree or the AST of the source program, the semantic analyzer should translate it to the appropriate *IR*, like *Portable C Compiler* [*PCC*] *trees*, *postfix notation*, or *triples*. Intermediate code is closer to the code of the target platform or of the abstract machine (like bytecode in Java technology, or Common Intermediate Language [CIL] on .NET);
- *Trustworthy semantic error diagnostics and error recovery.* If any type handling errors, nondefined identifiers, or other kinds of semantic analysis bugs are encountered, the compiler should provide reasonably detailed error diagnostics to the users, avoid a bunch of absurd error messages, and recover from the detected errors, to analyze the rest of the program in a trustworthy way.

It should be noted that algorithms of semantic analysis are especially important to be efficiently implemented. Modern compilers and compiler generators, for the purpose of generality and simplicity, often use nonefficient algorithms built into general-purpose compiler development tools when analyzing complicated structures related to semantic analysis: type denotations, declarations and definitions, AST, intermediate code, and so on. Inefficiency of such algorithms can be the reason for dramatic performance decrease of semantic analysis and of the whole front-end, which, in its turn, makes compiler nontrustworthy for the users who experience some "mysterious" compile-time delays. Usually, those delays are related to fatal inefficiency of semantic analysis using poor quality "visitors" or "resolvers" of exponential complexity. More details later in this chapter.

5.2 FORMAL MODEL OF SEMANTIC ANALYSIS: ATTRIBUTED GRAMMARS

The most common *formal model* of semantic analysis was invented by Knuth, as well as LR parsers. It is referred to as *attributed grammars* [64]. This model, as compared with others, is very simple to understand and very close to the practical style of thinking by compiler developers.

Briefly speaking, an *attributed grammar* is a CF grammar specifying the syntax, enhanced by some specific *semantic rules* attached to each syntax rule.

In general, methods of attaching semantic rules to those of the grammar that defines the syntax of the language are referred to as *syntax-directed translation* [5].

Semantic rules of the attribute grammar define the algorithms of evaluating the *semantics* of the language in the form of *semantic attributes* attached to each *vertex of the parse tree* (or *AST*).

For a node corresponding to the *left part* of some rule, the so-called *synthesized attributes* are defined by an attributed grammar and should be evaluated by the semantic analyzer. Synthesized attributes are semantic properties of the *left-hand part symbol* whose values depend on the attributes of the *right-hand part symbols*.

For a node corresponding to a symbol from the *right-hand part* of some rule, we evaluate the so-called *inherited attributes*—semantic properties whose values depend on attributes of the left-hand part and may also depend on other attributes of symbols of the right-hand part.

Realistic examples of semantic attributes used in compilers will be considered below in this chapter.

Actually, the phase of semantic analysis can be regarded as *semantic evaluation*—in other words, the process of evaluating the *semantic attributes* for all the nodes on the parse tree.

Let's consider a more formal definition of attributed grammars.

Let G be a CF grammar to define the syntax of the language.

Let $X \rightarrow X_1 X_2 \ldots X_n$ be a rule of the grammar G.

For the *occurrence* of X into the left part, a finite set of *synthesized attributes* $S(X)$ is defined.

For each *occurrence* of X_k into the right part, a finite set of *inherited attributes* $I(X_k)$ is defined.

Each syntax rule is augmented by a set of *semantic* rules. Each of the semantic rules defines a particular attribute as a function of some other semantic attributes.

The whole construct is referred to as *attributed grammar*.

For each attributed grammar, each of the semantic attributes shall be evaluable: There shouldn't be cyclic dependencies, and there should be enough semantic rules to evaluate each of the attributes. It is checked by the analysis of the *attribute dependency graph* (usually abbreviated as *DAG*).

Example:

```
digit -> 0  { Val(digit) = 0 }
...
digit -> 9  { Val(digit) = 9 }
number -> digit   { Val(number) = Val(digit) }
number -> number digit
         { Val(number₁) = Val(number₂) * 10 + Val(digit) }
```

This attributed grammar defines the syntax and semantics of the *integral number denotation* concept. Its semantics is the *value* of the number that should be evaluated, based on the syntax, according to the semantic rules. To support such evaluation, we define the *synthesized attribute Val* for the nonterminal symbols *number* and *digit*. Please note that different occurrences of nonterminal symbols into the same rule are numbered, to distinguish between them.

We emphasize again that semantic attributes define properties of each *occurrence* of a nonterminal symbol into some rule, rather than properties of the nonterminal symbol itself. So, from another viewpoint, we can regard the semantic attributes as properties of the *nodes of the (abstract) syntax tree*.

Evaluating semantic attributes on the parse tree. Now let's discuss the process of semantic evaluation in terms of the parse tree (see Fig. 5.1).

Since *inherited* attributes are those of the right-hand side symbols that depend on the left-hand side symbol's attributes, the process of their evaluation, generally speaking, is top-down.

As for *synthesized* attributes, they are attributes of the left-hand side symbol that depend on attributes of right-hand side symbols. That means, the process of their evaluation goes bottom-up.

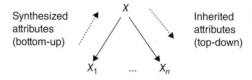

Figure 5.1. *The process of evaluation of synthesized and inherited attributes on a parse tree.*

So, synthesized attributes are intended to pass information bottom-up across the parse tree, and inherited attributes are suitable to pass information top-down.

In both cases, the process of information transfer via attributes goes by *local* steps closely tied to the appropriate syntax rules and parse tree nodes.

Synthesized, inherited, and global attributes. A typical example of a *synthesized* attribute is the *value* of a constant expression. The value of any expression depends on the values of its operands and on the operator.

A typical example of an *inherited* attribute is an *offset* of a local variable—its relative address in a stack frame. It depends on the context, that is, on the position of the variable definition within the sequence of all local variable definitions of a block (or routine).

So, the advantage of the attributed scheme of semantic analysis is that the whole process of semantic analysis can be represented as a sequence of local steps attached to the syntax of the source program. Each of the steps is easily intuitively understandable.

Based on our own experience, we should say that semantic attributes are a very convenient, not "too theoretical" but easy-to-understand, mechanism to formulate algorithms of semantic analysis.

The syntax-directed nature of semantic attributes is comfortable for their application in compiler development tools like *yacc*.

However, the "pure" synthesized/inherited attribute scheme may appear inconvenient to express any kind of global information transfer. For example, try to formulate, using synthesized and inherited attributes, the process of accumulating local definitions within some scope (block), and passing the information on the local scope to all other parts of the block—statements and expressions. From a formal viewpoint, to find the defining occurrence for some applied occurrence of an identifier into an expression, it is necessary, first, to evaluate the synthesized attribute *scope*—a list of all local definitions, and, next, to pass its value by many local steps as an inherited attribute to any appropriate node of the parse tree representing an applied occurrence of an identifier. This is surely uncomfortable and inefficient.

So, based on compiler development practice, another kind of semantic attributes appears to be necessary—*global attributes* [65], in addition to synthesized and inherited attributes.

A *global attribute* of a nonterminal X is a function not dependent on local attributes. It is a value taken from some global table. For example, according to our own principles of compilation, to make the lookup process efficient, we keep for any applied occurrence of an identifier, denoted by *id*, its global attribute *CED(id)*—the current effective definition (CED) of the identifier *id* taken, when necessary, from the identifier table *id_tab* (see Chapter 3 and Fig. 3.1). So, *CED* is an example of a global attribute.

The concept of global attribute was formalized by the Moscow compiler group from the Computing Center of the Russian Academy of Sciences [65].

L-attributed grammars. Another important concept related to the attributed scheme of semantic analysis is *L-attributed grammar.*

Speaking informally, an L-attributed grammar is an attributed grammar whose semantic attributes can be evaluated during LL(1) parsing or recursive descent parsing during one pass of the source program.

In more formal terms, it means the following. Given a syntax rule of the grammar:

$$X \rightarrow X_1 \dots X_k \, X_{k+1} \dots X_n$$

the *syntax* part of the attributed grammar should be *LL(1)*, and the dependencies of the semantic attributes should be such that any inherited attribute of a right-hand side symbol X_k depends only on the attributes of the left-hand side symbol X and (or) on the attributes of the right-hand side symbols located *on the left* from the symbol X_k—attributes of the symbols $X, X_1 \dots X_{k-1}$. This condition is referred to as *Bochmann's condition*, formulated in his classical paper [66].

Specifics of non-L-attributed languages. As the reader may have guessed, from a formal viewpoint, *none* of the real programming languages is L-attributed, or, less formally, none of the real programming languages is a "one-pass" language.

The root of this issue lies in *multi-pass features* that always present in programming languages and cannot be restricted for principal reasons. Those are features of the language that cannot be analyzed by one pass.

Typical examples of such features are the use of an identifier before its definition, and the use of a label in a *goto* statement if the label is defined later in the source code.

Here is the Pascal code that demonstrates both of them:

```
type pElt= ^elt;
     elt = record info: integer; next: pElt end;
begin
  goto L;  ...
  goto L;  ...
  L: /* the label definition */
end
```

Below we propose techniques that help to work around these issues and make the process of parsing and semantic evaluation "almost L-attributed," without an extra pass of the source program.

The technique proposed is referred to as *applied occurrences lists*. Here are the main ideas:

- For each symbol *S*, which is used but not yet defined, its *applied occurrences list* is constructed. A pointer to this list is stored in a special *dummy entry* we create in the table of definitions for the not-yet-defined but used symbol *S*. The applied occurrences list links the appropriate nodes of the parse tree and the IR fragments containing applied occurrences of the undefined symbol *S*.

- When the definition of *S* is found, its applied occurrences list is scanned, and the semantic evaluation process is completed for each node of the applied occurrences list, based on the just defined symbol *S* and its attributes. The dummy entry for the symbol *S* in the table of definitions is converted to an ordinary entry. So, the whole process of semantic evaluation remains «almost L-attributed», except for scanning of (usually very small) applied occurrences lists. That is much more efficient than to make another pass of the whole program for the only purpose of resolving possible forward references.

5.3 DEFINITION SYSTEMS WITH FORWARD REFERENCES AND THE ALGORITHM OF THEIR ONE-PASS ANALYSIS

The algorithm of processing lists of applied occurrences discussed in Section 5.2 above works "as is" for processing label references prior to their definitions. For more complicated constructs, like compound-type definitions, this technique needs generalization.

For this purpose, we introduce the general concept of *definition system* [2] in a programming language—a sequence of *equates* of the kind:

$$\{i_k = t_k\}_{k=1,\ldots n}$$

where i_k is an identifier; t_k is some kind of *expression* or *type expression (denotation)*. The expressions t_k may contain applied occurrences of any identifier i_j. The specific of the definition system is as follows: *Forward references* are within its sequence of definitions. In other words, any expression t_k may contain references to other symbols defined later within the same definition system.

Examples of definition systems are as follows: type definitions in Pascal; equates in CLU.

Let's assume the following properties to hold for a definition system *D*:

- The syntax of the right parts allows for deterministic LL(1) parsing.
- The scope of the definition for any identifier i_k is the entire code of the definition system, that is, the identifier i_k can be used in any of the right-hand parts t_j, including the case $j < k$, that is, *before* its definition.

Let T_k be the parse tree of the right-hand part t_k; I_j—nonterminal nodes of the parse trees T_k from which the applied occurrences of i_j are derived. The *dependency graph* $G(D)$ of the definition system D is defined to be a directed graph obtained from the union of all trees T_k by adding all possible edges from the terminal nodes corresponding to an applied occurrence of the identifier i_k to the root of the tree T_k depicting the right-hand part of the definition of i_k.

The definition system D is referred to be *correct* if and only if:

1   each of the identifiers i_k used in right-hand parts of D has its definition in D;
2   $i_k \neq i_j$ if $k \neq j$ (no repeated definition allowed);
3   the dependency graph $G(D)$ does not contain loops.

The third condition above holds for equates in the CLU language (it means that no explicit or implicit recursion in the definitions is allowed). In Pascal, for type definitions, the condition is relaxed: Any directed loop in $G(D)$ must contain a vertex marked by the "^" symbol (the pointer type denotation in Pascal). In ALGOL-68, the third condition is even more relaxed: The definition of a *mode* (the term *mode* is used in ALGOL-68 instead of the term *type*) is correct if the graph $G(D)$ contains a vertex marked by a nonterminal from the set:

$$D_1 = \{ref, procedure\text{-}with\text{-}no\text{-}arguments\}$$

and a vertex marked by a nonterminal from the set:

$$D_2 = \{struct, procedure\text{-}with\text{-}arguments\}$$

The set D_1 in the above definition denotes the condition of *finite memory size* in the representation of the mode, and the set D_2 denotes that the mode cannot be casted to itself.

Algorithm D for one-pass semantic analysis of a definition system. The idea of our algorithm (let's call it the *D algorithm*) to process a definition system in one pass [2] is as follows. We construct hierarchical lists of applied occurrences. When the definition appears, its applied occurrences list is traversed.

The algorithm works recursively because the right-hand side of the definition of X can contain references to symbol Y not yet defined, and the definition of Y, in its turn, may contain a reference to a not yet defined symbol (or symbols), for example, Z.

The principles of our algorithm for resolving such definitions are to construct lists of applied occurrences for each symbol, which is used but not yet defined, and to store the counter of uncompleted subconstructs for each parse tree node that contains undefined identifiers.

The purpose of the algorithm is to evaluate all the semantic attributes, to check the correctness of the definition system, and to issue error messages for all incorrect definitions in D.

The algorithm actually stores *the plan (path) for evaluating semantic attributes* for the expressions t_k that couldn't yet be evaluated because some of the identifiers used in the expression are not yet defined.

The algorithm uses the following tables and data structures:

- the table of the defined identifiers $D = \{i_k, T_k\}_{k=1,...n}$;
- the table of used but not yet defined identifiers $N = \{i_k, F_k\}$;
- the parse trees T_k for the right-hand sides of the definitions;
- the dummy parse trees F_k (consisting of the root only) for the identifiers i_k belonging to N (i.e., for the identifiers used but not yet defined).

For the purpose of the algorithm, we'll use two extra semantic attributes of an expression T, where T is t_k or its component (subexpression):

1   $a(T)$—*list of all applied occurrences of T*. If T is t_k, $a(T)$ is the pointer to the list of all the vertices representing the *applied occurrences* of i_k. If T is a component of t_k, $a(T)$ is a pointer to the *parent* of T in the parse tree.

2   $n(T)$—the number of children of T whose attributes are not yet evaluated.

The algorithm works by passing the definition system from left to right in the process of its LL(1) parsing or recursive descent parsing. The algorithm builds the dependency graph $G(D)$ and performs the following actions related to undefined identifiers:

1   When processing the first applied occurrences of an identifier i_k, which is undefined, its dummy parse tree F_k is constructed; the pair (i_k, F_k) is added to the table N, and the first applied occurrence of i_k is included into the list $a(F_k)$ of its applied occurrences.

2   When processing of further applied occurrences of a not yet defined identifier i_k, already included to N, or when processing of a *not completely defined* identifier i_k (whose right-hand part of the definition is not fully defined), such that $n(T_k) > 0$, the occurrence of the identifier i_k is included into the list of applied occurrences $a(T_k)$.

3   When processing an expression T with an undefined component S (such that $n(S) > 0$), the attribute $a(S)$ is set to be a pointer to T, and $n(T)$ is incremented by one.

4   When processing a definition $i_k = T_k$, we check whether the identifier i_k is in the N table. If so, the identifier is excluded from N. The pair (i_k, T_k) is stored into the table D. At that moment, we check that the definition of i_k is not repeatable. If it is, an error message is issued. If the attributes of T_k are now fully evaluated ($n(T_k) = 0$), and the list of applied occurrences $a(F_k)$ is non-empty, the algorithm calls the

recursive procedure $eval(a(F_k))$ of traversing the list of applied occurrences, which completes the evaluation of attributes for each element T of the list $a(F_k)$, and calls $eval(a(T))$. On evaluating the attributes of the subexpression T, the value of the attribute $n(T)$ is zeroed out, and the value of $n(a(T))$ is decremented by one. If $n(T_k)$ becomes zero, where T_k is the right part of the definition $i_k = T_k$, the procedure of traversal of the list $a(T_k)$ is called, and so on. Thus, the process of completion of attribute evaluation is spread in the directions pointed out by the values of the a attribute—pointers to the appropriate applied occurrences.

5   On completion of the analysis of the definition system D, the N table is scanned. For each element (i_k, F_k), the error diagnostic message is issued:

The identifier i_k is undefined.

Then, the table $D = \{(i_k, T_k)\}$ is scanned. For each identifier i_k such that $n(T_k) > 0$, the error diagnostic message is issued:

The definition of the identifier i_k is incorrect.

We leave to the readers the proof of correctness of the algorithm and its implementation (see Exercise 5.1).

We used this algorithm in a number of our compilers, in particular, in Pascal and CLU compilers for "Elbrus" computers [2].

In practice, lists of applied occurrences are very small, usually just one or two elements. It is clear that traversing such small lists is much more efficient than to undertake the whole second pass over the intermediate code of the program.

Example. Let's see how the algorithm D works when analyzing the system of constant definitions:

```
a = b + c - d;
b = d * 2;
c = a * 5 * d;
d = 3;
e = f + 1;
```

The semantic attribute to be evaluated is the value of each constant. In Figure 5.2, ASTs are shown for the right-hand parts of the definitions of a, b, c, d, e—$T_a, T_b, T_c, T_d,$ and T_e. The arrows show the values of the a attribute for the subtrees. The indexes of the constant names indicate the textual order of the applied occurrences of the identifiers. In nonterminal vertices, the values of the n attribute are shown. The sequence of steps

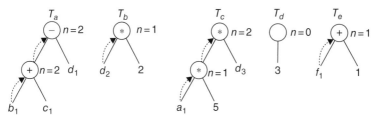

Figure 5.2. The abstract syntax trees of the sample definition system right-hand parts processed by the D algorithm.

Definition	D	N	Comment
a	(a, T_a)	$(b, (b_1))$ $(c, (c_1))$ $(d, (d_1))$	Dummy parse trees created for b, c, d
b	(a, T_a) $(b, T_b(b_1))$	$(c, (c_1))$ $(d, (d_1, d_2))$	b is moved from N to D but cannot be evaluated since
c	$(a, T_a(a_1))$ $(b, T_b(b_1))$ $(c, T_c(c_1))$	$(d, (d_1, d_2, d_3))$	$n(T_b) = 1$ $n(T_c) = 2$
d	$(a, T_a(a_1))$ (b, T_b^*) $(c, T_c(c_1))$ (d, T_d^*)	empty	The value of b is evaluated immediately, d – via the applied occurrences list
e	$(a, T_a(a_1))$ (b, T_b^*) $(c, T_c(c_1))$ (d, T_d^*) (e, T_e)	$(f, (f_1))$	Diagnostics: f undefined a defined incorrectly c defined incorrectly e defined incorrectly

Figure 5.3. The sequence of steps of the D algorithm for the sample definition system analysis.

of the algorithm is presented in Figure 5.3. The status of tables D and N is depicted after the analysis of the corresponding definition. In angular brackets, the applied occurrences lists are given. The parse trees with all attributes fully evaluated are marked by asterisks.

5.4 COMMONLY USED SEMANTIC ATTRIBUTES FOR PROGRAM CONSTRUCTS

Now let's consider the most commonly used semantic attributes to be evaluated for programming language constructs during the semantic analysis phase.

In each case, we'll make clear what kind of semantic attributes they are—*synthesized*, *inherited*, or *global*.

Semantic attributes of type (T). For the construct of *type* (let's denote it *T*), the following semantic attributes are to be evaluated.

$size(T)$—the size (in bytes) of the value of the type *T* in memory, if the size is a compile-time constant (like in Pascal). If not, $size(T)$ is the *size of the static part of T*, or its *head*, or *passport*. For example, for dynamically sized array in ALGOL-like languages, the size of the array, generally speaking, cannot be evaluated at compile time, since it can be specified by a variable or an expression containing variables, for example:

```
integer array a[m : n];
```

but the size of its *passport (dope vector)* [26], the structure representing the array variable on the runtime stack, can be evaluated at compile time and depends only on the *number of dimensions* of the array.

Size is clearly a *synthesized* attribute because the size of the compound type is purely determined by the *sort* of the type (*ARRAY*, *RECORD*, etc.) and the sizes of its *component types*.

$align(T)$—the *alignment* (in bytes) of a variable of the type allocated on the runtime stack or in heap memory. This attribute is necessary to enable correctness of hardware read and write instructions for primitive value types like long integers or floats. It is well known that in most hardware architectures, it is not possible to handle a misaligned long numeric value by a single hardware instruction. Misaligned data should be handled by special subroutines (*intrinsics*), which is much less efficient.

As well as the *size* attribute, *align* is also a *synthesized* attribute because it is purely determined by the *sort* of the type and by (alignment of) its *component types*.

$hasPointers(T)$ is an example of a *synthesized* attribute characteristic of Pascal types. This is a flag showing whether *T* has pointer type components. This attribute is necessary for checking correctness of some operations for compound types: In standard Pascal, it is not allowed to store in files the values of compound types with pointer components (i.e., speaking in modern terms, Pascal pointers are not persistent).

$sort(T)$, as already explained, is a *kind* of the type *T*—array, record, set, file, integer, float, and so on. This is obviously a *synthesized* attribute.

$componentType(T)$ for compound types like *array*, *set*, or *file* is a reference to the component type's entry in the table of all types. This is also a synthesized attribute, since its value depends only on the structure of the type and doesn't depend on the context of its use.

For example, for the Pascal type *ar*:

```
type
   compl = record re, im: integer end;
   ar = array [1..10] of compl;
```

representing an array of records, each of them representing a complex number, for 32-bit target machine architectures, the attributes considered above will have the following values:

size(ar) = 10 * size (compl) = 10 * 8 = 80 (bytes)
align(ar) = align(compl) = align(integer) = 4 (bytes)
sort(ar) = ARRAY
hasPointers(ar) = false

More details and formulas for evaluating the sizes and alignments of aggregate types are provided in Chapter 6, since they are closely related to code generation for accessing typed variables.

Semantic attributes of variable (V). For the construct of *variable definition* (let's denote it *V*), the following semantic attributes should be evaluated.

type(V)—the type of the variable (a pointer to the element of the table of all types that represents the type of *V*). This is a *synthesized* attribute, since it depends only on the structure of the definition, rather than on its context.

size(V)—the size of the value of *V*, when allocated on the stack or on the heap. That size is determined by the size of the *type(V)*, so it is also a *synthesized* attribute.

align(V)—the alignment of the value of the variable on a stack frame or on the heap. It depends on the alignment of *type(V)* and is also a *synthesized* attribute.

offset(V)—the *offset*, or *relative address*, of the variable *V* on the stack frame. Since it depends on the *context* of the variable definition and on the *position* of *V*'s definition in the sequence of the other definitions, it is an *inherited* attribute.

memoryClass(V)—the memory allocation class of the variable *V* usually specified in its definition, that is, specification of the memory area where the value of the variable will be allocated at runtime.

The typical kinds of memory classes of variables in programming languages are the following:

- *static*—the variable will be allocated on the global area, and its offset and symbol will be evaluated at compile time;
- *automatic*—the variable will be allocated on the stack, and its offset will be evaluated at compile time;

- *dynamic*—the variable will be allocated on the heap at runtime.

Since the *memoryClass* attribute depends on the context of *V*'s definition, it is an *inherited* attribute.

Semantic attributes of expression (E). For the construct of *expression* (let's denote it *E*), the following are the most important semantic attributes to be evaluated.

type(E)—the type of the expression. This is the most common attribute of expression, but not always evident how to evaluate.

Please note there are actually *two* (kinds of) types for an expression.

A priori type is the type of the expression without taking its context into account. This kind of type is a *synthesized* attribute purely determined by the components of the expression, their types, and the operators used in the expression. For example, if *i* is an integer variable, then the *a priori type* of the expression *i* + 1 is also integer.

A posteriori type of the expression is its final type *imposed* by the *context* where the expression is used. For that reason, the *a posteriori* type is an *inherited* attribute.

For example, in an assignment construct, the type of the right-hand side should be an assignment compatible to the type of the left-hand side.

For example, in Pascal:

```
var: x: real;  i: integer;
begin x := i + 1; end
```

In the assignment $x := i + 1$ where *x* is a variable of type *real*, a posteriori type of the right-hand part expression is also *real*, whereas its *a priori* type is *integer*.

In practice, that means the compiler should insert a coercion operation to convert the integer value to floating point format.

isConstant(E) is a *synthesized* attribute, a flag to indicate whether an expression is a constant expression or not. The value of the attribute depends on the kind of the expression, its operators, and operands only.

For constant expressions, the synthesized attribute *value(E)* should be evaluated—the *value* of the constant expression. The process of evaluating it can be referred to as *constant folding*. The attribute *value(E)* depends on *type(E)*. However, if the constant expression stands in a position where some *a posteriori* type is imposed to it, the value of the constant expression should be converted to this *a posteriori* type, like in the example in C below:

```
float f = 1 + 2;
```

The a priori type of the constant expression is *int*, but its a posteriori type imposed to the expression by its context is *float*, so the constant 3 evaluated by the compiler should be converted to its float format 3.0f.

5.5   DESIGN FLAWS OF THE SEMANTIC ATTRIBUTE EVALUATION AND OUR EFFICIENT METHODS TO SPEED IT UP

Surprising as it may seem, a typical design flaw of many compilers is poor efficiency of semantic analysis algorithms. It dramatically decreases the performance of the front-end. The reason can be just poor design, or using predefined general-purpose visitors or resolvers provided by compiler generation utilities, which are often inefficient, since they use general multi-pass or multi-traversal algorithms.

We found an example of such design flaw in the Sun Pascal compiler, version 3.0.1 (1992).

The customers complained that, for applications with compound expressions containing many operands and operators, the compilation time used by the front-end, for some unknown reason, increased almost exponentially.

Our analysis detected the following design flaw in semantic analysis, explained below.

The compiler was based on *yacc*. During bottom-up parsing, *no semantic attributes* were evaluated, so the "pure" AST was constructed only, in bottom-up direction, from terminal nodes to root, with no attempt to collect semantic attributes "on the fly" (on the way of parsing), and to store them in the AST.

All semantic attributes were evaluated subsequently, by multiple traversals of the parse tree, top-down, depth-first.

For example, to determine the type of an expression, the compiler had to make a special traversal of the expression AST, with no intermediate code generation.

For intermediate code generation, the compiler called the same routine that traversed the expression tree again, but also generated an intermediate code.

Let's estimate the complexity of such algorithm.

Let n be the depth of the expression tree, which can be considered to be a binary tree because most of the operators are binary.

So, because of using the strategy of visiting each subtree twice, to evaluate the type of the expression itself and of its any subexpression at each layer, the compiler had to make $O(2 ** n)$ steps, hence the exponential performance decrease noticed by the users.

Our methods of resolving such design flaws, and of efficient evaluation of semantic attributes we applied to Sun Pascal compiler, are based on the following principles:

1   *Pre-evaluation of synthesized attributes during LALR(1) parsing.* The compiler should evaluate all semantic attributes as early as possible and store them on the parse tree immediately after their evaluation. Strictly speaking, such tree enhanced by semantic attributes should be referred to as *attributed* (*abstract*) *syntax tree*.

   So, in bottom-up parsing based on *yacc* like in Sun Pascal, we can evaluate all synthesized attributes for a construct immediately before the reduce action to be performed according to the appropriate syntax rule [62].

For example, for expressions, we can evaluate and store on the AST the following synthesized semantic attributes during *yacc*-based LALR(1) parsing, before the reduce action of the parser:

Type (E)—a priori type of the expression;

ConstExpr (E)—the flag indicating this is a constant expression;

Val (E)—the a priori value (of the a priori type) of the constant expression.

To explain our method for pre-evaluating semantic attributes during LALR(1) parsing [62], let's consider an example of the Pascal source code:

```
var x: real;
x := 2 * 3;
```

The syntax of the assignment is defined by the following syntax rule:

```
E -> E '*' E
```

We augment this syntax rule by the following semantic rules:

```
Type (E₁)  =  Type  (E₂);
ConstExpr (E₁)  =  ConstExpr (E₂) && ConstExpr(E₃);
Val(E₁)  =  Val(E₂)  *  Val(E₃);
```

where, as above, E_1, E_2, and E_3 are the occurrences of the symbol E into the left-hand part and the right-hand part of the syntax rule.

Figure 5.4 depicts the attributed syntax tree for the above assignment construct. The tree is built bottom-up in the process of *yacc*-based LALR(1) parsing. The *Type* and *ConstExpr* attributes are shown for each tree node. Single-lined arrows indicate the syntax relationships in the parse tree. Double-lined arrows show the process of spreading the values of the synthesized attributes evaluated before the reduction according to the corresponding rule and stored on the parse tree. The dotted-lined arrow shows the process of further passing (imposing) the type of the left-hand part of the assignment to its right-hand part—the expression. Final evaluation of the expression's a posteriori type and value takes place in further tree traversal, top-down, during generation of the intermediate code.

Please note that now, due to the our *Type*, *ConstExpr*, and *Val* attributes already stored in the parse tree, there is no need for the compiler to make an extra traversal of the parse tree just to determine the type of the expression: That type is already known from the *Type*

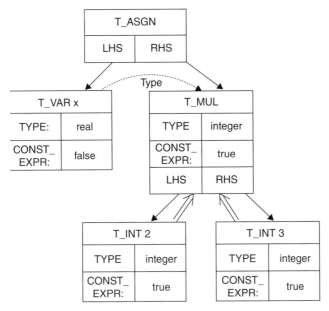

Figure 5.4. *The attributed syntax tree for the assignment construct x := 2 * 3.*

attribute. So, applying our method fixed the defect we found in Sun Pascal: no double traversals of parse trees any more. More formal and detailed definition of the method can be found in Reference 62.

2 *Using applied occurrences lists.* For evaluating inherited attributes, where necessary, the technique of applied occurrence lists discussed in Section 5.3 above should be used.

3 *Using CED pointer from the identifier table to the namelist (NL) table. The NL table*—the table of all definitions in the compilation unit, should be efficiently organized, based *on the CED* pointers discussed in Section 3.6. The basic idea is that the element in the *id*_tab table for the identifier always directly points to NL to its CED, if any. See also Figure 3.1 for our structure of the identifier table [61]. How this method works during different stages of processing definitions of identifiers and their lookup, is explained in the next section.

The methods described above work faster than those explained in classical compiler textbooks [5,26], which recommend, for lookup, to scan the local table of definitions, next, the outer block's table of definitions, and so on. The complexity of such algorithms is $O(N)$ where N is the total number of definitions in the compilation unit. The complexity of our lookup algorithm is $O(1)$—a constant.

We applied the above principles and methods to refurbish the Sun Pascal compiler.

As a result, the total performance increase of the front-end we achieved, due to application of these techniques, was, in average, 2–4 times, depending on the size and on the nature of the source program (the larger the Pascal source, the faster our algorithms work).

This is a practical proof of how important it is to make the semantic analysis really efficient and what happens if its algorithms are too straightforward.

Due to our work on the Sun Pascal compiler refurbishment, we issued the four U.S. patents [25,61–63] covering our efficient techniques of semantic analysis and their application to Sun Pascal.

5.6 LOOKUP—TRADITIONAL AND NOVEL TECHNIQUES

Lookup is one of the essential parts of semantic analysis.

To be able to perform type-checking and subsequent intermediate code generation, the compiler, at first, should find definitions (or *defining occurrences*) for each use (or *applied occurrence*) of an identifier or label.

This task (part of semantic analysis) is referred to as *lookup*. Another, older, term used in the same meaning is *identification*.

Actually, lookup can be viewed as the process of checking if the used identifier does have any definition at all, and, if so, what is its current definition.

In most languages, including the latest ones—Java and C#, identifier definitions and scopes of their visibility are bound to the static structure of a program. Identifiers can be defined as class names, method names, formal parameter names, local variable names, and so on, in some *scope* tied to some part of the program source. Beyond that part, the identifier does not make sense. Such approach is referred to as *static* identification.

Some languages, like LISP, SNOBOL, and other symbolic processing languages, are based on another approach—*dynamic* identification. For example, for a variable or an argument X in a LISP program, the *associative list* (in other terms—*dynamic chain*, i.e., chain of called functions on the stack) is scanned backward at runtime to find the latest definition of the variable.

In this book, we cover static identification as the most widely spread.

Since the definition of an identifier is attached to some *scope*—probably small (like the current block) or a larger, embracing piece of code (like the code of some routine), straightforward lookup algorithms described in classical textbooks [5,26] must somehow examine the local definitions of the nearest block, of the outer block, and so on (up to the outermost block of the whole compilation unit). So, the complexity of such algorithms can be estimated as $O(n)$ where n is the total number of definitions (declarations) in the program that can be very large—several hundred or even thousand identifiers may be defined in a large piece of source code.

So, since lookup is performed very often (when processing each identifier), lookup algorithms should be made as efficient as possible, and "blind" multi-layered linear search [5,26] is undesirable.

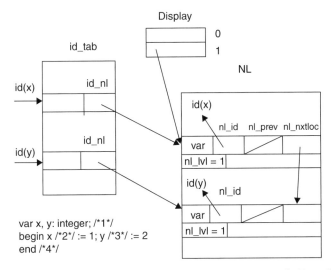

Figure 5.5. *Our efficient lookup technique and its use case (in Pascal).*

For efficient lookup, we offer the following technique [61] illustrated in Figure 5.5.

The basic idea is to keep a pointer to the *CED* directly in the *identifier table (id_tab)* entry for each identifier.

It is quite clear that, since we take this approach, no search will be needed at all during lookup—the compiler just looks into the *id_tab* entry for the identifier.

In Figure 5.4, that reference is denoted *id_nl*, as a reference from the *identifier table* to *namelist* table.

The *NL* table represents information on all available definitions and has an entry (element) for each of them.

Please recall that a pointer to *id_tab* is the way of representing the identifier during all phases after lexical analysis that generates *id_tab* (see Section 3.6).

The idea of the representation is simple; to support the *id_nl* reference that should always be up-to-date at any moment of the semantic analysis is more complicated.

The idea how to enable that is as follows.

In each *NL* entry (i.e., for each definition), we keep two pointers:

- *nl_prev*—a pointer to the *previous* definition of the same identifier in an outer scope, if any;
- *nl_nxtloc*—a pointer to the *next local definition* of some identifier in the same scope.

So, all local definitions of any block (scope) are linked to a list.

The pointer to the start of this list is stored in an array referred to as *display* (the initial idea of using display for addressing variables at runtime belongs to Dijkstra who coined it in the 1960s, in relation to ALGOL-60 implementation).

Each *display* element refers to a list of local definitions of some block, and the index in the *display* is referred to as *static (or nesting) level* of the block.

The scope of the predefined identifiers has static level 0; the scope of the whole compilation unit has static level 1.

Display works as *stack*, that is, on entry to a block, it is extended by one element, and on exiting a block, it is truncated by one element.

The *nl_lvl(D)* field keeps the scope level for the definition *D*.

Each NL entry also contains the field *nl_cat(T)* to denote the *category* of the definition—*variable declaration (VAR)*, *type definition (TYPE)*, and so on.

In addition, each *NL* entry has a backward reference (*nl_id*) to the *id_tab* entry for the identifier. It will be needed to restore the scope information on exiting the block.

Now let's consider how it works using a very simple example in Pascal (also shown in Fig. 5.4).

In the Pascal code example in Figure 5.4, the comments specify different points in the program:

1   the definitions of the variables *x* and *y*;
2   the use of *x*;
3   the use of *y*;
4   exiting the block where *x* and *y* are defined.

At point 1, two NL entries are created for the definitions of *x* and *y*. The pointers to them are assigned to the *id_nl* fields of their *id_tab* entries.

Before that, the *previous* values of *id_nl* (corresponding to outer scope definitions of the variable, if any) are stored to the *nl_prev* fields of the new *NL* entries:

$$nl\_prev(D) := id\_nl(X);$$

$$id\_nl(X) := D$$

where *D* is the entry for the new definition in *NL*.

So, if *x* or *y* is already defined in an outer scope, that information is not lost because the new definition keeps the reference to an outer one. If not, the *nl_prev* field is *nil*.

The pointer to the start of the list of local definitions of *x* and *y* is stored in the appropriate level (1) entry of the *display*.

At points 2 and 3, while processing the uses of *x* and *y*, the compiler looks into their *id_tab* entries and immediately retrieves the references to the appropriate *NL* entries, without any kind of search. Please note again the efficiency of this operation, with no search—this is the main advantage of our method.

At point 4, the compiler scans the list of all local definitions. For each of the local definitions *D*, the following simple swapping of references is performed:

- by using the *nl_id* pointer, the *id_tab* entry is found;
- the contents of the *nl_prev* field of *the NL* entry is assigned to the *id_nl* field of the *id_tab* entry:

$$id\_nl \ (nl\_id \ (D)) := nl\_prev(D);$$

This way, we restore information on the outer definitions (if there is no outer definition, *id_nl* becomes *nil*).

This scheme enables efficient lookup for many languages like Pascal.

It was successfully applied to the Sun Pascal compiler whose previous lookup algorithms were based on multilayered linear search [5,28].

Please note that for object-oriented languages, this scheme needs to be updated.

First, an *overload* is possible for method identifiers. So, for methods, the *id_nl* field should contain a reference not just to one definition but to a *list* of method overloading definitions, if any. Nevertheless, it is still much more efficient than scan the whole list of all definitions because in practice, the size of the overloading list is very small.

Second, if the same identifier can be defined within the same scope several times but in different name "universes" (for example, as a field and a method name in the same class, which is allowed in C#), the list of all such definitions should be accessible via *id_nl*.

Error diagnostics and error recovery in lookup is especially important for compiler trustworthiness.

A lot of compilers issue many "garbage" error messages related to undefined identifiers.

Due to our technique, we can easily handle the errors of repeated definition and of lacking definition for an identifier, and recover from such errors.

First, let a repeated definition of the same identifier in the same scope is detected, for example (in Pascal):

```
var x: integer; var x: real;
```

To check such kind of errors, any *NL* entry keeps the *level* of nesting for the appropriate scope in the *nl_lvl* field. The compiler issues an error message and either ignores the second definition or resets the *id_nl* reference to the new definition.

Second, if an identifier is used but not defined, the compiler detects that at once, due to *id_nl* field, issues an error message, and *creates a dummy NL entry* for the identifier, as if it were defined at this point. That dummy entry keeps information on all uses of the undefined identifier within the current scope, including their line numbers. On exiting the scope, when scanning its list of local definitions, the compiler issues one message with the list of all uses of the undefined identifier at once.

Such technique helps to avoid hundreds of error messages on using the same undefined identifier in different lines of the source code (the latter behavior of the compiler would be annoying for the users).

5.7   TYPING AND TYPE-CHECKING: BASIC CONCEPTS

Typing and *type-checking* are yet another key parts of semantic analysis.

In general, the concept of a type plays a very important role in programming languages and software engineering. Types are used to make programs more trustworthy—reliable and secure, since typing mechanisms enable to check if the use of any operations is correct, that is, corresponds to the data processed by the operations. Also, types make it possible to avoid security flaws in programs, in particular, to check that the indexes are always within the bounds of arrays, and that the fields of structures and objects being addressed do exist within the corresponding type.

The concept of type has evolved over 50 years of development of programming languages.

In FORTRAN, the first programming language, there were only primitive types and arrays of primitive types (in later versions of FORTRAN, its type system was enhanced).

In Pascal, types specify the sets of values that a variable can take. Pascal, invented in 1970, still remains a good example of *strong typing*. It provides a reasonable set of types—primitive types, including strictly typed *enumerations*, *arrays*, *records* (structures), *sets* (with elements of primitive types), and *files*. Pascal allows the programmers to always perform type-checking at compile time or at runtime, with the appropriate implementation (more details later).

In C, it is possible to cast (convert) the type of any structured data to any other type, without any limitations, so it becomes possible to arbitrarily handle any data belonging to any type, which may be insecure and unreliable. The most criticized (but, nevertheless, one of the most widely used) feature of C is *pointer arithmetic*—C allows to handle pointers by adding or subtracting numerical values (like *p++*—incrementing a pointer by one), which is quite comfortable for sequential data processing, but may appear unsafe since it actually allows to address an arbitrary memory area, with no bounds checks.

In modern object-oriented languages, type is considered to be an aggregate of its (hidden) *concrete representation* (data) and public *operations* (functions or methods) to handle those data. In other words, the concept of type in modern programming languages follows the concept of *abstract data types* introduced by Hoare [67]. Another major feature of types in modern object-oriented languages is *inheritance*—relationship between *classes* (types), such that the descendant type inherits nonstatic fields and methods from the ancestor type. Please note that inheritance is a powerful "weapon" that enables the programmers to easily add to their classes a lot of inherited functionality (often implemented by other developers), which may be dangerous and may lead to confusions, because the inherited functionality is not always documented and understood well by the author of the class [1].

Another important feature of types in modern languages is a tendency to use *dynamic typing*, in the sense that the set of members (fiends and methods) of classes and objects in some languages used for Web programming (e.g., Python, Ruby, JavaScript) can be changed at runtime. For example, it is possible in such a language to make an assignment like $p.x = V$ where p is an object reference, and x is a *new*, *nonexistent* field of the object p (defined by this assignment), and V is the value of the new field x. Surely such constructs are convenient for software developers. However, such dynamic typing feature poses specific requirements to the implementation of types, which stimulate new runtime architectures (like *dynamic language runtime* [*DLR*] [68] supporting such dynamic typing, an enhancement of *Common Language Runtime* [*CLR*], implemented on the .NET platform, but not quite suitable for Python-style dynamic types).

Theoretical models of types are covered in Chapter 2. The most adequate of them seems to be *algebraic specification* of types, since, in that model, a type is considered as a *multi-sorted algebra* with the *carrier* (finite set of *sorts*—domains and ranges for the type's operations) and the *signature*—set of operations of the type. Algebraic approach to type specification allows the programmers to easily specify the properties of the type's operations, in terms of algebraic equates involving their calls.

Below in this book we'll be mostly interested in the concepts of types and typing especially important for compilers: How a type is denoted; how it can be assigned a name (identifier); how can types be represented in memory; which types are considered to be identical (equivalent) and compatible (similar).

Type-checking in compilers can be regarded as the process of checking that the type of each operand corresponds to the operation used.

First let's consider the basic notions related to type-checking.

Strong typing means that the type is indicated in the variable's definition; type-checking is performed at compile time. Examples of programming languages based on strong typing are Pascal (of classical languages), Java, and C# (of modern ones).

Weak typing, on the contrary, means that the types are *not* specified in the definitions of variables; type-checking of objects (or values) is performed at runtime. Examples of programming languages to follow this typing model are mostly *symbolic manipulation* languages, like LISP and SNOBOL.

Type identifier is the name of a type introduced by a *type definition*, for example, by the following Pascal code:

```
type TArray = array [1..10] of integer;
```

All earlier languages, starting from PL/1, ALGOL-68, Pascal, and C, provide such or similar kinds of type definitions (as already noted above, in ALGOL-68, the term *mode* is used instead of the term *type*).

In modern object-oriented languages, there are no such kinds of type definitions, but similar role is played by the names of the interfaces and classes that have no aliases (synonyms).

Type denotation is a type identifier, or an explicit anonymous *type expression* (like the right-hand part of the Pascal array type definition above).

Though both forms of type denotations (via type identifier, or directly using anonymous type denotation constructs like the array type expression above) are allowed in programming languages, the use of type identifiers is strongly recommended, to avoid type confusions or errors because there can be various approaches to *type identity*, that is, with the issue of determining which two types denoted by two given type denotations should be considered "the same type."

Checking two types for their identity can be regarded as the function (predicate) *type_ident (T1, T2)*. The efficiency of its implementation plays a critical role in compilers.

The different approaches to the notion of type identity taken in different programming languages are the following.

Name identity of types is the approach to consider two types to be identical only if they are denoted by the *same type identifier*.

Structural identity of types is the approach to consider two types to be identical if their *structures* (type expressions, trees, or graphs) *are identical*, in some sense, to be precisely specified in the language definition.

For example, Pascal has an "almost" name identity—"almost" because of the fact that synonyms to already defined types are allowed. For example, it is possible, in addition to the *TArray* type definition above, to make yet another definition providing an *alias* (synonym) to the *same type*:

```
type T = TArray;
var a : TArray; b: T;
```

With the above definition, the types *TArray* and *T* are considered to be identical in Pascal, so it is possible, for example, to make assignments like $a := b$, or $b := a$, or to compare the values of those variables: $a = b$. The Pascal model of strong typing allows doing so.

When using Pascal-like languages, one should keep in mind that "similar" explicit type expressions repeated twice denote *different* types in Pascal.

So, to avoid confusions, any compound type should be given a name, desirably a unique one.

Not for the purpose of confusing the readers, but just for information, we should warn that in standard Pascal, it is quite legal to make such type redefinition as:

```
type integer = real; /* surely not recommended! */
```

In ALGOL-68 and CLU, the purely structural type identity model is taken. Actually, it means that the specification of the language should precisely define what does the phrase "the structures of the types are identical" actually mean, in terms of tree- or graph-like type representations, and the compiler should provide a mechanism of efficient implementation of such type-checking.

In modern languages like C# and Java, basically, name equivalence approach is taken. Any type, a class or an interface, is considered to be different from the others.

From the viewpoint of software reliability and security [1], the name identity model is much more attractive, since it prevents from occasional or intended "coincidence" of types. On the contrary, the structural identity model is dangerous in this respect, since it allows hackers to "guess" the structure of the type (in similar style as they guess passwords), and to "intrude" into the data structure with malicious goals. The name identity model fully prevents from that.

Also, the structural identity model may cause issues with module-to-module interoperability, since both interacting modules should "understand" the structure of their common typed data the same way. Again, name equivalence is more attractive in this respect, since it helps to avoid confusions: The software developer should just denote the "same" types by the same type identifier.

From a compiler implementation viewpoint, name identity is simpler to implement, since there is no need to use potentially slow algorithms to compare type trees and graphs. However, below we propose an efficient method of representing types in structural identity languages (we used in CLU compiler for "Elbrus" [2]), which allows the compiler to handle types for structural identity languages as efficiently as types for name identity languages.

5.8 REPRESENTING TYPES AT COMPILE TIME

How can types be represented efficiently and comfortably, and how can they be processed during semantic analysis?

We recommend the following approach we used in a number of our compilers.

All type denotations (expressions) are stored in a separate table, referred to as *types*.

Creating and handling the *types* table is performed during semantic analysis.

Each type denotation has a separate entry in the *types* table.

The entry contains the *semantic attributes* of the type T including its *sort*, *component types*, *size*, and *align*.

Our basic principles of efficient type-checking are as follows:

- a type should be represented as a pointer to its *types* entry;
- regardless of the type identity approach taken in the language to be implemented (either name or structural), the basic type-checking routine *type_ident(T1, T2)* should be implemented just as a comparison of references (addresses), rather than trees;
- for the latter purpose, if type identity is structural, the compiler should keep *only one copy* of each type denotation in the *types* table (the same principle as for the identifiers in *id_tab*—see Section 3.6).

For languages with name identity, there is no problem in following these principles. Each explicit type denotation (expression) is considered to be a *new* type, so it is just stored in a new entry of the *types* table, and the principle of *compare types by comparing references* holds.

But if the model of type identity is structural, the compiler should keep only one copy of each type denotation in the *types* table. In this case, the efficiency of the basic *type_ident* operation will be guaranteed. Only this way the principle "compare types by comparing references" can be efficiently implemented.

Surely, for efficient search in the *types* table, an appropriate hash function should be selected.

We think that, for hashing types, the *sort* of the type is the most suitable hash code. It means, in the hashed *types* structure, all array types are linked into one hash list, all record types to another hash list, and so on.

A little later, we'll show how type expressions can be efficiently handled in a language with structural identity.

Here we just note that most of the other compilers demonstrate nonefficient type processing and checking, especially for languages with structural type identity.

Figure 5.6 illustrates our approach to representing types by an example of representing a Pascal array type expression in the *types* table.

Please note that *three* tables take part in adequate representation of the array type *T* with its identifier:

- the *types* table stores the type expression (the right-hand part of the type definition);
- the *id_tab* table entry for *T* keeps a reference to the *NL* table entry representing the current definition of *T* as a *type identifier*;
- the *NL* table keeps the information that the identifier is defined as a type name.

The field *nl_cat* of the NL entry is referred to as the *category* of the definition. It stores the *TYPE* tag specifying that *T* is a *type identifier*.

Another field *nl_type* of the NL entry points to the appropriate entry in the *types* table that represents the array type expression of the right-hand side of type definition.

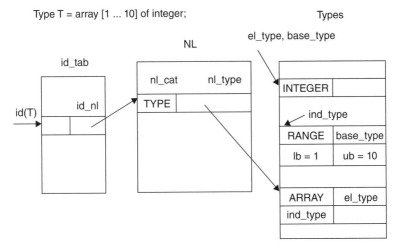

Figure 5.6. *Representing types at compile time in the types table.*

Please note at this point that, if a *synonym* (say, *S*) to the same type is defined by the definition of the kind:

```
type S = T;
```

the definition of *S* will be represented by a new NL entry, pointing to *the same entry* in the *types* table, so there is no need to copy type expression information in *types*.

The array type is represented in *types* by three entries—an entry for the array type itself, an entry for the *index type* and an entry to the *elements type*.

The elements type is *integer*, so the array type entry just refers to *integer* entry located somewhere in the "predefined" part of *types*.

The index type is the *subrange type*, 1 … 10 (an integer from 1 to 10). That type is represented in *types* by a separate entry containing the *lower and upper bounds* and the *base type* of the subrange—the type of both bounds (*integer*).

5.9 EFFICIENT METHOD AND ALGORITHM TO REPRESENT AND HANDLE TYPES WITH STRUCTURAL IDENTITY

For languages with structural identity of types, we propose an efficient algorithm for processing type expressions so that, in the *types* table, only one copy of each type or subtype will be stored, similar to identifiers in the *id_tab* table (see Section 3.6).

Please note that the *types* table for structural identity languages should be hashed by the *sort* of the type, which plays the role of the hash function. It means that, on one hash list, all array type denotations will be stored, on the other hash list—all subrange type denotations and so on.

Here is the scheme of our recursive algorithm (referred to as *ST*, for *S*tructured *T*ypes) we offer for efficient handling type expressions for languages with structural type identity:

1 *sort(T)* is used as a hash function: *types* entries with the same sort are linked to distinct hash lists. That helps to avoid, for example, absurd searching of an array type expression among record types.
2 Each explicit type expression is processed as follows.

Its subtypes are handled bottom-up, left to right.

3 For each of the *primitive* subtypes (for example, RANGE), linear search is made in the appropriate hash list of all types of such sort.
4 If the type is found (let's denote it *T*), we use *T* as the type representation.
5 If the type is not found, create a new entry (let's refer to it as *NewT*), link it to the hash list, and use it as the type representation.
6 The same action is performed for each of the structured subtypes of the type being processed, if its component types are already found or created.
7 The result (let's refer to it as *ResT*) is either a new *types* entry *NewT* (if the type is not found) or some already existing *types* entry *T* (if the type is found).

The algorithm guarantees that each of the references to the *types* table points to a unique type.

So, the basic type-checking routine *is_ident(T1, T2)* can be implemented as comparing references *(T1 == T2)*.

The algorithm was used in the CLU compiler for "Elbrus" computers [2].

Example. To illustrate the above algorithm, let's consider an example of type denotation in CLU and its processing by our algorithm.

The sample type denotation we use is a denotation of the following type:

```
proctype (array [int], array[int]) returns (record
[re, im: int])
```

The above is a CLU type of a procedure taking two arrays of integers as arguments, and returning a record with two fields, *re* and *im*, of type *int*.

To simplify our considerations, let's assume that initially the *types* table contains only one predefined type *int* at index 1, denoted as follows:

⟨1⟩ int

In a real CLU compiler, the *types* table is initialized by hundreds of predefined types of the CLU language.

Below, to make the algorithm clear, we use a self-evident form of depicting the content of elements of the *types* table using the syntax of the language.

The steps of the algorithm to process the example type are as follows:

1   Starting to process the type. The type is processed during its syntax analysis by recursive descent. To record the detected types for further hashed search in the *types* table, an auxiliary "buffer" table *buf_types* is used.

2   Detect the outer *proctype* (referred to as *p1*). Start to create its element in *buf_types*.

3   Detect the first inner *array [int]* type—the first argument type of the procedure type. Create an element in *buf_types* for that type (referred to as *a1*).

4   Search the *a1* type in the *types* table. To do that, retrieve from the *hash_hdr* hash header the hash list of all arrays. The list is empty; the type *a1* is not found in *types*, so this is a new type.

5   Move the *a1* type from the *buf_types* to the *types* table. So, the state of the *types* table is now as follows:

```
⟨1⟩ int
⟨2⟩ array [ ⟨1⟩ ]
```

Store in *buf_types*, in the element for the *p1* type, the reference to its first argument type to be ⟨2⟩.

6   Detect the second inner *array [int]* type—the second argument type of the procedure type. As before for the first argument type, create an element in *buf_types* for this newly detected type (referred to as *a2*).

7   Search *a2* in *types*, according to our hashing principle, among the list of all array types stored in the *types* table. Find an array type ⟨2⟩ in types. Compare it to *a2*: their element types ⟨1⟩ compared, so *a2* is considered to be the same type as ⟨2⟩.
     Store in the *buf_types*, in the element for the *p1* type, its second argument type as ⟨2⟩, a reference to the *same* element of the *types* table. Delete the *a2* element from the *buf_types*.

8   Detect the end of the argument types of the *p1* type and the beginning of the *returns* part.

9   Detect the start of the first (and the only) result type—a *record* type (referred to as *r1*). Start to create in the *buf_types* table the element for the record type *r1*.

10   Process the fields of the record. Their types appear to be the same, the predefined type *int*, stored at index ⟨1⟩ in the types table.

11   Finish creating an element for *r1* in the *buf_types* table. Search *r1* in types on the list all record types. There are no record types in the *types*

table yet, so *r1* is a new record type. Move it from *buf_types* to *types*. So now the status of the *types* table is as follows:

```
⟨1⟩ int
⟨2⟩ array [ ⟨1⟩ ]
⟨3⟩ record [ re: ⟨1⟩; im: ⟨1⟩ ]
```

For simplicity, we depict the *record* as just one table element; in a real compiler, the fields *re* and *im* are represented by separate elements of *types* each, linked to a list, and the pointer to the head of the fields list is stored in the element ⟨3⟩.

12 Detect the end of the *returns* part of the procedure type *p1*, and the end of the type in whole. Store in the *p1* element of *buf_types* the reference ⟨3⟩ as the result type. Search the type *p1* in *types* on the list of all procedure types. There are no procedure types on the *types* table yet, so this is a new procedure type. Move it from *buf_types* to *types*. So now *buf_types* is completely empty (actually it works as a stack), and the final status of the *types* table is as follows:

```
⟨1⟩ int
⟨2⟩ array [ ⟨1⟩ ]
⟨3⟩ record [ re: ⟨1⟩; im: ⟨1⟩ ]
⟨4⟩ proctype ( ⟨2⟩, ⟨2⟩ ) returns ( ⟨3⟩ )
```

Please note that, according to the principles of our algorithm, in further processing of more type denotations, if for example, the same (structurally equivalent) record type ⟨3⟩ or procedure type ⟨4⟩ is found on the source code, we guarantee that the newly detected type will be recognized as an already known type, and found on the *types* table.

This is an important advantage of our algorithm and our method to process types in a language with structural type identity. We are not aware of any other compiler from such kind of language that used a similar technique. Instead, other compilers use complicated type graphs comparison algorithms each time it's necessary to compare the types of, say, two variables, which is a far more often performed operation than processing a new explicit type denotation.

5.10 TYPE IDENTITY AND TYPE COMPATIBILITY

Besides type identity, there are two other concepts related to type-checking— *type compatibility* and *assignment compatibility*.

Type identity in Pascal is used for type-checking reference parameters and structured type assignments.

Type compatibility in Pascal is used to type-check subrange types and set types.

Two subrange types are compatible if they have the same *base type* (the type of each of the constants). For example, the types 1 ... 10 and –1 ... 5 are compatible.

A similar rule holds for set types.

For example, the two *set* types *set of 'a' .. 'z'* and *set of '0' .. '9'* are also compatible.

The type compatibility rule is used to check operands of arithmetic or set expressions. For example, in the Pascal expression:

```
['a' .. 'z' ] + ['0' .. '9' ] ,
```

evaluating the set of all letters and digits, the types of the operands are compatible.

The *assignment compatibility* rule is used for type-checking in assignments and passing value parameters.

In assignment $V := E$, the type $T2$ and the value of the expression E are *assignment compatible* to the type $T1$ of the variable V if $T1$ and $T2$ are *compatible*, and the value of the expression E belongs to the set of possible values of $T1$.

Such rule actually means that, generally speaking, *assignment compatibility should be checked at runtime*.

For example (in Pascal):

```
var x: 1..10;  y, z: integer;
begin
    y := 3;
    z := 20;
    x:= y;
    x:= z
end
```

The latter assignment is incorrect: $type(x) = 1 ... 10$; $value(z) = 20$, and that can be detected at compile time, since the statement part is a basic block, with sequential control flow.

However, it can be discussable whether such checks are really performed in Pascal implementations. The standard of Pascal treats such situation as an "error," to be handled by the "Pascal processor." Most Pascal compilers usually don't detect such errors at compile time, but generate code to do that at runtime when the corresponding option is turned on.

In practice, such checks are switched off by default for efficiency reasons, but can be explicitly switched on as a compiler option.

5.11   TYPE-CHECKING, TYPING ERROR DIAGNOSTICS, AND RECOVERY

Type-checking and type error recovery can be organized as follows.

For each construct such as expression, a variable component selection, and so on, a *type evaluation (typing)* routine is implemented. Its goal is to check the correctness of using types in the construct and to deliver, as the result, the *type of the construct.*

> *Typing for expressions.* For each kind of expressions (for example, for the "+" operation), a *type-checking semantic routine* is implemented. Its result is the *result type* of the operation. Such routine usually looks like a big *switch* statement where all allowed combinations of operand types should be considered. The choice between the alternatives should be done using *sorts* of operand types.
>
> So, if in the operation *a OP b* there are *m* allowed alternatives of *sort(type(a))*, and *n* allowed alternatives of *sort(type(b))*, there should be up to *m * n* alternatives in the *switch* statement of the semantic type-checking routine for that operation, plus the *default* alternative to handle and diagnose improper combinations of operand types.
>
> For example, in Pascal, the "+" operation may denote addition for integer or real numbers, set union, or (in Turbo or Borland Pascal) string concatenation. So, the type-checking routine can have 4 * 4 = 16 *switch* alternatives and a *default* alternative for error diagnostics.
>
> *Typing error recovery.* This is based on the idea to use the dummy *T_UNIV* type entry considered to be identical and compatible to any other type, so as not to generate silly error messages.
>
> If any type-related error is detected in an operation (for example, in the operation *s + i*, where *s* is a set, and *i* is an integer), the compiler should issue an error message of improper combination of operand types, and the resulting type of the expression is set to be *T_UNIV*.
>
> In all subsequent type checks, the dummy *T_UNIV* type is successfully compared with any other types, so it is guaranteed that, for one expression, only one type error message is issued, rather than a bunch of absurd error messages.
>
> So, using our approach to typing, we can efficiently implement one of the main operations of typing, *is_ident(T1, T2)*—checking that the types *T1* and *T2*, represented by their references to the *types* table, are identical (with type errors taken into account), as follows:

$$is\_ident\ (T1,\ T2) = ((T1 = T2)\ or\ (T1 = T\_UNIV)\ or\ (T2 = T\_UNIV))$$

This variant also works for structural type identity languages, if our approach is taken to keep a unique copy of each type and subtype in the *types* table.

Typing for record (structure) and object members. For constructs like *p.x*, where *p* is a pointer to a record, structure, or object, and *x* is a *member* of this structure or object—a field or a method—typing is based on *linear search* of the member *x* in the representation of *type (p)*, if it is possible to do at compile time. A record or class type is represented according to the same principles as classical Pascal types (see Section 5.8). The representation of *t = type(p)* should contain a reference like *first_member(t)* to the list of entries of the *type* table, each representing a member of the type.

The entry for each type member *m* contains the following fields:

- *name(m)*—reference to *id_tab* to the members identifier;
- *type(m)*—the type of the member;
- *offset(m)*—the *offset* of the member—its relative address (in bytes) in the representation of the structure (object) *p* in memory; more details on evaluating offsets in Chapter 7;
- *next_member(m)*—a reference to the next member, or *NIL*.

So, the type-checking routine scans the list of members, starting from *first_member(t)*, for the purpose of finding the member *x*. If *x* is not found, an error message is issued, and the type of the member is set to be *T_UNIV*, for error recovery.

For class and interface types in object-oriented languages, we should take into account the *inheritance* of object-oriented types. So, each class type entry *t* in the *types* table should have the field *parent (t)*—a reference to the entry for the parent type (or to a list of parent types, if the source language allows multiple inheritance). So, for class types, if the member *x* is not found in the type *t*, the search is continued in *parent(t)*, and so on. Only if the member is not found, but there is no parent type, an error is diagnosed.

Moreover, as we've noted before, the source language (like Python or Ruby) can have a dynamic typing feature: The member *x* can be absent in the initial definition of *type(p)* but is dynamically *added* to *type(p)* by an assignment like *p.x = E*. So, in this case, the syntax context of the expression *p.x* should be defined, and if it is an assignment to the lacking field, the compiler and the runtime support system should treat such situation as a *dynamic extension* of the object's type. To implement such dynamic features, traditional representation of an object in a contiguous segment of memory is not suitable, and list-like representations should be used. These ideas are implemented in the DLR [68] on the .NET platform.

Typing for indexed variables. For constructs like *a [i]*, where *a* is an array and *i* is the index expression, the compiler should evaluate *at = type(a)*, *it = type(i)*, and check if the *index_type(at)* and the type *it* are compatible. If so, the type of the construct is defined to be *element_type(at)*. If not, the type of the construct is defined to be *T_UNIV*, and the error message is issued. Moreover, a trustworthy compiler in some cases can check the correctness of the index *value* at compile time: for example, if *index_ type(at)* is 1 ... 10, and the index $i = 5$, or i is a variable of type 1 ... 10 or of a narrower range of integer type, the compiler can detect that no runtime code is necessary to generate to check that the index value is within bounds of the range type. If, in the above example, $i = 20$, the compiler can issue an error message that index is out of bounds. It is interesting to note that in modern languages like Java and C#, according to the semantics of the language, the runtime support system *must* generate an exception *at runtime* if the index is out of bounds, so, even if it is statically known that the index is within bounds, the compiler should just issue a warning message (if it detects index out of bounds) and generate the general intermediate code for the construct, with possible exception at runtime. This situation is corrected by just-in-time (JIT) compiler that optimizes the native code for the construct to exclude the redundant runtime checks (see Chapter 6).

Typing for generic (parameterized) types and their instantiations. In languages with abstract data types like CLU, and in modern object-oriented languages like Java and C#, it is possible to use *parameterized types* (in CLU terms), or *generics* (in modern Java or C# terms). A generic type can have *static parameter*, usually the type of the element of the collection defined by this type. Using generics allows software developers to write one "generalized" module of code using type parameters, instead of several similar code modules differed only by the concrete type of the collection's element. For example, in Java, the following code is possible:

```
class Stack ⟨t extends Comparable⟩ ...
```

It means that stack is defined to be a *generic type* whose type parameter *t* is the type of an element of the stack. Any actual type parameter corresponding to the formal type parameter *t* is required to implement the *comparable* interface that contains the *compare* operation (which can be used within the generic type to compare two elements of the stack). If we need to define a stack with concrete element types (e.g., *int* or *String*), we can use *instantiations* (concretizations) of the generic type: *Stack⟨int⟩* or *Stack⟨String⟩*. The task of the compiler when handling instantiations is to check that the requirements for the parameter type hold.

It is very important that, from a typing viewpoint, each two instantiations with different parameters (e.g., *Stack⟨int⟩* or *Stack⟨String⟩*) are considered to be *different* (nonidentical) types, so assignments of variables of such types to each other is a compile-time error. On the other hand, if the instantiation with the same parameter (like *Stack⟨int⟩*) is used several times, it denotes *the same type* (identical types) each time it is used.

Generic types are an important addition to the type identity model covered above in this chapter.

5.12 CODE TRUSTWORTHINESS CHECKS DURING SEMANTIC ANALYSIS

The two tasks and techniques of semantic analysis already considered above, lookup and typing, are intended to exclude semantic bugs in the source program, and to help the program developer make the code more trustworthy by fixing the bugs the compiler found.

However, not all possible kinds of bugs or vulnerabilities in the program code are covered by traditional semantic analysis. There are kinds of possible (or real) bugs and the appropriate semantic checks to be done by a language processor tool, but not covered by most compilers.

Since compilers appear not to be enough to catch and diagnose those bugs, special *source code checkers* are developed that, in addition to compilers, analyze the source code and catch much more potential bugs than traditional compilers. A classical example of such tool is the *lint* code checker [69].

We do think all or most of the problems in the source code listed above should be detected by trustworthy compilers.

Detecting such issues sometimes requires ingenuous algorithms that fully or partially perform at compile time data flow and control flow analysis of the source code.

To leave the detection of such bugs to runtime support system is impractical and nontrustworthy: We do know practical situations when detection of such kind of bugs in large code at runtime took several working days of an experienced programmer.

Also, in this section, we present our method to perform one of such nontrivial static trustworthiness checks we implemented in the Sun Pascal compiler—static checking for proper and improper use of noninitialized record fields [63].

Here are code trustworthiness issues that should be covered by semantic analysis:

1 *Using noninitialized variables.* Most compilers for earlier languages, like FORTRAN, Pascal, or C, don't detect such bugs. Typical example in Pascal:

```
var a: integer;
begin
    writeln('This is garbage: ', a);
end
```

However, the Sun Pascal compiler detects such bugs by the following simple method. For each local variable definition *d* in the NL table, two special fields (flags) are stored and set when appropriate: *nl_mod (d)*—meaning that the variable was modified within the code of its block, and *nl_used (d)*—meaning that the variable was used. At the end of the block, if *nl_mod (d)* is false but *nl_used (d)* is true, a warning message is issued:

The variable ⟨name⟩ was used but never set.

In compilers from modern languages, for example, Java, using non-initialized local variables is checked, so, to keep the Java compiler quiet, we highly recommend to Java programmers to initialize all local variables in their definitions.

Please note that, in general, the compiler cannot be 100% sure whether, according to the control and data flow at runtime, the variable is actually used or actually assigned, since that can happen in an alternative of a conditional statement. But the compiler can detect that within a *basic block*—purely sequential piece of code, without any branches or exceptions. Anyway, performing such kind of checks makes the compiler and the source code more trustworthy.

If the task of the compiler is to check for potential use of noninitialized *component variables* (e.g., record fields), it is much more complicated to do. Below in this section, we describe our method how to do that, implemented in the Sun Pascal compiler.

2   *Defining variables that are never used in the source code.* Such defect is not dangerous and cannot be a potential source of bugs or attacks, but detecting such issue by the compiler can help the program developer to save memory, which is critical if the code is to be executed in the environment with strict limitation of resources (e.g., on a mobile device). Again, the Sun Pascal compiler detects such issue and generates a warning message. The method how to implement such kind of checks in a compiler should be clear from our explanation above how similar checks are implemented for using noninitialized variables.

3   *Array index potentially out of bounds.* In some situations, it is quite possible to detect at compile time that the index of an array can be out of bounds, in particular, when the index is a constant expression.

4   *Incorrect (unreachable) logical conditions.* This is a typical kind of logical mistakes made by programmers in complicated conditions. Example in C:

```
if (x == 1 && x == 2) {
    printf("This is impossible!\n");
}
```

Surely the programmer wanted to use the "||" operation, rather than "&&." Most C compilers don't detect such bugs. *Lint* does.

5   *"Fall through" in switch statements:*

```
switch (a) {
  case 1: S1; /* fall through to alternative 2 */;
  case 2: S2;
}
```

To break the alternative 1, the *break* statement after *S1* is needed. Most C compilers don't warn uses of a potential bug; *lint* does.

6 *Dangerous use of weak typing features* (in particular, in the conditions of *if* statements):

```
int i = 0; …
if (i)
{ printf("Executed if bit 0 of i equals 1\n"); }
```

C and C++ allow the programmers to relax typing in conditions of *if* statements: Instead of Boolean expressions, integer expressions can be used. The condition is considered to be *true* if the lowest bit of the integer resulting value is 1. This is quite a dangerous feature that can lead to a bug: Probably the programmer wanted to write *if (i == 0)* but forgot the tail of the expression.

Most C compilers don't warn users of a potential bug; *lint* does.

7 *Potentially incorrect string comparison using the* == *operator.* This is typical of Java, considered to be one of the most trustworthy languages. Many Java beginners use to compare strings like this:

```
String s1 = System.in.readLine();
String s2 = System.in.readLine();
if (s1 == s2) {
    System.out.printLine
         ("This is true only if s1 and s2 are
      the same object");
}
```

The correct version of string comparison is:

```
if (s1.equals(s2)) { … }
```

None of the Java compilers we know and use detects this potential bug and warns the users, but a really trustworthy compiler should do that.

8 *Synchronization bugs in multi-threading (potential deadlock).* As well known, most synchronization techniques for parallel threads or processes are based on *synchronization brackets*—calls like *wait()* and *signal()* used as brackets for *critical sections* of the code, to be made mutual exclusive for several parallel threads. Example of a synchronization bug:

```
public void run() { // The executable code of the thread
   wait();
   critical_section();
} // the signal() call is forgotten - potential deadlock
```

None of the Java compilers we know detects such potential bugs and warns the users, but it should have done that to be trustworthy.

The above list could be much longer. We hope it will encourage compiler developers to make the compilers really more trustworthy, once the present compilers don't yet detect such potential bugs, evident when the source is examined visually by an experienced programmer.

Our method of compile-time checking for use of non-initialized record fields [63]. Consider an example in Pascal:

```
program p;
procedure qq;
type
  compl = record re, im: integer end;
  arc = array [1..2] of compl;
var
  z: compl;
  a: arc;
begin
  writeln(z.im);
  writeln(a[1].re);
end; /* qq */
begin
end.
```

The program contains two bugs: The field *z.im* is used but never assigned; the field *a[1].re* is also used but never assigned.

None of the Pascal compilers we know, except for the Sun Pascal with our enhancements, detects such bugs at compile time. If the source code is large, detecting such bugs at runtime may be too time-consuming.

So, we implemented in the Sun Pascal compiler our method [63] of detecting such kind of bugs as the *–Rw* option (for *R*ecord *w*arnings).

The method is based on the following ideas. For any kind of local record variable definition, we create two extra fields in its NL table entry *d*:

- *flist (d)*—the list of the fields, used and/or assigned, and
- *clist (d)*—the list of the components assigned,

and use in NL table elements an extra flag *ASSIGNED* showing whether the record variable has been assigned or not.

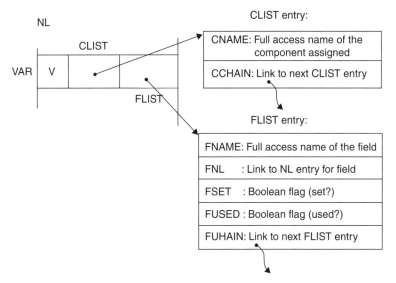

Figure 5.7. *The structure of the namelist table entry for a record variable in the first code example.*

Figure 5.7 illustrates the structure of the NL entry for a record variable. A *clist* entry contains full access name of the record's component assigned *(CNAME)*. A *flist* entry contains full access name of the field (e.g., *"z.im"*), the flags *FUSED* (the field was used) and *FSET* (the field was set), and a backward pointer *(FNL)* to the NL table entry for the record field.

Here is another example in Pascal, with correct and incorrect usage of record fields. We'll demonstrate the use of the above structures using this example:

```
program p;
procedure q;
  type
    R = record a, b: integer end;
    RR = record c: R; d: integer end;
  var
    V: R;
    VV: RR;
  begin
    V.a := 0; { * }
    writeln(V.a); { 1 }
    writeln(V.b); { 2 }
    VV.c := V; { ** }
    writeln(VV.c.a); { 3 }
    writeln(VV.d); { 4 }
  end; { q }
```

```
begin
  q;
end.
```

In the code example, usage {1} and {3} are correct. Usage {3} is correct, since *VV.c* is assigned prior, so *VV.c.a* is also considered to be assigned. Usage {2} and {4} are incorrect and should be diagnosed as bugs, since values of *V.b* and *VV.d* are undefined. Figure 5.8 illustrates the state of the NL table and the corresponding *clist* and *flist* entries for the record fields.

For a record field assignment, a *flist* entry is created, if one does not already exist; the *FSET* field for the *flist* entry is set to *true*, and a *clist* entry is created, if one does not already exist.

For a record variable assignment, the *ASSIGNED* flag of its NL entry is set to true.

For a record field use, a *flist* entry is created, if one does not already exist. The *FUSED* field of the *flist* entry is set to *true*. If the *FSET* field of the *flist* entry is *false*, there is no *clist* entry for the field, the record variable was not assigned (the *ASSIGNED* flag of its NL entry is *false*), and there are no possible control flow changes, this is a bug: A record field is assigned but never used. The compiler issues a warning message.

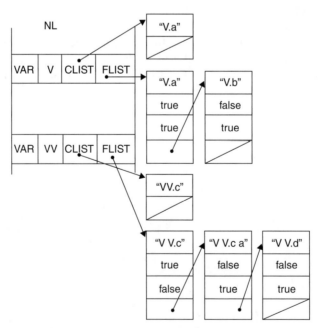

Figure 5.8. *The state of the namelist table and the clist and flist entries for the record fields in the second code example.*

An important idea is used in the algorithm: All record field names are stored in the *clist* and *flist* entries as *strings*, for example, "*V.a*," "*VV. c.a*," and so on, with no spaces. If a record field is accessed by a more complicated construct containing indexed variables, like *R.f [1].x*, its access name is stored in the form "*R.f[...].x*."

So, in searching for the appropriate *clist* or *flist* entries, the identity of the two access names is recognized as the result of string comparison, which is simpler to implement and more efficient than constructing and comparing full ASTs for the record field access operations.

Here is yet another Pascal example that illustrates more complicated cases of assignments and usage of record fields, and their checking by our algorithm:

```
program p3;
  procedure q;
    type
      R = record a, b: integer end;
      AR = array [1..2] or R;
      PAR = ^R;
      FR = file of R;
    var
      V: R;
      A: AR;
      P: PAR;
      F: FR;
    begin
      new (P);   { 1 }
      reset (F); { 2 }
      V := F^; { 3 }
      A [1] := V; { 4 }
      writeln(V.a); { 5 }
      writeln(A[1].b); { 6 }
      writeln(F^.a); { 7 }
      writeln(P^[2].b); { 8 }
      close(F);
    end; { q }
  begin
    q;
  end.
```

This Pascal program contains typical cases of assigning and using record fields, in combination with array, pointer, and file types.

The status of NL, *clist*, and *flist* entries for this example are shown in Figure 5.9.

Here are comments to the numbered points 1–8 in the above program and to the corresponding actions of our algorithm:

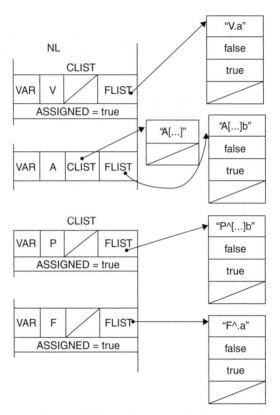

Figure 5.9. *The state of the name table and the clist and flist entries for the record fields in the third code example.*

1   *P* is implicitly initialized by the predefined procedure *new*, which allocates a new dynamic variable on the heap, and assigns its address to *P*. The whole variable is marked as assigned by the *ASSIGNED* flag in *P*'s NL entry, so any of the component fields will be considered assigned. No warning is printed.

2   The predefined procedure *reset* implicitly assigns the content of the first file's block to the buffer variable *F^* of the file *F*. So *F* is also marked as assigned in the NL table. All its components are considered to be assigned. No warning issued.

3   The record variable *V* is explicitly assigned. It is marked as assigned by the *ASSIGNED* flag in the NL table. No warning issued. Please note that the *whole* variables (like *V*) are not recorded into *clist* or *flist*; only record fields are.

4   The indexed variable *A[1]* is assigned. Its full access name is transformed into "generalized" form "*A[...]*," and the corresponding *clist(A)* entry is created. No warning issued.

5 *V.a* usage is not a bug, since the whole variable *V* is assigned. No warning issued.

6 *A[1].b* usage is not a bug, since *A[…]* is assigned. The access name is transformed into a "generalized" form "*A[…].b*" and added to *flist(A)*. On adding, the compiler checks whether there is a prefix of the field access on the *clist(A)*. The "*A[…]*" entry is found on the *clist(A)*. No warning issued.

7 *F^.a* usage is not a bug, since *F* is marked as *ASSIGNED* in NL. No warning issued.

8 *P^[2].b* usage (transformed into "*P^[…].b*") is not a bug, since *P* is marked as *ASSIGNED* in NL table. No warning issued.

The algorithm works only in case the *–Rw* option is passed to the compiler. By default, static record field checking is switched off.

The work on enhancing the existing Sun Pascal compiler by static record field checking was done by the order of a customer who was satisfied with the quality of the checking and warnings implemented.

This example shows how an existing commercial compiler can be made more trustworthy, without substantial changes in the code, and without any extra tools developed. The efficiency of the algorithm is clear: No extra passed on the source code made; no high complexity algorithms like comparison of trees used; the algorithm works as part of the semantic pass of the source program.

5.13 CHECKS FOR CONTEXT RESTRICTIONS IN SEMANTIC ANALYSIS

As we noted before, in real programming languages, there can be situations when some context restrictions cannot be expressed by the CF syntax specified by the grammar of the language. So such kinds of checks are forced to be done during the semantic analysis phase.

Here is just a funny example of such situation in our practice of the Sun Pascal compiler maintenance in the 1990s. A customer filed a bug with the following description. The buggy "kindergarten-style" Pascal program given below was successfully compiled, with no errors or warnings:

```
program p;
begin
  read (10 numbers);
end.
```

When analyzing the *yacc* grammar of the language, and the compiler code, we found the reason of this bug. A fragment of the grammar for procedure calls used in the compiler before fixing the bug is given below. Some unimportant rules or alternatives, and semantic action parts are omitted. For the readers to quickly understand the meanings of syntax notions, we added some comments:

```
stat:  … /* syntax of Pascal statement */
    |
         qual_var '(' wexpr_list ')' /* procedure call
*/
    …
    ;
…

wexpr_list: /* list of expressions with width fields
             for output */
    /* empty */
        |
    wexpr
        |
    wexpr_list ',' wexpr
        ;
wexpr:  /* expression with width fields for output */
    expr
        |
    expr YID /* actually YID can only be 'oct' or
                'hex' */
        | …
        ;
```

The problem with the context restrictions was as follows. The source language, extension of Pascal, allowed to output (by *write* or *writeln* predefined procedures) values of integer type expressions in octal or hexadecimal form. For that purpose, the modifiers *oct* or *hex* after are used after the expressions to output, for example:

```
writeln('i (hexadecimal)= ', i hex, ', i (octal)' = i oct);
```

To specify this syntax by CF grammar in *yacc*, the developers introduced the extra syntax notion *wexpr* that can be of the following format: *expression identifier*, as can be seen from the above grammar. But general framework of CF syntax didn't allow the compiler developers to formulate the following important context restrictions:

- *wexpr* can be used only in a call of the predefined *write* or *writeln* procedure;

- the *YID* (identifier) in *wexpr* does make sense only if the expression is of *integer* type;
- when the two above conditions hold, the identifier can only be *hex* or *oct*.

So, checking for the above conditions to hold should have been done by the appropriate semantic analysis routines. But the developers of the initial version of the compiler just forgot to make those semantic checks.

We fixed this bug by adding the appropriate semantic checks to the appropriate semantic analysis routine. In case the above conditions don't hold (like in the "10 numbers" example above), we added an error message of the kind: *The operator symbol in the expression missed*, to make the compiler behavior trustworthy in all possible cases.

5.14 INTERMEDIATE CODE GENERATION—PRINCIPLES AND ARCHITECTURAL MODELS

Intermediate code generation is the concluding part of semantic analysis.

Intermediate code is generated as the result of semantic analysis, if there is no lexical, syntax, or semantic errors (i.e., for semantically correct programs only).

Then, the intermediate code is passed to the next phases of the compiler—to code optimizer and object code generator. Those phases constitute the back-end of the compiler.

If the phases of the compiler, except for lexical analysis, are organized as a set of independent programs, with the compiler driver to invoke them in turn, the intermediate code is stored in a temporary file whose path is passed to the next phases via command line.

For example, Sun Studio [14] compilers are organized that way, and the IR is stored in a temporary file with the *.ir* extension.

Please note that, in many compilers, *several* forms of intermediate code are used during semantic analysis and the subsequent phases.

Requirements to IR, also referred to as *intermediate language* (IL), are determined by the role of the intermediate code. They are as follows:

- *Simplicity.* The intermediate code should be easily understandable and analyzable.
- *Ease of subsequent object code generation.* The intermediate code should be based on a simple model (for example, reverse Polish notation) that supports easy and efficient algorithms to convert the IR into any of the target platform instruction sets.
- *Ease of optimization.* Optimization phase is usually performed using IR. It takes as input nonoptimized IR and generates optimized IR. During program transformations performed by the optimizer, typical operations are code insertion, deletion, replacement, or moving code back and forth.

So, from this viewpoint, any reference-based tree-like form of the IR is preferable, and linear forms of the IR are less suitable. For that reason, for example, in Sun Studio compilers, the optimizer takes linear IR (organized as *triples*), converts it to tree-like format (*PCC trees*), performs code transformations, and then converts the resulting IR back to triples.

- *Language independence.* IR is an IL that can be regarded as an instruction set of some *abstract machine*. But it should not, if possible, depend on the source language being implemented by the compiler, because in this case, the compiler developers can organize the front-end and the back-end as completely independent parts, related only by the IR, and, due to that, use one common back-end with several language-dependent compiler front-ends. Several families of compilers (e.g., Sun Studio, GNU compilers) are organized according to this principle.

Approaches to IR architecture models can be the following:

- *IR is an «abstract machine» code.* A possible method of implementing such kind of IR architecture is *postfix notation*, like Microsoft.NET Intermediate Language (MSIL) or Java bytecode. The other method is to use *triples*, each of them containing an *abstract operation code*, first and second operands, similar to machine code of target hardware platforms.
- *IR is a tree-like representation of the program.* We already explained why trees are convenient for this purpose. As a higher-level form of intermediate code used in earlier phases of compilation, *attributed syntax trees* are used in many compilers. Also, *PCC trees*—a form of binary trees—are very popular in compilers now. *B-trees* and *B+ trees* are also used as IR in some compilers, due to a number of their efficient analysis and transformation algorithms known in computer science.
- *IR is the basic IL for the common back-end* of a family of compilers, or for a compiler design system. One of the most famous of them is Sun IR designed by Muchnick [70]. There was also an interesting Russian project of this kind, implemented in 1980s in Novosibirsk in BETA [29] compiler development system with the IL VYAZ (in Russian, the latter acronym means both "internal language" and "elm tree"). One of the latest examples of such approach is Microsoft Phoenix [3]—a toolkit for compiler development, a kind of universal optimizing multi-targeting back-end. It uses three kinds of common IRs: high-level IR (HIR), medium-level IR (MIR), and lower-level IR (LIR). Phoenix is discussed in Chapter 10.

5.15 POSTFIX (REVERSE POLISH) NOTATION

The most popular kind of IR is *postfix notation* (or *reverse Polish notation*).

The origin of the latter name is as follows: The idea of similar prefix notation was proposed in 1920 by Polish mathematician Jan Łukasievicz.

Each expression in postfix notation is represented in the following way: the operands first, then the operator. This principle is applied recursively, for all subexpressions. For example:

Expression:

```
(a + b) * (c - d)
```

Its postfix notation:

```
a b + c d - *
```

The advantages of using postfix notation as an IR are:

- *Simplicity.* The structure of the postfix notation is even simpler than that of the traditional infix notation. There is no need for brackets.
- *Ease of extraction from the source code or from the parse tree (or AST).* Well known is the classical algorithm by Dijkstra for translating expressions to postfix notation [5]. We'll outline this algorithm and offer the readers to implement it as Exercise 5.5 to this chapter.

    There are two stacks used in Dijkstra's algorithm: *stack of operands* and *stack of operators*. At each step, the algorithm reads the current symbol from the input. If it is an operand, it is pushed onto the stack of operands. If it is an operator, the precedence of the operator is compared with that of the operator on top of the operator stack. If the current operator on the input has lower precedence, the two operands are popped from their stack, and then the operator is popped from the operator stack to the output. Left parentheses, if any, are also pushed onto the stack of operators, and popped from that stack when the pairing right parenthesis is encountered. Parenthesized expressions are considered to be primary expressions, as well as identifiers or constants.

    For the above example of expression, Dijkstra's algorithm of its conversion into postfix notation works as follows:

Step 1:

Input: $(a + b) * (c - d)$
Stack of operators: *Empty*
Stack of operands: *Empty*
Actions:
Shifting "(" onto the operator stack;
shifting the operand a onto the operand stack

Step 2:

Input: $+ b) * (c - d)$

Stack of operators: (
Stack of operands: *a*
Actions:
Shifting "+" onto the operator stack

Step 3:

Input: *b) * (c – d)*
Stack of operators: (+
Stack of operands: *a*
Actions:
Shifting *b* onto the operand stack

Step 4:

Input: *) * (c – d)*
Stack of operators: (+
Stack of operands: *a b*
Actions:
The input symbol is ")" considered as the end of subexpression whose operands *a* and *b* are on the operand stack, and whose operator "+" are on the operator stack.

So we shift the symbol ")," output "*a b* +" as part of the postfix notation, and pop "+" and "(," and the operands *a* and *b* from their stacks.

Step 5:

Input: * *(c – d)*
Stack of operators: (+
Stack of operands: *a b*
Actions:
Shift the operator "*" onto the operator stack.

Steps 6–9:

Input: *(c – d)*
Stack of operators: *
Stack of operands: *Empty*
Actions:
Work similar to steps 1–4 when processing *(a + b)*, that is, output "*c d –*" as part of the postfix notation.

Step 10:

Input: ⟨*EOF*⟩
Stack of operands: *
Stack of operators: *Empty*
Action:

Output "*" as the concluding part of the postfix notation.
Stop.

- *Ease of conversion to tree-like representation and vice versa.* Using simple algorithm similar to Dijkstra's algorithm above, postfix notation can be transformed into a binary tree representation. Similarly, tree-like representation can be easily transformed into postfix notation. We offer the readers to implement these two transformation algorithms as Exercise 5.6 to this chapter.
- *Ease of interpretation (emulation).* Postfix notation can be interpreted using just one stack and the following algorithm. Each operand is pushed onto the stack. When an operator is encountered, its one or two operands are popped from the stack (they should be on top of the stack to be easily seen), the operation performs, and the result is pushed onto the stack. This algorithm is used in all hardware-implemented and virtual stack-based machines.

A notable use of Postfix notation in compilers was *p-code*—a Pascal intermediate code, based on postfix notation, designed by Wirth [71] in early 1970s. Wirth designed and used p-code for the purpose of easily porting his Pascal implementation to a variety of target platforms. The influence of p-code not only to software but even to hardware development was deep. There appeared hardware platforms on which the p-code was *hardware implemented*.

James Gosling, the author of Java, stated in an interview that p-code and its hardware implementation on some workstations inspired him to design *Java bytecode*—the IR used in Java technology, also based on postfix notation.

On the Microsoft.NET platform, its IL—CIL (also known as MSIL), is similar to Java bytecode and is also based on postfix notation.

As for the Russian hardware and software engineering, an interesting example of hardware architecture from late 1970s to early 1980s based on postfix notation was "Elbrus," a family of Soviet computers [2] whose architecture supported basic features of high-level languages. The "Elbrus" instruction set was based on postfix notation. But actually those stack machine instructions were used as *intermediate code*, since the "Elbrus" hardware performed (speaking in modern terms) JIT compilation of stack-based instructions to three-address register machine code.

For reasons already clear to us, postfix notation has been used in a lot of interpreters for a variety of languages.

The following *issues of postfix notation* should be taken into account.

First, postfix notation is hardly human readable, and, for this reason, nontrustworthy and not suitable as a programming language.

Surprising as it may seem, postfix notation actually has been used for about 20 years as the basis of the programming language FORTH [72]. Speaking straightforward, we don't consider FORTH to be a comfortable and safe language because, in our opinion, programming "on the stack," without using any named variables, by hand, is too tricky and can lead to hardly recognizable bugs. Actually, programming in a stack-based language requires usage of a dynamically changing image of the current state of the whole stack at each step of programming.

Fortunately, MSIL and Java bytecode, in addition to their model of evaluation of expressions on the stack, also have local variables addressed by integer numbers. Such addition to postfix notation substantially increased readability and trustworthiness of the postfix code.

The second issue of the postfix notation is that it's not quite comfortable for program transformations because of its linear structure.

5.16 PCC TREES

Another popular form of IR is referred to as *PCC trees* [54]. The PCC acronym comes from Portable C Compiler—the first compiler by Johnson developed in the late 1970s where this kind of IR was used.

Essentially, PCC trees are a kind of *binary trees*.

They are not explicitly dependent on the source language, but nevertheless, they are much more suitable for C than, for example, for Pascal.

PCC trees are still being used in many commercial and research compilers, for example, in Sun Studio compilers. So, we'll consider their structure in more detail.

An advantage of PCC trees, and the main reason why they have been so popular for about 30 years, is their suitability for various program optimizations and transformations. It is much easier and much more efficient to update a tree than a linear sequence of postfix or prefix instructions.

The main issue of PCC trees is as follows: They don't contain sufficient information on data types (so to say, «metadata»), even for languages like Pascal. In particular, there is no adequate way of representing a Pascal compound type by PCC trees.

So, some of the terminal PCC tree nodes have to keep references to NL table entries during the phases of semantic analysis, optimization, and code generation. When doing Sun Pascal compiler, we had to use such a technique.

An interesting idea implemented in PCC trees is a compact representation of types in a 32-bit word referred to as *TWORD* (for *Type WORD*).

This encoding of types is based on C language. Other language compilers have to map their language types onto PCC types.

A type is encoded as «TWORD» (32 bits, or 4 bytes long) that contains packed representation of the type. The principle of encoding is as follows.

There is the *base type* encoded by 6 bits, and there are *type modifiers* added to the base type, each of the modifiers occupying 2 bits. The modifiers are PCC_PTR (*pointer*) and PCC_FTN (*function*).

So, there can be no more than 13 type modifiers in a TWORD, but, in practice, this restriction would never be exceeded.

For example, the C type:

```
(* int) ()   ,
```

the type of a function returning a pointer to *int*, will be represented as the following TWORD:

(PCC_FTN (2 bits), PCC_PTR (2 bits), PCC_INT (6 bits))

The "senior" modifier comes first.

Here are two other base type codes corresponding to the ways of type structuring: PCC_STRTY (*structure type*) and PCC_UNION (*union type*).

The plus of such representation of a type is its small and fixed size—a 32-bit word. It does not require extra memory for any internal pointers and intermediate table entries.

The minus of this representation is as follows: It does not contain explicit information on size and alignment for structured types. So, the designers of TWORD had to add a special PCC *structure node* (*stn*), which should be used for structured types and should contain their *size* and alignment—(*stsize*, *stalign*).

For the rest of the types like PCC_PTR and PCC_FTN, the size and alignment is assumed implicitly.

Here is C code to define the kinds of notes and the layout of PCC trees:

```c
union p2node {
    struct {
            int         op;
            TWORD        type;
            NODE        *left;
            NODE        *right;
            char        *name;
    }            in;    /* interior node */
    struct {
        /*
         * this structure is the same as above
         * but is used when
         * a value, rather than address, is stored
           in "left"
         */
            int         op;
            TWORD       type;
            long        lval;
            int         rval;
            char        *name;
    }            tn;    /* terminal node */
  struct {
        /*
         * used when a floating point constant is
```

```
                * being computed
                */
            int            op;
            TWORD          type;
            double         dval;
    }            fpn;    /* floating point node */
    struct {
            /*
             * used for operations on structures
             */
            int            op;
            TWORD          type;
            NODE           *left;
            NODE           *right;
            int            stalign;
                       /* alignment of structure
                          objects */
            int            stsize;
                       /* size of structure objects */
    }            stn;    /* structure node */
struct {
            int            op;
            TWORD          type;
            int            cdim;
            int            csiz;
            int            bfwidth;     /* bit field width
*/
            int            bfoffset;    /* bit field
                           offset */
    }              fn;    /* front-end node */
/* * TIP-style interface to P2 trees, see Section 1.1
 */
 #define P2_OP(p)      /* Operator tag */ \
     ((p)->in.op)
#define P2_NAME(p)     /* Node (symbol) name */ \
     ((p)->in.name)

#define P2_LHS(p)      /* Left operand */ \
     ((p)->in.left)

#define P2_RHS(p)      /* Left operand */ \
     ((p)->in.right)

#define P2_TYPE(p)       /* P2-type of the terminal
                            node */ \
     ((p)->tn.type)
```

All kinds of PCC nodes defined above contain the following fields:

- *op*—the code of the (abstract) operation related to this node;
- *type*—the resulting type of the node (in the form of *TWORD*).

Interior nodes (*in*) are intended to represent unary or binary operations.
They contain the pointers to PCC trees representing the *left* and the *right*
operand, and the *name*, if any, associated to the expression.

Terminal nodes (*tn*) represent terminal nodes of expression trees: variables,
constants, formal parameters, and all other cases of identifier usage. Please
note that an explicit constant literal is also represented by a terminal node.

So the specific fields of terminal node are as follows:

- *rval*—the value of the constant (if any);
- *lval*—the location or a global symbol of a variable or constant, if any.

Floating-point nodes (*fpn*) are a special kind of node to represent floating-
point (float or double) constant literals. So, the specific field of a floating-point
node is *dval*—the value of the constant.

Structure nodes (*stn*) are used to represent an operation whose result is of
a structured type. So, they are organized similar to interior nodes but also have
the fields *stsize* and *stalign* to keep the size and the alignment of the structured
result.

The so-called *front-end nodes* (*fn*) are actually *bit field nodes*. They are used
to represent bit field operations characteristic for C-like languages. So, they
contain the specific *bfwidth* and *bfoffset* operations to represent the offset and
the width of the bit field.

After the definitions of PCC structures in C, we placed our code of some
useful macros in technological instrumental package (TIP) technology [2] style
we use for accessing and updating PCC tree nodes.

5.17 TRIPLES

Triples, as well as postfix notation, is another form of linear IR.

It is based on a model of an abstract two-address machine, so each triple
has the following structure:

```
⟨n⟩ type   op_code   first_operand   second_operand
```

where *n* is the number of the triple; *type* is the type of the triple (the type of
the result delivered by the *op_code* operation). The type can be represented
by a *TWORD* (see Section 5.16), augmented by the *size* and the *align* of the
type; this enables all information on the type necessary for the subsequent
optimizations and code generation.

Since the triples are numbered, one triple can refer to another triple (e.g., representing one of the operands) by its number.

For example, the expression $a + b * c$ (where the type of a, b, and c is int) can be represented by triples as follows:

```
⟨1⟩ int  add  a_var_leaf   ⟨2⟩
⟨2⟩ int  mul  b_var_leaf   c_var_leaf
```

where *a_var_leaf*, *b_var_leaf*, and *c_var_leaf* are references to the *leaves* representing the variables a, b, and c (see below).

The structure of the triples is close to «two-address» machine code characteristic of Reduced Instruction Set Computer (RISC) machines.

Triples are organized into *blocks*. A block is a list of triples representing a *basic block*, a sequential part of a program with purely linear flow of control.

Operands of triples can be:

- references to other triples, for example, ⟨2⟩;
- references to *leaves*—terminal nodes representing constants or variables.

Leaves (or terminal nodes) represent *variables* (VAR_LEAF)—the offset and the size of a local variable, or the assembly symbol for a global variable; *constants* (CONST_LEAF)—the type and the value of a constant; or *address constants* (ADDR_CONST_LEAF), the address of a variable.

Each leaf belongs to some *segment*—abstraction of a class and the area of memory where the leaf is allocated. Segments can be of many kinds, corresponding to real classes of memory on a target machine, in particular:

- AUTO_SEG—stack activation record or its contiguous part;
- BSS_SEG—static global memory. In BSS section, all noninitialized global data are allocated.

Blocks (containing triples) and segments (containing leaves) are tied to *modules*. *Module* corresponds to a procedure or function. A module contains the list of its blocks and the list of its segments.

So actually, no matter triples are a linear form of IR, they are linked into a tree-like structure, to reflect the structure of the program.

Triples and leaves are used in many compilers, including Sun Studio compilers [70].

5.18 SUMMARY OF THE CHAPTER

In this chapter, we have shown how to make algorithms of semantic analysis more efficient, using our innovative ideas and approaches. We have seen that, in many cases, straightforward implementation of traditional schemes of semantic analysis, or "blind" use of multiple traversals (passes) of tree-like IRs of the source program may lead to dramatic inefficiencies, and have explained how to resolve such issues by reasonable use of semantic attributes, applied occurrences lists, and hashed tables.

To conclude the chapter, we should summarize that semantic analysis is still an attractive and evolving part of compiler development, since the semantics and typing of modern languages are getting more and more complicated, so compiler researchers and developers still have a good chance to invent new, yet more efficient algorithms.

We'll refer to the material of this chapter and will actually enhance this material later on in Chapter 6 on optimization and in Chapter 7 on code generation. In particular, Chapter 7 covers runtime representation of various data types, and the ways to handle the variables (objects) of various types and their components at runtime. This is because the phases of compilation are closely interrelated, in particular, IRs, optimization, and code generation.

EXERCISES TO CHAPTER 5

5.1 Prove correctness of the algorithm D of one-pass analysis of definition systems from Section 5.4, and implement this algorithm.

5.2 Define an attributed grammar for very simple, Pascal-like language containing *integer* type, variable definitions, assignments, and blocks. Test this grammar using *yacc*.

5.3 Implement the algorithm ST to process type expressions for structural type identity languages from Section 5.9.

5.4 Implement a type-checking algorithm for Pascal expression of the kind $a + b$.

5.5 Implement Dijkstra's algorithm to convert an expression into postfix notation.

5.6 Implement an algorithm to convert a binary tree representation of an expression to its postfix notation, and, vice versa, the algorithm to convert postfix notation of an expression to its binary tree representation.

5.7 Implement the structure of the IR consisting of triples, leaves, and segments covered in Section 5.17.

Chapter 6

Trustworthy Optimizations

Optimizations are program transformations preserving the program functionality but improving its runtime performance against some *criteria* (*speed, memory use*, etc.).

This chapter is only a brief overview of compiler optimizations, which is so serious a subject that it deserves many special courses and many books.

The classical book on compilers, actually devoted to optimizations, is the excellent book [13] we recommend for advanced study of compiler optimizations.

The novel features of this chapter, as compared with other compiler books, are our analysis of trustworthiness of compiler optimizations (Section 6.1), an overview of the concept of optimization as a kind of mixed computations, and an overview of optimizations in Java and .NET, and of just-in-time (JIT) compiler optimizations.

6.1 BASIC CONCEPTS AND TRUSTWORTHINESS OF OPTIMIZATIONS

In compilers, the phase of optimization usually follows the phase of semantic analysis and precedes the phase of code generation.

The optimization phase of the compiler is usually implemented as optional, that is, optimizations are switched off by default, and the user can switch on the appropriate level of optimizations as compiler options.

From the viewpoint of our book and approach, optimizations should be trustworthy. The trustworthiness of optimizations can be considered twofold. On the one hand, optimizations should fully preserve the functionality of the program, that is, they should not be buggy, for example, deleting an assignment to a variable that is used in an outer procedure (more details later in Section 6.3). On the other hand, optimizations should not make it hard for the user to understand his or her program's optimized code (at the source level, at some intermediate level, or at the object code level). The optimized code should remain readable, understandable, and debuggable.

Please note that, according to the dialectical nature of programming, it's not possible to meet all optimization criteria at once. For example, if a program is optimized to run at minimum possible time, this optimization is likely to use, in an explicit or implicit way, some extra memory (either for the program data or for the code) to achieve the performance boost.

One of the best examples of optimizing compilers is Sun Studio compilers [14,70]. Sun Studio provides a unique set of optimizations, subdivided into five levels (more details in Section 6.7). Optimization mode in Sun Studio is turned on by $-xO1, \dots, -xO5$ options, according to one of the five desirable levels of optimization to be done.

Usually, compiler optimizations are performed at the intermediate code level. That means, the optimizer takes nonoptimized intermediate representation (IR) as input and generates optimized IR.

From a more general viewpoint, the task of optimization can be regarded apart from the compiler, as a separate task, performed as *conversion*, or *optimizing transformations*, at the source code level.

At very high levels of optimization, sometimes the so-called "*over-optimization*," or "*pessimization*" can happen. That is, too high level of optimization, or optimizations nonsuitable for some particular program, can make total runtime performance worse than just some reasonable middle-level optimizations.

From the target hardware or virtual platform viewpoint, optimizations are subdivided to *platform-independent* and *platform-dependent*.

Platform-independent optimizations are performed by a special optimizer phase at the intermediate code level.

Platform-dependent optimizations are performed by the code generator at the target hardware platform or abstract machine code level.

On the Microsoft.NET platform, all the compilers generate the Microsoft. NET Intermediate Language (MSIL) code actually with *no optimizations* (except *constant folding*—calculating constant expressions at compile time). All optimizations are performed on-the-fly by the JIT compiler (more details in Section 6.10).

According to the region of the program where optimizations are made, they are subdivided to:

- *local*—optimizations within a *procedure (method)*, or, more locally, within a *basic block*, that is, a linear part of the program with no calls, branches, or exceptions;
- *global*—optimizations taking into account the whole program structure and interprocedural relationships;
- *peephole*—a kind of local optimizations, performed by the optimizer or the code generator, as if looking at the code through a "peephole" of fixed size—two to five statements or machine instructions, that is, performing optimizations only within such small fixed-size pieces of code.

6.2 OPTIMIZATIONS AS MIXED COMPUTATIONS

A more general concept worth considering when speaking about optimizations, is *mixed (partial) computation* invented by Russian academician Ershov in 1977 [73].

Mixed computation M is a program transformation of the kind:

$$M: (P, D) \rightarrow (P_1, D_1)$$

where:

- P is the source program,
- D is P's initial data (or input),
- P_1 is the *residual program*, and
- D_1 is the *residual data*.

The mixed computation system M performs program transformations, taking into account both the program structure and its concrete data (the latter may allow some simplifications or optimizations).

In particular, M can substitute some of the data from D into the program P, generate the program P_1, simplified or somewhat transformed due to taking D into account, and leave the residual part of D as D_1.

The input D is not necessary to be the input data themselves. It can also be some extra information on the program P, in particular, the initial values of some of its variables, some assertions based on program analysis or on the practical experience, and so on.

The process of converting D to D_1 is also referred to as *concretization*.

From this general viewpoint, optimization is just some specialized form of mixed computations. Other forms of mixed computations include *compilation* itself, *JIT compilation*, *interpretation*, and *conversion* from one high-level language to another, or to the same language.

Please note that mixed computation systems can be conveniently and efficiently implemented on the Microsoft.NET platform, due to its functionality to load new assemblies at runtime, reflection (*System.Reflection*), and to runtime generation of MSIL and new assemblies (*System.Reflection.Emit*).

6.3 OVERVIEW OF THE MOST COMMON KINDS OF OPTIMIZATIONS

Optimizations within a basic block. A *basic block* is a linear control flow part of a program, with no *if* or *switch* statements, calls, branches, or exceptions, that is, with no control transfers, except for implicit control transfer to the next statement.

Typically, a basic block consists of assignments (containing expressions) and probably system calls like data input (semantically similar to assignment) and output.

The basic block optimizations take into account its linear control flow ("as textually written"), so the optimizer can be sure that, if some variable X is assigned a value as the result of some earlier statement, the value is preserved until the next assignment to X.

Please note that, even if applying just one of the optimizations considered below may have no effect on program performance, the local optimizations can make proper effect when used together.

The first, most common, kind of optimizations (usually performed by the front-end rather that by a separate optimizer) is *constant folding*— evaluation of constant expressions at compile time. We already discussed in Chapter 5 how to implement it efficiently using two special synthesized attributes evaluated as early as possible and stored in the abstract syntax tree (AST).

Example:

```
x:=  1+2+3;        ->          x:=  6;
```

The second one is *constant propagation*. That means, when a variable is assigned a constant value, say 0, all its subsequent uses are replaced by that constant.

Taken as is, this optimization may have no effect, but using this optimization, followed by constant folding, can simplify and optimize the program because, due to constant substitutions, more expressions can actually become constant expressions that may be evaluated at compile time.

Example:

```
a:=  0;  b:=  1;   ... a  ... b  ... a+b   ->     a:=  0;  b:=  1;
                                                  ... 0  ... 1  ... 1
```

The third one is *copy propagation*. That means, when a variable X is assigned the value of the variable Y, all subsequent uses of Y can be replaced by X.

Again, taken by itself, this transformation could be useless, but followed by constant propagation as in the example below, and then followed by constant folding, those optimizations together can make the program more efficient.

Example:

```
y:= z;  … y … y            ->    y:= z;  … z … z
```

Here we are replacing the variable *y* by the variable *z* if the assignment *y* := *z* takes place prior, and the value of *y* remains unchanged within the basic block. By itself, this kind of transformation may have no effect, but it may be efficient when applied together with constant propagation, for example:

```
x:= 1; y:= x;  … x … y … x … y ->
x:= 1; y:= 1;  … 1 … 1 … 1 … 1
```

Arithmetic simplifications. A number of local optimizations are related to various *arithmetic simplifications*. Such optimizations are a kind of *peephole optimizations*, since, to perform them, it's enough to "see" only a small fixed-size piece of code.

First, a number of *strength reductions* can be applied to replace slower operations (like *multiplication*) to sequences of faster ones. For example, *integer multiplication to a power of 2* can be replaced by a *left shift*, as shown in the example:

```
x * 2     ->    x << 1
x * 4     ->    x << 2
```

Multiplication to a small constant can be replaced by *several additions*, for example:

```
a * 1 ->  a
a * 3 ->  a + a + a
a * 0 -> 0
```

The "add one" or "subtract one" operations can be replaced by pseudo-calls of *inc* or *dec* routines that are hardware implemented on a number of platforms and may be more efficient:

```
z := z+1;  -> inc(z);
z:= z-1;   -> dec(z);
```

Common subexpression elimination. Either in a complicated expression or even in a whole basic block containing such expressions, *common sub-*

expression elimination can be applied. It means, each of the subexpressions occurring several times is evaluated once only, and its value is assigned to a temporary variable or register. Later on, all the subsequent occurrences of the same subexpression are replaced by the use of that temporary variable (register).

This optimization is more difficult to implement because it requires analysis and comparison of the expression trees within the basic blocks.

Surely, such optimization can be performed if the values of all the variable operands of the expressions are unchanged since their single assignment. The latter condition means that implementing this optimization requires *data flow analysis* [5,70] within the basic block.

Example:

```
a := (b+c)*(d+e) + f;  x:= (b+c)*(d+e);    ->
tmp:= (b+c)*(d+e);  a := tmp + f;  x:=  tmp;
```

Code elimination. There is another important class of local optimizations—*code elimination*. They are subdivided into *dead code elimination* and *unreachable code elimination*.

Dead code elimination is deleting part of the basic block's code if, on the optimizer's opinion, it is useless for the effect of that block. Typical example shown below is assigning a value to a local variable, which is not used subsequently, by the end of the basic block. The deleted code in the examples below is marked by self-evident comments.

It is very important for optimizer's developer to take into account that eliminating an assignment to *a nonlocal (uplevel) variable* is dangerous and may appear to be an optimizer bug. In our practice with the Sun Pascal front-end, some situations happened when the optimizer mistakenly deleted an assignment to a nonlocal variable from a Pascal procedure because it did not take into account that the variable was *uplevel addressed*, that is, used in an outer procedure (though not used in the current one).

Example:

```
procedure p; /* outer */
  var x: integer;
  procedure q; /* inner, embedded to p */
  var y: integer;
  begin /* q */
    y := 1; /* assignment to a local variable */
    x:= y; /* assignment to uplevel variable x
- don't delete */
  end; /* q */
begin /* p */
  q; /* assigns x */
```

```
writeln('x=', x);
end; /* p */
```

In the above code, the assignment to the uplevel variable *x* within the inner procedure *q* (embedded to *p*) shouldn't be deleted by the optimizer, since *x* is used in *p* after the call of *q*.

To take this into account, the optimizer should mark the leaf corresponding to the variable applied occurrence as *possibly uplevel addressed* and do not apply dead code elimination optimizations for the code of assignment to any variables marked in such a way.

Here is an example of correct code elimination:

```
var x, y: integer;
begin
  /* dead code - deleted by the optimizer */
  x:= 1;
  /*end of dead code */
  y:= 0;
  writeln(y);
end
```

In the above example, the assignment *x* := 1 is considered to be a dead code because its result is not used in the current block. So it can be eliminated by the optimizer. This optimization is correct only if *x* is a local variable.

Unreachable code elimination is detecting pieces of code that will not be executed because they are unreachable (e.g., because of some specific use of *goto* statements, as shown in the example). This optimization requires *control flow analysis*, at least for procedure or a method body. Again, the code to be deleted is marked by appropriate comments:

```
begin
    a:= 0;
    goto M;
    /* unreachable code - can be deleted by the
       optimizer */
    writeln('Not reached!');
    /* end of unreachable code */
    M: writeln('I am alive!');
end
```

Loop optimizations: Invariant code motion. There are a number of specific *loop optimizations* that make the most positive effect for *scientific computing* programs, especially for programs that sequentially process vectors and matrices. Surely, the more loop iterations are performed, the more effective these optimizations are.

The first one is *invariant code motion*. The optimizer analyses the body of the loop and detects the code that does not depend on the *loop parameter* (also referred to as *loop induction variable*).

Such code can be moved outside the body of the loop and thus executed once only before the loop instead, for example, a million times within its body.

Example. The code:

```
. for i := 1 to n do
  begin
    x:= y+z;
    a[i] := x * i;
  end;
```

due to code motion, can be replaced by the following code:

```
x:= y+z; /* moved from the loop */
for i:= 1 to n do
begin
    a[i]:= x * i;
end
```

The invariant expression does not depend on the loop induction variable, so it is moved outside the loop, to be executed once before the loop.

Loop optimizations: Induction variable elimination. Another important group of loop optimizations is related to using multidimensional arrays in the bodies of the loops.

Since a two-dimensional slice takes, on average, 10–20 machine instructions, the optimizer tries to replace it by *one-dimensional slice*, based on the facts that arrays are represented in *linearized form*, that is, in a linear piece of memory, and addressing of an array element is based on its *passport* that consists of *the address of the initial element* and the so-called *dimension steps*—the factors each index should be multiplied to. The expression for calculating the address of an array element is a *linear form* depending on the indexes. More details on representation of arrays later in Section 7.5.

So the basic idea is for the optimizer to find all multidimensional slices within the loop body and to try to replace them to one-dimensional slices, by constructing, prior to the loop, a passport for one-dimensional array with the appropriate initial address and the dimension step.

It can be easily shown that such optimization is possible if each array index expression within the loop is a *linear form of the indexes*. For example, if an index expression is the sum of loop parameters, the appropriate one-dimension passport can be constructed, but if the index expression is the product of the loop parameters, such passport *cannot* be constructed.

On average, 5–10 machine instructions can be saved for each two-dimensional slice, due to such optimization. Please multiply this number by the number of loop iterations (say 1 million), then you can realize how dramatic its effect can be for programs that process arrays in a *linear* (or *regular*) way.

Example. The following code:

```
for i:= 1 to n do
    for j:= 1 to m do
        a[i*2+1, j*3+2] := i+j;
```

can be transformed by an optimization to the following much more efficient code where a two-dimensional slice is replaced by indexing of a vector:

```
k := c1;
for i:= 1 to n do
begin
  for j:= 1 to m do
  begin
    b[k] := i+j;
    inc (k, c2); /* move to the next element in
    the row of a */
  end;
  inc (k, c3); /* move to the next row of a */
end;
```

where:

- b is the vector that stores the linearized representation of the array a; and
- $c1$, $c2$, and $c3$ are constants that depend on the size of a but don't depend on the loop parameters i and j (induction variables).

Loop optimizations: Loop unrolling. As any other control transfer statement, a loop changes the flow of control. It takes time to execute extra *branch* commands and breaks the hardware *pipeline*—optimizations performed by most hardware architectures (parallel execution of several data-independent machine instructions). So optimizations that transform a piece of program code into a basic block without any changes of control flow may appear to be very effective. Among those optimizations is *loop unrolling*. Its idea is as follows. If a loop has only k iterations, or is likely to be repeated only k times where k is a small constant, the optimizer can "unroll" those k iterations of the loop into a basic block, and thus save execution time.

Examples:

```
1) for i := 1 to 3 do S    -> S; S; S

2) for k := 1 to n do S ->
     S; S; S;
     for k := 4 to n do S; /* this code is likely
                 to be skipped */
```

Inlining. Inlining is another kind of optimizations that can produce substantial effect, in case an application contains a lot of calls of very small routines.

The essence of inlining is to implement small routines as macro extensions, that is, to substitute the code of the routine body instead of its call.

The routines subject to inlining can be detected by the optimizer using some criteria (e.g., the total small number of instructions is less than 100, and the absence of the other calls in the body of the routine).

Inlining can be switched on either by special compiler options, for example, by the C/C++ "pragma" of the kind:

#pragma inline.

The effect of inlining can be substantial because it eliminates the instructions of passing parameters, control transfer to the routine, and return.

Typical examples when inlining can take a lot of effect are *getter* and *setter* methods in object-oriented languages, for example, C# and Java. Their bodies do not contain other calls and are actually as small as to consist of less than 10 instructions. For example:

```
public class C {
   int x;
   public int getX() /* a getter method */
   { return x; }
   ...
}
 C p = new C(); ...
C.getX()    /*    this code can be replaced by p.x */
```

The only issue of inlining, but a serious one, is its confusion with the principles of abstract data types (ADTs) and object-oriented programming (OOP). One of the key principles of these programming techniques is *data encapsulation*. But, for efficient application of inlining, the optimizer has to "disclose" the implementation, or *body* of the underlying function or method. Moreover, when processing some compilation unit, the implementations of methods from other classes it calls are likely to be unknown yet.

Nevertheless, inlining can be efficient at the phase of *JIT compilation* because at runtime, when the JIT compiler works, all the implementations working as parts of an application are known and accessible. More details on optimizations in JIT compilations later in Section 6.10.

6.4   CONTROL FLOW AND DATA FLOW DEPENDENCIES

To be able to optimize the source program code, the optimizer performs *control flow analysis* and *data flow analysis* of the program and of each basic block. It constructs *control flow* and *data flow graphs* in some forms, specific for the optimizer, that specify control and data dependencies between the elements of the program. Here are the most important kinds of such dependencies [13].

The statement *S2* is *control dependent* on the statement *S1* if the execution of *S2* depends on the conditions evaluated in *S1*. For example:

```
S1   if i > 0 then goto L1;
S2   a := 1;
S3   L1: c := a + 2;
```

Here, *S2* is control dependent of *S1*, since the fact whether *S2* will be executed or not depends on whether the condition evaluated in *S1* is true or not.

The statement *S2* is *data flow dependent* on the statement *S1* if *S1* assigns a variable used by *S2*, and *S1* precedes *S2* in the control flow of the program. For example:

```
S1   a := 0;
S2   b := a + 1;
```

In the above example, *S2* is data flow dependent on *S1*.

A statement *S2* is *antidependent* on *S1* if *S2* assigns a variable that *S1* uses, and *S1* precedes *S2* in the control flow. For example:

```
S1    a := b + 1
S2    b := 2
```

In the above example, *S2* assigns the value of the variable *b*, but *S1* uses the value of *b* prior to the assignment.

A statement *S2* is *output dependent* on *S1* if *S1* and *S2* assign the same variable, and *S1* precedes *S2* in the control flow. For example:

```
S1    a := 1
S2    a := 2
```

In the above example, *S2* and *S1* both assign to the variable *a*.

A statement *S2* is *input dependent* on *S1* if *S1* and *S2* use the same variable, and *S1* precedes *S2* in the control flow. For example:

```
S1        a  :=  b  +  1
S2        c  :=  b  +  2
```

In the example above, *S2* and *S1* use the same variable *b*. Actually, such dependence is not a dependence in the same sense as those defined above, since it doesn't prevent from any kind of reordering the statements.

More details are found in Reference 13.

6.5   STATIC SINGLE ASSIGNMENT (SSA)

From our considerations and definitions above, it should be clear that a number of optimizations on basic blocks (e.g., constant propagation, copy propagation) can be done only if the optimizer is sure that a variable *a* is assigned a value that is *not changed* within some further code of the basic block. From this viewpoint, it would be the most comfortable for the optimizer if any variable would be assigned *once* only within some piece of code.

For the purpose of transforming the source program to such format, the *SSA* form of IR is used. SSA is a form of program in which each variable is assigned once only. If, in reality, any variable is assigned several times within a piece of code, when transforming to SSA form, the variable is *renamed* each time its new assignment is found. For example:

```
a  :=  0;
a  :=  a  +  2;
a  :=  3;
a  :=  a  +  4;
```

In this code, the variable *a* is assigned twice. The SSA form for this code can be as follows:

```
a  :=  0;
a  :=  a  +  2;
a1  :=  3;
a1  :=  a1  +  4;
```

So, in the SSA form, all occurrences of the variable *a* are renamed to *a1*, starting from the second assignment to it.

In case there are changes of control flow, for example, in conditional statements, if the flow of control and the values of the variables cannot be fully tracked at compile time, the φ function is used to specify the cases where the value of the variable can be different in the different branches of control flow. For example:

```
if x > 0
then a := 1
else a := 2;
```

In the above code, the value of the variable *a* after executing the conditional statement depends on the condition that cannot be evaluated at compile time. To "hide" such specifics, the φ function is used in the SSA form of the above code, as follows:

```
if x > 0
then a1 := 1
else a2 := 2;
a3 := φ (a1, a2);
```

The SSA form is used in many compiler optimizers, including the Microsoft Phoenix toolkit [3]. Phoenix constructs *SSA graphs* that model the dependencies of use and assignment for the variables. An example of an SSA graph for the variable *a* and the code like the above is shown in Figure 6.1. Dotted edges indicate *Use* dependencies; contiguous edges depict *Def* dependencies.

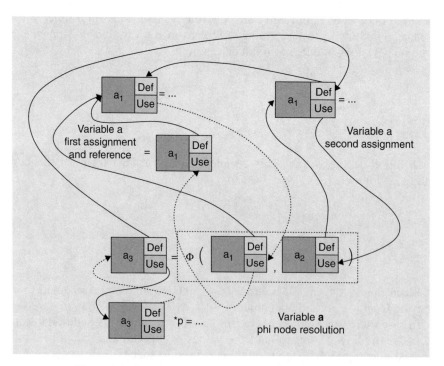

Figure 6.1. *Example of an SSA graph constructed by Phoenix.*

6.6 DATA STRUCTURES CONSTRUCTED AND USED BY THE OPTIMIZER

This section summarizes informational structures constructed and used for the purpose of compiler optimizations.

The *SSA* form of program IR is explained in Section 6.5.

Data flow graph is a graph of informational dependencies between variables. Each variable is represented by a vertex, and an edge from the vertex A to the vertex B shows that the value of the variable B depends on the value of the variable A (like in the assignment: $B = A + 1$).

Control flow graph represents all control flow dependencies between *basic blocks* of the program. Each control flow branch (like a *goto*, call, exception throw, etc.) is represented by an edge of this graph. Vertices typically represent *basic blocks*.

Basic blocks are fragments of the program with purely linear control flow—without any control flow branches. Within basic blocks (in Sun IR—just *blocks*), as we've seen before, a lot of optimizations are possible, based on the assumption that the control flow is linear.

For each statement S, an optimizer usually constructs and uses two sets of variables:

- *In(S)*—set of all input variables of the statement (i.e., the set of variables whose values are used in the statement);
- *Out(S)*—set of all output variables of the statement (i.e., the set of variables whose values are defined, or assigned, by the statement).

In Phoenix IR, these two lists are parts of the internal representation for each IR instruction. An overview of the optimization techniques in Phoenix will be given later on in Chapter 10.

The best references related to optimizing compiler techniques are References 13, 74, and 75.

6.7 OPTIMIZATION IN SUN STUDIO COMPILERS

Sun Studio [14] is a family of compilers by Sun Microsystems, Inc. It currently includes the C, C++, and FORTRAN compilers that work on the following platforms:

- Solaris/Scalable Processor ARChitecture (SPARC);
- Solaris/×86/×64;
- Linux/×86/×64.

Back in the 1990s, Sun compilers also included Pascal and Ada compilers. As explained in Chapter 5, our role in the development of Sun compilers was maintenance and enhancement of the Sun Pascal compiler that was actively used by many customers in the 1990s.

Sun Studio compilers are organized according to the classical UNIX scheme. A compiler (say, the C compiler—*cc*) can be used from the command line in the following style:

```
cc mycode.c
```

where *mycode.c* is the C source code file to be compiled.

Each of the Sun Studio compilers has got a *compiler driver*—the control program that invokes, in turn, the phases of the compiler as separate programs, using the classical UNIX *exec*/*execve* system calls.

Here are, for example, the phases of the C compiler invoked as separate programs:

- *acomp*—the front-end, comprising lexical analysis, parsing, and semantic analysis, which generates Sun IR (see Chapter 5) in a separate intermediate *.ir* file;
- *iropt (the IR optimizer)*—the optimizer of Sun IR, which takes nonoptimized IR and generates optimized one. The *iropt* is called only in case the *–xO*, *–xO1*, *–xO2*, *–xO3*, *–xO4*, or *–xO5* option is switched on. The number in the option is the *level* of optimizations. By default, there is no optimization. With the *–xO* option, optimization level 3 is performed;
- *cg*—the code generator that takes the IR and generates the object code (in *.o* file).

The Sun optimizer, *iropt*, is one of the most advanced optimizers among many compilers we have ever used. Algorithms used in *iropt* became classics of optimizing compilers. The foundation of *iropt* was laid by Dr. Steven Muchnick in the 1980s and 1990s [13,70] who invented the Sun IR (intended for multilevel optimization) and most of the optimizations still used in Sun Studio compilers.

Internally, *iropt* uses both Sun IR and Portable C Compiler (PCC) trees as IR. The resulting IR can look very different from the original one: *iropt* renumbers and reorders triples and leaves.

The following *levels of optimizations* are implemented in Sun Studio compilers.

Optimization level 1 (–xO1 option). Peephole optimizations are performed. Peephole optimizations are optimizations via some fixed-size "window" through which the optimizer "sees" only a limited number of instructions (triples). An example of an architecture-dependent peephole optimization (for SPARC hardware platform) is *filling out the delay slots.* SPARC architecture allows a control transfer (e.g., *call*) two-cycle instruction and the next one-cycle instruction (typically, load register) to be executed in parallel. So, the optimizer can generate optimal code for routine calls like

$p(x)$ with one argument: The call of p (taking two hardware cycles) and loading to the output register the value of the argument x (taking one cycle) can be executed in parallel. By default, with no optimizations, loading the register comes first, then goes the call command, and the delay slot after that command is occupied by a placeholder—the *nop* (no operation) instruction. More details on SPARC architecture in Chapter 7.

Optimization level 2 (the –xO2 option). Basic local and global optimizations are performed at this level (see Section 6.3 for the overview of most of them): Induction variable elimination, algebraic simplifications (e.g., replacing multiply by degree of two by shift operations), constant propagation and copy propagation, loop-invariant optimizations (e.g., code motion from the loop if the code doesn't depend on the loop parameter), dead code elimination, and tail recursion and tail call elimination. Level 2 doesn't allocate in registers the results of global, external, or indirect references. Instead, all such references are treated as *volatile* (not subject to optimization). With level 2, the optimized code is at the minimum possible size.

Optimization level 3 (the –xO3 option). At this level, all level 2 optimization are performed, and a number of extra ones: optimizing references to external variables, loop unrolling, and software pipelining. So, with level 3 optimization, the size of the code may increase (e.g., as the result of loop unrolling). The external variables not to be optimized should be marked by the *volatile* type specifier, to avoid optimizations.

Optimization level 4 (the –xO4 option). This optimization level not only works as level 3 but also performs *inlining* (see Section 6.3) of the functions contained in the same file. This decreases execution time but increases the size of the resulting code. Inlining can be controlled by special options and pragmas (like *#pragma inline*), to more concretely specify the set of the functions to be inlined.

Optimization level 5 (–xO5 option) is the highest level of optimization. It uses the results of prior *profiling* the program that can be obtained by the *–xprofile=collect* option. Next, the *–xprofile=use* option should be used together with *–xO5* to enable the highest level of optimizations. Please note that using profiler results doesn't always help to improve performance, so, with level 5, the code performance can sometimes appear to be worse, as compared with level 4; so level 5 optimizations should be used carefully.

6.8 OPTIMIZATIONS OF THE JAVA BYTECODE

The Java bytecode is the platform-independent binary representation of executable Java code, based on postfix notation of the program. In general, the task of optimizing Java applications is very important, since Java is used worldwide, but its performance is still far from the ideal. Since Java technology is not the subject of this book, the goal of this section is to summarize some interesting methods of optimizing Java applications.

The traditional scheme of compiling and executing Java programs by Sun is based on the following steps:

- compilation of the Java source (*.java*) to bytecode (*.class*);
- JIT compilation of Java methods in the process of executing Java programs by the Java Virtual Machine (JVM). Each method is JIT compiled from the bytecode to the native code on its first call by the JVM;
- dynamic profiling, optimization, and de-optimization of Java programs by the HotSpot Performance Engine, part of JVM.

So, there are several opportunities of optimizing Java programs: during their compilation to bytecode; at the bytecode level (conversion from nonoptimized bytecode to optimized bytecode); and at runtime, by the JIT compiler. This section summarizes the first and the second alternatives; Section 6.10 covers the third one.

In general, all the optimization techniques summarized above (constant and copy propagation, common subexpression elimination, loop unrolling, etc.) are applicable to Java. The Sun's Java compiler *javac* has got the *−O* option to switch on some minor level of optimizations (peephole) when generating the Java bytecode. The *−O* option appears to be undocumented in the Java Development Kit (JDK) documentation.

However, there are many opportunities how to optimize the Java bytecode. For mobile devices and personal digital assistants (PDAs), with their strict memory limitations, the most important is *optimization for size.*

To more deeply understand how to decrease the size of the Java bytecode (more exactly, of a Java *.class* file that contains the bytecode), let's make an overview of the class file representation.

The Java class file consists of the *constant pool* and the bytecode of a Java class (method-by-method). The constant pool is a kind of "universal" constant and type repository in Java technology. It contains not only string and numerical constants used by the Java program but also the *types* and the *names* of all entities defined and used in the Java program. Please note that, in Java technology, *local* variables (defined in methods), as represented in the *.class* file, don't have names; they are represented by their *numbers*, starting with 0. The Java class represented by the *.class* file has *public* members—fields and methods—whose names are necessary to be known from outside of the class. On the other hand, *private* fields and methods of the class are only visible inside the class, so their names (though they are kept in the *.class* file) are unimportant to the rest of the Java program.

So, to optimize the size of a *.class* file, the better way is to optimize the size of the constant pool [76,77]. On average, the constant pool occupies about 60% of a Java *.class* file.

Here are some useful ideas and methods that can be used to decrease the size of the constant pool in a Java *.class* file [76,77]:

- deleting unnecessary records in the constant pool, by prior marking really useful records, with further constant pool compaction and deleting unnecessary records (a kind of "mark-and-sweep" garbage collection for the constant pool). Unnecessary records may appear in many situations, for example, when the bytecode refers to predefined *constants* (in Java, *public static final* fields of predefined classes). For example, if a class uses the predefined constant *Math.PI*, its constant pool contains a reference to the predefined class *Math*, though the Java compiler replaces the access *Math. PI* to the value of the constant, so the reference to *Math* becomes an unnecessary record in the constant pool that could be deleted during the constant pool compaction. There are many kinds of such situations in Java [78,79];
- renaming private methods (invisible to other classes) to shorter names;
- reusing records in the constant pool by using already existing method names (represented in the constant pool) as the new names of private methods. For example, let a class (and the constant pool) uses the predefined method *Double.isNaN*. Then, the constant pool contains the corresponding record to refer to it. Let also the same class has a private method *MyMethod*. Since the name of a private method is not visible from outside the class, and is not important for the JVM to correctly call the private method, the Java bytecode optimizer can formally rename *MyMethod* to *isNaN*, so the record for *MyMethod* in the constant pool appears to be unused, and can be deleted during the constant pool compaction.

Another interesting approach to reduce the size of the Java bytecode [80] is *pattern-based peephole bytecode optimization*. The optimizer works using a number of patterns for typical small fixed-size fragments of Java bytecode to be replaced by shorter ones. For example, the following Java code:

```
int a, b; ...
a = b;
```

by default is compiled to nonoptimal bytecode like this:

```
iload_2; // load to the stack the value of b
dup; // copy it to the stack
istore_1; // save the stack top to a
pop; // delete the current stack top value
```

The optimizer [81] finds in the input *.class* file the code fragments like the above, and replaces them to more optimal and shorter ones:

```
iload_2; // load to the stack the value of b
istore_1; // save the stack top to a
```

6.9   OPTIMIZATIONS OF THE .NET COMMON INTERMEDIATE LANGUAGE (CIL) CODE

As already noted in Chapter 1, usually .NET compilers, when generating a CIL code, don't make almost any optimizations (except for the simplest ones, like constant folding), and leave the favor of optimizing the program to the JIT compiler. The latest Microsoft.NET development environment available, Visual Studio.NET 2008, doesn't have explicit optimization options or CIL code optimization tools. To our knowledge, there are no other commonly used tools specifically for CIL code optimization (as opposed to the Java bytecode optimization—see Section 6.8). However, we do think such tools will be developed in the future, since the common optimization techniques like those summarized in Section 6.3, are applicable to the CIL code.

A good basis for the CIL code optimization tools could be Microsoft Phoenix [3] covered in detail in Chapter 10. From the CIL code processing viewpoint, Phoenix follows the strategy explained below. Among Phoenix tools, there is the *MSIL code reader* that converts MSIL code to *Phoenix IR*. Phoenix IR represents the program code as triples, with the set of *input* and *output* variables explicitly stored for each triple. All optimizations are performed by Phoenix at the IR level, as more suitable for optimizing transformations. Then, Phoenix can convert the optimized IR back to (optimized) MSIL code, with its component referred to as *portable executable (PE) writer*.

6.10   OPTIMIZATIONS DURING JIT COMPILATION

JIT compiler, as already explained in Chapter 1, is a runtime support component of modern software development platforms, like Java and .NET. The role of the JIT compiler is as follows: When a method is first called by the runtime support system (according to newly established tradition, let's use a shorter term *runtime*), the runtime calls the JIT compiler that compiles the method to a *native code* of the target hardware platform—×84, ×84, SPARC, and so on. Subsequently, when the JIT-compiled method is called repeatedly, the runtime transfers control directly to the native code generated by the JIT compiler. Such runtime strategy greatly reduces the execution time of the program, in case JIT-compiled methods are called more than once. However, if a method is called just once, its JIT compilation doesn't increase total runtime performance of the program, since a lot of time is spent to the JIT compilation itself.

The idea of the JIT compiler is not new and was coined long before Java or .NET appeared. Many programming systems of the past approached the idea of JIT compilation, but, to our knowledge, the first JIT compiler was developed by ParcPlace Systems, Inc., as part of the VisualWorks programming system, the implementation of Smalltalk. Here is the citation from the VisualWorks system manual [82] dated 1994, kindly presented to us by Dr. Coleman, one of the developers of that system:

When you enter a method in a code view and choose accept, the method is immediately parsed for syntax errors and then compiled into byte codes. At runtime, invoking the method causes the byte codes to be translated to native machine code appropriate to the run-time platform. This native code is then cached so that subsequent invocations of the method do not require translation. Consequently, the performance of Smalltalk applications is comparable to that of statically compiled languages, but the code is portable to any supported platform without recompilation.

Please note that the language and the terminology of this document written 15 years ago look quite contemporary, as if it were part of modern documentation on the latest versions of Java or .NET.

The terms *native code* and *byte code*, key terms of Java and .NET, are used in the above fragment. The term *JIT compilation* is not explicitly used. It appeared some years later, in mid-1990s, when the first JIT compilers for Java were developed by Symantec and by IBM (the latter—as part of IBM DK for Java system [78,79]). JIT compilers in both systems performed optimizations based on the results of dynamic profiling of the program.

The other major project, one of the first Java implementations that included an optimizing JIT compiler, is Jikes RVM (initially referred to as Jalapeňo) [81,83].

Microsoft.NET, since its first version, stated JIT compilation to be one of its keystones. The commercial version of .NET includes optimizing JIT compiler.

Here are the principles and most typical kinds of optimizations performed by modern JIT compilers:

1   *Selective JIT compilation based on profiling.* We have already seen that JIT compilation of all methods is not always justifiable and may even lead to overall runtime performance decrease, if JIT compiled methods are called once only. So, one of the key ideas of JIT compilers is to collect profiling information on method calls. For the purpose of profiling, pure interpretation of all methods can be used by the virtual machine. A threshold value T—the number of method calls (typically $T = 10$)—is set by the JIT compiler. When JIT compilation is turned on, the JIT compiler analyses the number of calls $nCalls(M)$ for the method M it attempts to compile. If $nCalls(M) > T$, the method M is considered to be *hot*, and is JIT compiled, with a number of optimizations performed. If not, the method remains in bytecode form. Similar strategy is used by the HotSpot performance engine, part of Sun's JVM. The practice of the use of modern object-oriented software development platform shows that this principle enables the most dramatic performance increase effect.

2   *Inlining.* We have already noted in Section 6.3 that *inlining*, substitution of the code of method call to the point in the program where it is called, plays an especially important role in OOP systems. Due to the principle of *data encapsulation*, OOP recommends to define the fields of a class

as *private* (hidden in the class definition) and to provide *getter/setter methods* to access and update the information represented by the field, for example:

```
class C {
  private int counter = 0;
  public getCounter() // getter method
  { return Counter; }
  public setCounter(int c) // setter method
  { counter = c; }
}
```

So, a call of the method *p.getCounter()*, where *p* is the object reference to an object of the class *C*, is actually equivalent to just one instruction of the virtual machine—loading to the stack the value of the field *counter*. A call of the method *p.setCounter(c)* is equivalent to the assignment *p.counter* = *c*. So, principles of OOP may lead to the situation when, in a large application, a lot of code will be split into very small parts like getter/setter methods, which may cause performance decrease, since it requires the execution of a lot of redundant call/return commands, taking much more time than the above reading or assigning fields. So, JIT compilers usually perform *inlining* of such short methods. This optimization, when performed at runtime by the JIT compiler, doesn't contradict to the principles of data encapsulation, since the user cannot see the JIT compiled native code, which is normally *not persistent*, that is, not saved on finishing the program execution.

3   *Devirtualization.* Virtual method calls work much slower than calls of static or instance methods. The reason is as follows: Virtual methods are represented by their pointers in the *virtual method table (VMT)* of the host class (more details in Section 7.6). Such implementation of virtual methods cannot be changed, since it enables the dynamic selection of the method to be actually called. The main idea of implementing virtual methods is the following: For a virtual method *M*, in ancestor and descendant classes, the offset of the pointer to *M* in their VMTs is the same. The situation with virtual methods may seem critical because in Java, all nonstatic methods are virtual by default, and there is no way to define an instance nonvirtual method. But please don't forget that a JIT compiler that works at runtime exists. Its advantage is that, unlike ordinary compiler, it "sees" all actual references to methods, and can determine which implementation code of the virtual method *M* is actually called by the constructs like *p.M()* where *p* is the object reference. So, a JIT compiler, typically, performs *devirtualization* of methods: For each virtual method call, it evaluates the actual address of the code of the method *p.M* and, in the native code generated, instead of generating an indirect call command, generates an ordinary call, which is much

faster. The JIT compiler can store and use the table of the addresses of code of the kind *p.M* for each method it compiles to native code. Such optimization helps to save a lot of execution time and avoid substantial slowdown that might occur because of the use of virtual methods.

4 *Basic block optimizations by JIT compilers.* Typical basic block optimizations considered in Section 6.2—constant propagation and copy propagation—are also performed by JIT compilers.

5 *Elimination of redundant runtime checks.* In many cases, the JIT compiler that "sees" not only the types and definitions in the program but also all runtime structures can generate a native code without runtime checks that appear to be redundant (typically for indexing arrays). For example, consider the following typical fragment of a Java code:

```
int [] a = new int [100];
for (int i = 0; i < 100; i++) {
  a[i] = i+1;
}
```

Though it is evident that no *ArrayIndexOutOfBoundsException* will be thrown (since the index *i* is guaranteed to be within the bounds of the array *a*), the Java compiler *javac* must generate the common case of the Java bytecode for the construct *a[i]*, with the array indexing JVM command to check the value of the index at runtime, since the Java compiler should preserve Java semantics. However, such check is redundant, and the JIT compiler is in a good position to generate more optimal native code for this construct, without bound checks for the index *i*.

More details on JIT compilers later in Chapter 8.

EXERCISES TO CHAPTER 6

6.1 Design and implement a suitable representation of basic blocks, and implement the typical basic block optimizations: constant folding, constant propagation, copy propagation, and dead code elimination summarized in Section 6.3.

6.2 Design and implement an algorithm of transforming the program to its SSA form.

6.3 Implement the algorithm of compaction of the constant pool of a Java .class file outlined in Section 6.9.

6.4 Practice with some existing open source JIT compiler, for example, the FJIT compiler in Shared Source CLI/Rotor—noncommercial version of .NET), or the JIT Java compiler in Sun's OpenJDK: Add to the code of the compiler any optimizations (e.g., basic block optimization, devirtualization, etc.) outlined in Section 6.10.

Chapter *7*

Code Generation and Runtime Data Representation

Code generation is the concluding phase of compilation. Its purpose is to generate a *native object code* of the target platform (e.g., ×86/Windows, Itanium/ Windows, SPARC [Scalable Processor ARChitecture]/Solaris, etc.) or *virtual machine object code* (e.g., Java bytecode or Microsoft.NET Intermediate Language [MSIL]).

Generally speaking, code generation, as well as code optimization, deserves a separate course. We devote to it just a chapter in our book.

The novel material in this chapter is the detailed discussion of runtime data representation for various types and code generation for SPARC architecture. It reflects our own experience and results in compilers.

7.1 TARGET PLATFORMS FOR CODE GENERATION

Code generation techniques should take into account the specifics of the target platform.

Evolution of target platforms since the 1980s leads from the *Reduced Instruction Set Computer (RISC)* to the *Very Long Instruction Word (VLIW)* and the *Explicit Parallelism Instruction Computer (EPIC)* hardware architectures, and, recently, to multi-core architectures.

Basic features of RISC architectures are simplified instruction set, register operations only, large register file, and pipelining. They are still widely used.

Trustworthy Compilers, by Vladimir O. Safonov
Copyright © 2010 John Wiley & Sons, Inc.

More details on RISC architectures are discussed below in this chapter, in relation to SPARC architecture that belongs to the RISC type.

The main features of the VLIW/EPIC architecture are wide instruction word containing several *subinstructions* for all of the units—arithmetic units, logical units, and so on. The compiler should statically plan optimal loading of each unit for each wide instruction.

The main idea of *multi-core* architectures is that the program execution can be parallelized by using several *cores* of the CPU located in the same chip and by sharing the same memory.

The code generator may perform platform-dependent optimizations.

The simplest of them are peephole optimizations, like *filling the delay slot* in RISC architecture, that is, parallelizing execution of the *call* instruction and loading the argument of the function to be called.

Due to widespread Internet programming and programming for embedded (mobile, etc.) systems, there is an evident trend in modern programming systems and platforms (Java, .NET) to postpone native code generation up to the runtime phase and to perform it as *just-in-time (JIT) compilation*, which actually means compiling from the Java bytecode or MSIL to a native code at runtime ("on-the-fly"). Java technology started using JIT compilation technology since Java 1.1 in 1996, and .NET has made it ubiquitous.

7.2 OVERVIEW OF CODE GENERATION TASKS AND GOALS

The code generator performs a variety of tasks. They are summarized in this section.

Parsing the intermediate representation (IR). As we saw in Chapter 6, the structure of the IR is simple enough to make this task easier. Some complicated code generators, in their turn, use their own internal representation (or representations) of the program, most convenient to perform different stages of code generation. In this case, a code generator also performs conversion of the IR to its favorite internal code.

Platform-dependent optimizations. This task is optional and can be controlled by compiler options. The specific kinds of optimization depend on the specifics of the hardware platform. Examples of platform-dependent optimizations are the following:

- filling delay slots for RISC architecture;
- planning 100% load of each operational unit in VLIW/EPIC architecture at each machine cycle;
- using a specific kind of machine instructions to support loops and induction variables, increment and decrement, and so on;

- using specific machine instructions to prefetch next elements of arrays during their sequential processing, for example, in matrix multiplication.

Memory allocation and data representation. Based on the information retrieved from the IR generated by the front-end, the code generator plans *stack, heap,* and *static* memory areas allocation and assigns to local and global variables and their components the corresponding *global symbols* or *offsets.* For components of variables of compound types, like records, arrays or objects, the code generator provides the object code that implements the appropriate formulas to evaluate the address of the component. For example, if R is a record variable and F is its field, the address of F equals to the address of R plus the offset of F within the R record. Data representation and formulas to evaluate the sizes, offsets, and addresses are discussed in Section 7.5.

Register allocation. The essence of this task is planning the use of the minimum possible number of registers to evaluate all the expressions. The simplest algorithm to do that is to use the postfix notation of the expression and the *list of free registers.* Also, a *stack of temporary values* is used. The scheme of the algorithm is similar to that of evaluating postfix notation on the stack. Postfix notation is processed from left to right. If the current element is an operand, a new free register is taken from the list and an instruction to load the register by the value of the operand is generated.

On the same step, the current register number is pushed onto the temporary values stack.

If the current element is an operator, the two upper elements (register numbers) are popped from the temporary values stack, the new register number is taken from the free list, and an instruction is generated to perform the operation on the two popped numbers of registers from the temporary stack and to store the result in the new register. Then, the numbers of registers used for the operands are returned back to the list of free registers.

Let's consider in more detail the algorithm (referred to as G) outlined above. The input of the algorithm is the postfix notation for an expression (*Expr*). The algorithm uses the list of free registers (*Reg*) and the stack of register numbers for temporary values (*Val*). The task of the algorithm is to generate a code for evaluating the expression for a RISC machine (e.g., SPARC) using the minimum possible number of registers. Let the instructions to be used be:

- ld %r a—load the value of the variable (or constant) a to the register %r;
- add %r1 %r2—add the values from registers %r1 and %r2 and store the result into %r1 (also, the *sub* and *mul* instructions are available, with the format similar to *add*).

Here is the scheme of the algorithm *G*:

```
G1. Repeat the following steps until the end of Expr
G2. x = Next_Expr();
G3. If x is a variable or a constant
        r = New_Reg();
        Gen("ld %r x ");
        Push_Val(r);
G4. (assert: x is a binary operator)
        c = Instr(x); // the instruction corresponding
                             to x
        r2 = Pop_Val(); // the second operand (register)
        r1 = Pop_Val(); // the first operand (register)
        Gen("c %r1 %r2");
        Free_Reg(r2); // r1 is busy with the result
        Push_Val(r1); // the result
G5. Go to G1
```

In the above pseudocode of the algorithm, we used the following denotations:

- *Next_Expr()*—the next element of the input postfix notation of the expression;
- *New_Reg()*—find and return the new free register number;
- *Free_Reg(r)*—put back the register *r* into the list of free register numbers;
- *Push_Val(r)*—push the register *r* onto to the stack of temporary values (stored in registers);
- *Pop_Val()*—pop a register number from the stack of temporary values;
- *Instr(x)*—the machine instruction corresponding to the operator *x* (*add, sub,* or *mul*);
- *Gen(c)*—generate the instruction *c*.

Please note that the complexity of this algorithm is $O(n)$, where n is the length of the (postfix notation of) expression, since the algorithm allocates registers and generates code for the expression at one pass of the input expression.

Example of the use of the algorithm:

Let the input expression be: *a b + c d - **.
Let the register file *Reg* be: *(%r1, %r2, %r3, %r4)*.

The algorithm *G* will work as follows:

Step 1. $x = a$ (variable); $r = \%r1$; $Val = (\%r1)$; **generate**: *ld %r1 a*;

Step 2. $x = b$ (variable); $r = \%r2$; $Val = (\%r1 \ \%r2)$; **generate**: *ld %r2 b*;

Step 3. $x = +$ (operator); $r2 = \%r2$; $r1 = \%r1$; **generate**: *add %r1 %r2*;
$Reg = (\%r2, \%r3, \%r4)$; $Val = (\%r1)$

Step 4. $x = c$ (variable); $r = \%r2$; $Val = (\%r1, \%r2)$; **generate**: *ld %r2 c*;

Step 5. $x = d$ (variable); $r = \%r3$; $Val = (\%r1, \%r2, \%r3)$; **generate**:
ld %r3 d;

Step 6. $x = -$ (operator); $r2 = \%r3$; $r1 = \%r2$; **generate**: *sub %r2 %r3*;
$Reg = (\%r3, \%r4)$; $Val = (\%r1, \%r2)$

Step 7. $x = *$ (operator); $r2 = \%r2$; $r1 = \%r1$; **generate**: *mul %r1 %r2*;
$Reg = (\%r2, \%r3, \%r4)$; $Val = (\%r1)$

Step 8. End of *Expr* and of the algorithm. The value of the expression
is in register $\%r1$.

For the above example, the algorithm used three registers to
store the intermediate results and generated the instructions to store
the value of the expression in the first free register—$\%r1$. Three
registers $\%r2$, $\%r3$, and $\%r4$ are pushed back onto the list of free
registers and can be used to generate a code for evaluating the next
expression.

More optimal but more complicated algorithms of register allocation
are based on constructing a graph of dependencies for all the variables
and coloring the graph nodes into minimum number of colors so that
each neighbor nodes have different colors [5,13].

*Mapping variables of the source language (or intermediate language [IL])
to the global symbols, local symbols (in static sections), stack frame offsets,
and registers.* This task is actually part of the task of memory allocation
already considered above.

Static planning of parallel execution. For RISC architectures, code generator plans the pipeline and enables filling out the delay slots. For VLIW/
EPIC architectures, code generator plans full load of very long instructions for each machine cycle.

Generating proper object code for each kind of source code constructs. For
accessing variables, the sequences of instructions to evaluate their
addresses are generated. For expressions, register-based evaluation
instructions are generated, using the minimum possible number of registers. For statements, simple control transfer schemes are used based on
conditional and unconditional branches. More details below in this
chapter.

Generating debugging information. Debugging information is generated
together with the code, usually by a specific option (e.g., –g in Sun
Studio compilers). The goal of generating debugging information is

to enable backward mapping from the generated binary code to the source code, necessary to debug the program in terms of the line numbers and definitions of the source code. More details below in Section 7.9.

Generating object file in a proper format. On different hardware platforms and for different operating systems, a variety of object code file formats are used.

For the SPARC/Solaris platform, the common object code file format is *executable and linkage format* (*ELF*). For portable executable (PE) files in Microsoft.NET, the *common object file format* (*COFF*) is used. For Java technology, the *.class* file format is generated.

7.3   SPECIFICS OF CODE GENERATION FOR .NET

Common Type System (CTS). The most complicated task for a compiler developer for .NET is to map the language types onto *CTS* types.

.NET architecture is based on the idea of multi-language programming. For this purpose, it provides a CTS containing the most common kinds of types used in modern object-oriented languages—primitive types, enumerations, structures, interfaces, classes, managed pointers, delegates, and so on.

But the specifics of source language types may be different even for object-oriented languages, moreover for procedural-, functional-, or production-based (rule) languages.

So the developers of the front-end, especially the MSIL code generator, have to solve this complicated task whose difficulty depends on how much the language type system differs from CTS.

Easy MSIL code generation. Due to postfix notation structure of MSIL, it is much less difficult for a code generator to create this kind of code, as compared with a native code of any hardware platforms.

For example, since the evaluation model in MSIL is based on stack, there is no need to solve the problem of register allocation. Actually, the MSIL code generation algorithms are very close to those of translating expressions to postfix notation.

No optimizations when generating MSIL. Due to the two-step architecture of code generation on Microsoft.NET—compile-time generation of MSIL code and runtime generation (JIT compilation) of native target platform code—the developers of the compiler from a source language to MSIL may not take care of any optimizations. All optimizations are delayed until runtime and JIT compilation. Such decision is recommended by .NET experts.

For more details, please consult the book [84] on compiler development for Microsoft.NET.

7.4 SPECIFICS OF CODE GENERATION FOR SPARC ARCHITECTURE

Now let's consider the specifics of code generation for *SPARC architecture*—one of the popular RISC hardware architectures—and for *SPARC/Solaris platform*.

We've had 10 years experience of compiler development for SPARC architecture.

The overall scheme of compiler organization for SPARC/Solaris is as follows (let's consider it taking the C compiler as an example).

The *source code* is stored in a text file with .*c* extension, say *test.c*.

The compiler is a set of independent programs, each implementing some phase of the compiler.

The *compiler driver* (referred to as *cc*) is a program that parses the compiler options and calls the compiler phases with appropriate options and other command-line arguments.

The compiler phases pass information to each other only in temporary files, no shared memory is used.

The first phase of compilation is *preprocessing*. The C preprocessor, referred to as *cpp*, takes the *test.c* file, processes all directives like #*define* and #*ifdef*/#*endif*, and generates the preprocessed version of the C source—*test.i* (in modern versions of the C compiler, *cpp* for efficiency is merged with the front-end).

The second phase is the *front-end* (referred to as *acomp*, for *A*NSI C *COMP*iler). It takes the *test.i* (or *test.c*) file and generates the IR in the temporary file, say *test.ir*.

Then, the *IR optimizer (iropt)* comes into stage, if the –*O* option is on.

It takes the *IR* from the *test.ir* and generates its optimized version, also in the IR form.

Next, the *code generation* works. It translates the IR contained in the *test.ir* file to the *object code file*, *test.o*.

The concluding step to generate an *executable file* is *linking*, performed by the *ld* or *ild* (incremental version of the linker). The linker takes one or more object files (.o) and links them with *libraries* (.*a* files, for *Archive*). The result of linking is an executable, by default named *a.out*—a traditional abbreviation for *assembler output*.

Actually, the *assembler* (*as*) can be called as independent phase.

In this case, the code generator should be called with an –*S* option as shown, to produce the *assembler source code (test.s)*.

In Sun Studio compilers, for efficiency reasons, the assembler is part of the code generator *cg*.

See more details on SPARC architecture below in Section 7.7.

7.5 REPRESENTING TYPES AND ADDRESSING VARIABLES

Now let's proceed with another, especially important section of the chapter closely related to code generation—*representing types and addressing variables*.

To feel the specifics of code generation, the readers should better understand how the data types are represented and what kind of code the code generator is to create to access variables and their components.

Primitive types. For a *primitive type* (*int*, *float*, etc.), its value is allocated in a word. The size of a primitive type is the size of the machine word, and typically, the alignment of the type equals to the word size in bytes.

Since a local variable within some procedure or method is allocated on the *stack frame* (or *activation record*) when the procedure/method is called, the *address* of the variable is calculated at runtime as a sum of the *address of the (start of the) stack frame* and the *offset* (relative address) of the variable in the stack frame. The offset is calculated by the compiler at compile time:

$Size(T) = W$

$Align(T) = W$ (where W is the word size in bytes)

$Addr(V) = Addr(StackFrame) + Offset(V)$

Compound types. For *compound types*, as well known, there are two models of semantics, representation, and memory allocation—*container* model and *reference* model.

With the *container model* (Pascal, C, C++), the variable is considered a *container* of its value. Its declaration (definition) itself causes (stack) memory allocation for the variable. The value of the variable V is stored *on the stack frame* if possible (except for arrays and "dynamic" variables, speaking in Pascal terms).

Addressing a component of the variable with the container model is more efficient:

$$Addr(Component) = Addr(V) + Offset(Component)$$

The *reference model* (followed by most object-oriented languages—Java, C#, Smalltalk, etc.) assumes that the variable definition just creates a placeholder for a *pointer (object reference)* to a dynamic structure generated at runtime whose pointer is stored in the variable. So, the characteristic feature of the container model is *implicit pointers*, like in Java. Addressing of such variable's component requires one more layer of indirection:

$$Addr(Component) = Value(V) + Offset(Component)$$

Records (structures). For *records (structures)* of the kind:

```
var V : record F1: T1; … FN: TN end;
```

straightforward representation method is to allocate all the record's fields in textual order. The advantage of this method is that it's intuitively more understandable at the *application binary interface (ABI)* layer, in particular, in debugging the program. The drawback of this approach is that memory loss is possible, in case a short-sized (e.g., byte) field is followed by a more long-sized and more strictly aligned (e.g., double) one, since *padding* is required between the two fields to enable proper alignment of the second one.

More efficient representation method is as follows: The fields are sorted and allocated in the *descending order of their sizes.* For example, the record:

```
var r: record b: byte; r: real; s: short end;
```

when represented the ordinary way, with all fields allocated in textual order, on 32-bit machine, will have size 12 bytes (b is allocated in one byte; then padding 3 bytes to enable the proper alignment of r; then $r - 4$ bytes, $s - 2$ bytes, and then padding 2 bytes again).

When this record is represented in the decreasing order of the fields' sizes:

$$(r, s, b),$$

its size will be 8 bytes.

So, the advantage of such record allocation method is saving memory space.

Its drawback is that such allocation is less understandable at the ABI layer, for example, when debugging the program.

An alternative form of record is a *packed record*, like in Pascal.

According to the language specification, all fields of such record should be "packed" into the minimum whole number of bytes (or bits, if possible). For example, the following packed record:

```
var pr: packed record a: 1..5; b: 0..3 end;
```

can be represented in a minimal number of bits: the field a—in 3 bits, and the field b—in 2 bits; so the size of the record will be just 1 byte, rather than 8 bytes, in case the ordinary unpacked representation is applied. Similar structures in C are referred to as *bit fields*.

Surely, packed records can help to save a lot of memory. But the *minus* of this method is dramatic efficiency loss: Accessing such "misaligned" data is much less efficient (it requires shifts, performing logical *and* to a bit mask, etc.). So, accessing a field of a packed record is often implemented by a subroutine.

Here are the formulas for calculating the size, align, and address of the record and its components (fields):

```
var V: record F₁: T₁; … Fₙ: Tₙ end;
```

$Align(V) = max [Align(F_k)]$

$Size(V) = Padding(Size*(F_1) + … + Size*(F_n), Align(V))$

$Size*(F_k) = Padding(Size(F_k), Align(F_{k+1}))$

$Size(F_k) = Size(T_k)$

$Offset(F_1) = 0$

$Offset(F_{k+1})) = Offset(F_k) + Size*(F_k)$

$Addr(V.F_k) = Addr(V) + Offset(F_k)$

Here, *Padding(size, align)* is the function that pads the *size* to fit the alignment *align*; *Size*(F)* is the size of the field padded to fit the alignment of the next field.

The alignment of the record is a maximum of the alignment of its fields. Between the fields with less strict and stricter alignment, padding is required. The address of a field is calculated as a sum of the address of the record and the *offset* of the field. The offset is calculated at compile time.

Please note that, if a record is allocated on the stack, its field can be addressed as efficient as a simple (whole) variable, since its offset is known to the code generator.

Variant records and unions. Variant records (in Pascal) or *unions* (in C) have the same purpose: to store data of *one of* the types (*variants*) explicitly listed in the type definition. The form of a variant record in Pascal is as follows:

```
var V: record case T of
          C₁: (<Variant1>); … Cₙ: ( <VariantN>) end;
```

where each variant is a list of fields specific for this variant.

If a variant record is allocated on the stack, its size should be suitable to allocate any variant (maximum):

$Align(V) = max [Align (Variant_k)]$

$Size (V) = max [Size (Variant_k)]$

If a variant record is allocated on the heap at runtime, there is an opportunity to save memory and allocate on the heap exactly the variant indicated by its *case label* (as shown above). Its size is exactly the size of the variant to be allocated.

C-style *union* types are processed in the same way.

Addressing variant record fields is performed similarly to addressing ordinary record fields.

The main problem with variant records is to check or not to check the correctness of addressing the appropriate variant. Checking the variant should be performed at runtime and requires storing and checking at runtime a (explicit or implicit) *tag field* to specify the case label of the current variant.

Arrays. Arrays can be one-dimensional (vectors) or multidimensional.

Multidimensional arrays should be *linearized*, that is, stored in a linear memory area in some appropriate way.

The most common way is to linearize arrays "row-by-row," as shown in the example:

```
var V: array [1..2, 1..2] of integer;
```

Linearization (row-by-row): *V[1,1], V[1,2], V[2,1], V[2,2]*

The only language that contradicts to this rule is FORTRAN whose tradition is to linearize arrays "column-by-column." The latter specifics of FORTRAN may cause an issue when passing an array from a module in FORTRAN to a module written in another language, or vice versa.

When linearizing arrays row-by-row, the last index is changing faster.

To represent and address arrays, it is convenient to define and calculate, for each k from 1 to n (where n is the number of array dimensions), the d_k distance between the elements whose kth indexes are differed by 1, and the rest of the indexes are the same.

The formulas to calculate the size of the array, the distances d_k, and the address of an indexed variable are given below:

```
var V: array [l₁..u₁ ..., lₙ..uₙ] of T;
```

$size_k = u_k - l_k + 1$

$d_n = size(T); dk = d_{k+1} * size_{k+1}, k = 1, \ldots, n - 1$

$Align\ (V) = Align\ (T)$

$Size\ (V) = size_1 * \ldots * size_n * Size(T)$

$Addr\ (V[i_i, \ldots, i_n]) = a_0 + i_1 * d_1 + \ldots + i_n * d_n$

where $a_0 = Addr\ (V[0, \ldots, 0])$—initial address (of the zero's element, if any).

It is important to emphasize that the address of the indexed array element is calculated as a *linear form*, depending on the d_k coefficients and on the initial ("zero's element") address.

This fact is the basis of a lot of array indexing optimizations within loops.

If the array's index bounds are all constants (like in Pascal), all the d_k and the zero element address are calculated at compile time and used by the compiler for generating code to evaluate this linear form.

If not (i.e., if the size of the array depends on the values of some variables), representing an array requires storing its *passport* (also referred to as *dope vector*), which is also an array, represented at runtime and comprised by the values of the initial address and the distances d_k. So the size of the passport is $n + 1$ words where n is the dimension of the array.

If the programming system needs to check at runtime that each of the indexes is within its allowed bounds, the passport of an array should also contain the *lower and upper bounds* of the index for each dimension—l_k and u_k. In this case, the size of the passport is $3 * n + 1$ words, where n is the dimension of the array.

Pointers. *Pointers* can be *managed (safe)* or *unmanaged (unsafe)*.

Unmanaged pointer, like in C or C++, is represented just by an address of some data (variable). So it requires a 32-bit or a 64-bit word of memory, depending on the architecture. It is not possible to check at runtime whether a cast of the pointer to any data type is correct or not. So incorrect cast for an unmanaged pointer may cause a lot of bugs to be very difficult to detect, or may be the source of security break attack, like buffer overrun.

For type safety reasons, in modern platforms (like Microsoft.NET), *managed pointers* are used. It is very important to realize (and, in my teaching experience, is not always quite understandable by students) that a managed pointer is actually a *pair*: (*address of data*, *address of metadata*), where the metadata address points to the *data type* of this pointer. Actually, in .NET's internal representation of objects, the managed pointer is just one word (the address of the object), but the starting word of the runtime representation of the object contains the address of the metadata, so in total, the Common Language Runtime (CLR) system of .NET spends two words to represent a managed pointer. Spending extra memory word can be regarded as a drawback of managed pointers—this is the price of their safety.

But the important advantage is that managed pointers enable type-safe execution, since the runtime support system at each moment can check the correctness of data retrieval, data store, and type casting operations related to this pointer.

With managed pointers, no address arithmetic is allowed, either no invalid casting possible.

On old tag-based hardware platforms like Burroughs 5000 and "Elbrus" [2], a pointer was represented as a *descriptor*—a 64-bit word with a special *desc* tag, to protect it from invalid operations (e.g., from attempts to perform pointer arithmetic). The descriptor contained the *address* of the data, the *size* of their memory area, and the *protection bits*—protection of the array content from reading, writing, and (or) execution. So, descriptors enabled hardware protection of data from attacks like buffer overruns, and from occasional or buggy indexing out of bounds. But all of their trustworthiness was gained at the expense of hardware-based tag checking when executing each machine instruction. So tag-based architectures, even if they enable better security support, are not used in popular hardware architectures now, for reasons of their inefficiency.

7.6   REPRESENTING PROCEDURES, FUNCTIONS, AND METHODS

Now let's consider how to represent procedures, functions, and methods, and organize and address their runtime data.

Ordinary procedures, functions, and nonvirtual methods typically don't require explicit runtime representation as pointers. For their calls, in *call* instructions, their *assembler symbols* are specified that contain the address of the procedure's code. More details later in this chapter, in relation to code generation for SPARC.

Explicit storing and manipulating pointers to procedures or methods at runtime are required for:

- representing *procedural parameters*, for example, for the following Pascal code typical for procedural languages:

```
function integral
    (a, b: real; /* the range of integration */
    function f (x: real): real
    /* the function to be integrated; represented
    by a pointer */
    ): real;
```

- representing *values of procedural types* or *delegates*; for example (in Turbo Pascal):

```
type prt = procedure (x: real);
var v: prt;
procedure p(x: real); begin … end;
begin
    v:= p; /* the procedure pointer assigned to v */
```

```
      v(1); /* indirect procedure call using
      procedural variable */
  end
```

- representing *virtual methods*; for example (in Java):

```
  class C {
      void M () /* virtual by default in Java */
      { ... } /* C-specific implementation of M */
  }
  class D extends C {
      void M () /* inherited by D; implementation
      redefined */
      { ... } /* D-specific implementation of M */
  }
  public static void main(String[] args)
  {
      D p = new D();
      p.M(); /* indirect call of the virtual method */
  }
```

Virtual methods for a class (e.g., *C* or *D* in the above example) are represented at runtime by their pointers stored in the *virtual method table (VMT)* for the class. Each class has its own VMT, but the *offset* (index) is the same for any virtual method (e.g., *M* in the example) in the VMTs of the ancestor and the descendant classes. Let's denote *offset(M)* the offset of the virtual method in the VMT of the ancestor and the descendant classes. So, when a virtual method of an object *p* is called, the reference to the VMT of the *p*'s class is retrieved, and indexed by *offset(M)*. This is the basic idea of runtime representation of virtual methods for all object-oriented languages since SIMULA until Java and C#.

Pointers to procedures, functions, and methods, as well as pointers to data, can be *managed* or *unmanaged*. In Java and .NET, they are managed, that is, the type information on any method pointer is always available at runtime, which enables trustworthiness of the code execution, with full type-checking at runtime. In C and C++, on the contrary, pointers to functions are unmanaged, so any "trick" with their type casting (like passing invalid number of arguments in the indirect call) is possible; so the code execution is not trustworthy, and the programmer "pays" for using such tricks by hardly detectable bugs.

If procedures can be nested, pointer to a procedure should contain the *address of stack frame of the enclosing procedure*, referred to as *context*, or *static link*. More detailed explanation and an example are given below.

So, the most general form of a managed pointer to a procedure or method is as follows:

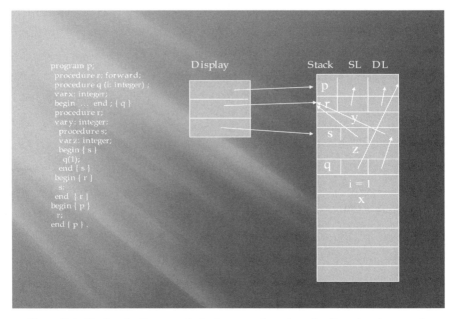

Figure 7.1. *Stack activation records for the procedures from the Pascal code example.*

(code address, metadata address, static link address)

The most important concepts to understand, in relation to representing procedures at runtime, are *static chain and dynamic chain* [5,26]. Both of them are represented on the stack of the current thread of the executable program.

Static chain is the list (in reverse order) of currently active *scopes* represented by *stack activation records*, each of them containing arguments and local variables of a procedure (or function) activation (call).

Dynamic chain is the list (in reverse order) of all stack activation records, starting from the most recently called procedure.

To appropriately control the stack of activation records, both chains should be explicitly stored in procedural pointers and on the stack.

Example of Pascal code with intensive use of procedures and the related runtime representation of the stack activation records are shown in Figure 7.1. Let's consider in more detail the principles of representing procedures using this example.

Implementation of procedure (method) calls is based on the following principles.

For each thread of execution, a *stack* is allocated to store *activation records* of procedures called within the thread.

Each activation record contains *linking information (static and dynamic links), arguments, local (automatic) variables* of the procedure, and *implicit save area* for saving the values of registers.

In addition, a *display* should be explicitly stored (the idea of using display belongs to Dijkstra who coined it in the early 1960s, in relation to ALGOL-60 implementation). From an abstract viewpoint, the display is an array that stores the references to activation records of the currently active *chain of statically nested procedures*.

In the example (see Fig. 7.1), when the procedure *s* is called, the state of the display will be as follows:

display[0] -> p

display[1] -> r

display[2] -> s

When *q* is called from *s*, the state of the display changes:

display[0] -> p

display[1] -> q

Addressing local variables and parameters, for the most general case of nested procedures, is based on the following principle.

Any local variable X is mapped to an *address pair: (level, offset)*, where *level* is the static nesting level of the procedure; *offset* is the relative address of X in the corresponding activation record.

A procedure pointer is represented as a pair: *(address of code, static link)*.

When a procedure is called by its pointer, the state of the display changes, if necessary.

In earlier Complicated Instruction Set Computer (CISC) hardware architectures, Burroughs 5000 and "Elbrus" [2], the above concepts of procedures, address pairs, and display update were fully supported by hardware, which surely caused its overcomplication. In "Elbrus," the call instruction execution required 100–150 CPU cycles, which is surely too long, since in most cases, a procedure or function call does not require updating the display (or require its minor updates). In addition, in Burroughs 5000 and "Elbrus," there were specialized *display registers* to represent the display by hardware.

On the contrary, in RISC architectures (like SPARC), there is a large pool of general-purpose registers, but there are *no* specific *display registers*.

The question arises: How can the display for RISC architectures be represented?

The answer is: If a procedure needs a display to address uplevel variables (variables of enclosing procedures), the code generated for that procedure should have a special *prologue* to create and store the display in the *stack activation record* of this procedure call. This idea was used in Sun's SPARC Pascal compiler we were responsible for in the 1990s.

7.7 PRINCIPLES OF SPARC ARCHITECTURE

To be more concrete regarding code generation target platform, let's consider code generation for *SPARC architecture* [85] developed by Sun Microsystems.

SPARC architecture is a kind of *RISC architecture* [86]. So, to better understand its main features, we summarize the principles of RISC.

RISC is the acronym for *Reduced Instruction Set Computer*. This term is a kind of antithesis to *CISCs*, a common name for most hardware architectures of the 1960s and 1970s; a typical example is IBM 360.

The origin of RISC is considered to be the design and development of the processor named *RISC-1* in the early 1980s.

The most famous and widely spread RISC architectures in the history of computing are SPARC, PowerPC, MIPS, PA-RISC, and Digital Alpha.

Here is an overview of the specifics of RISC architecture.

Simplified and unified format of code instructions. Each instruction occupies a 32-bit word, so all machine instructions have the same size. This dramatically simplifies hardware algorithms of decoding instructions. In RISC, there is no variable length instructions whose lengths are measured in bytes (unlike, for example, IBM 360 or "Elbrus").

No "storage/storage" instructions. Unlike IBM 360, there are no instructions whose operands are in memory. All arithmetic and other calculation operations are performed on values stored in registers. Accordingly, there are *register* load and *register* store instructions to exchange values between registers and memory.

No specialized registers (e.g., no display registers). There are common (general-purpose) registers, unlike, for example, "Elbrus" architecture that had many kinds of specialized registers (e.g., display registers). In RISC, only registers for integer and float values and operations are different (except for very few control registers necessary for each kind of processor).

Large "register file." Since in RISC a lot of attention is paid to general-purpose registers, the total number of registers (referred to as *register file*) is increased up to 512 or 2048 or even more.

Simple pipelining. RISC architectures have a few ways of parallelizing execution of instructions that should be taken into account for platform-dependent optimizations. Among them are *delay slots*. A delay slot is the next instruction after *call* and the other kind of control transfer. According to RISC principles, instruction executes in parallel to a control transfer instruction whose execution takes two machine cycles.

So in a very common case, if the called routine has one argument, for example, *p(x)*, the delay slot should be filled out by an instruction that passed to *p* the only argument *x* via a register.

SPARC architecture was designed by Sun Microsystems in 1985. More exactly, SPARC is a set of hardware architecture standards, and a number of hardware vendor companies, including Sun, produce such computers. SPARC is an acronym for *Scalable Processor ARChitecture*.

Besides the common features of RISC we already considered, the main specifics of SPARC are *register windows*.

Register window is a set of eight registers. From the logical "viewpoint" of any function called on SPARC, there are three register windows:

- *in (total of eight registers)*—the registers containing the *arguments* of the function;
- *local (total of eight registers)*—the registers the function can use for its calculations;
- *out (total of eight registers)*—the registers where the function should store the outgoing arguments for any called function, and its own result, if any.

When calling a function, the eight *out* registers of the caller become the eight *in* registers of the called function (i.e., the register windows are *shifted*).

In SPARC, the following denotations and conventions shown below are used for all the registers:

%r0–%r31—integer registers;
%i0–%i7—the same as *%r24–%r31* (the *in* registers);
%l0–%l7—the same as *%r16–%r23* (the *local* registers);
%o0–%o7—the same as *%r8–%r15* (the *out* registers);
%f0–%f31—floating point registers;
%sp (=%o6)—current stack pointer;
%fp (=%i6)—the frame pointer (the same as the previous stack pointer *%sp*).

All local variables are addressed relative to the frame pointer *%fp*.

The *stack pointer (%o6, or %sp)* and the *frame pointer (%i6, or %fp)* registers require special explanations.

Due to register windows shift, since the *out* registers of the caller become the *in* registers of the called function, the former *stack pointer* becomes the *previous stack pointer* (in other words, the current *frame pointer*).

So, according to SPARC *ABI* convention, all local variables allocated on a stack frame are addressed via *frame* pointer.

Other SPARC ABI conventions on the structure of stack activation records are as follows:

%fp + 68 – %fp + 92–the arguments of the function;
%fp + 64–the address of the structured result, if any;
since *%fp – 4*–local variables of the function;
since *%sp + 92*–the outgoing arguments (if the called function has more than six arguments);

%*sp* + 68 –...–six words for saving the *out* registers;

%*sp* + 64–address of the structured result, if any;

since %sp–10 words: register save area.

Even if the arguments of a function (if there are no more than six arguments) are passed via registers, the memory for the arguments is reserved on the stack, as shown above.

Also, a word is reserved for the address of the structured result of a function, if any.

According to SPARC ABI conventions, the caller should allocate memory for that structure and pass via that register to the called function the address where the called function should store the structured result.

Local variables on SPARC assembler level are characterized by negative offsets relative to *fp*, for example, %*fp* – 4.

For each routine, a register save area is reserved.

7.8   EXAMPLE OF CODE GENERATION FOR SPARC ARCHITECTURE

Let's now illustrate our overview of code generation by an example of code generation for SPARC architecture.

Below is a simple source code file in C:

```
#include <stdio.h>
void p(int x)
{
  int y;
  y = 1;
  printf("x=%d y=%d\n", x, y);
}
  int a;
  int main(int argc, char ** argv)
{
  a = 0;
  p(a);
  return 0;
} // Let the source file name be test.c
// The assembler source file name will be test.s
```

The above code has the *main* function and the *p* function with one integer argument *x*. The global variable *a* is defined in the C source. The *main* function calls *p* with a value argument, which is the value of *a*, initialized by 0 in *main*. The *p* routine prints out the values of its argument and its local variable *y* initialized by 1.

The *SPARC assembler source code* for that example, generated by the *GNU C Compiler*, is shown below:

```
.file "test.c"
gcc2_compiled.:
.section    ".rodata"
    .align 8
.LLC0:
    .asciz      "x=%d y=%d\n"
.section    ".text"
    .align 4
    .global p
    .type  p,#function
    .proc 020
p:
    !#PROLOGUE# 0
    save %sp, -120, %sp
    !#PROLOGUE# 1
    st   %i0, [%fp+68]
    mov  1, %o0
    st   %o0, [%fp-20]
    sethi %hi(.LLC0), %o1
    or   %o1, %lo(.LLC0), %o0
    ld   [%fp+68], %o1
    ld   [%fp-20], %o2
    call printf, 0
    nop
LL2:
    ret
    restore
.LLfe1:
    .size  p,.LLfe1-p
    .align 4
    .global main
    .type  main,#function
    .proc 04
main:
    !#PROLOGUE# 0
    save %sp, -112, %sp
    !#PROLOGUE# 1
    st   %i0, [%fp+68]    st   %i1, [%fp+72]
    sethi %hi(a), %o1
    or   %o1, %lo(a), %o0
    st   %g0, [%o0]
    sethi %hi(a), %o0
```

```
    or    %o0, %lo(a), %o1
    ld    [%o1], %o0
    call p, 0
    nop
    mov   0, %i0
    b     .LL3
    nop
.LL3:
    ret
    restore
.LLfe2:
    .size  main,.LLfe2-main
    .common    a,4,4
    .ident     "GCC: (GNU) 2.95 19990728 (release)"
```

As you can see from the above code example, the assembler file starts with the directive that specifies the name of the source.

The assembler file consists of several *sections*, corresponding to the sections of the binary *ELF* object code file. *Rodata* is the section that contains read-only data, that is, constants, like the format string used in *p*. *Text* is the section to contain the instructions of the object *code*. The constants in the *rodata* section and the routines in *text* sections are *labeled*. *BSS* is the section for allocating noninitialized global data.

The *.section* assembler directive switches the assembler to one of the following sections:

- *.bss*—the section containing the definitions of *global noninitialized variables*. In the example, the *common* directive defines the variable *a* allocated in the *.bss* section;
- *.rodata ("read-only data")*—the section containing the definitions of *constants and constant arrays*—the data that cannot be changed during the execution. The advantage of this section is that it can be allocated once and used by many concurrent applications or threads. In the example, the *format string* is allocated in the *rodata* section;
- *.text*—is, actually, the *executable code* section.

Each of the functions (*main* and *p*) has its *global symbols* defined in the code. In addition, the *type* directive is provided to specify that *main* and *p* are functions, and the *size* directive is provided for the assembler to calculate the size of the function's code.

In *p* routine, the prologue starts with shifting the frame pointer. Then, *ld* commands are used to load registers, *st* commands—to store the values from registers into memory.

The *call* command calls a routine; the *ret* command makes a return from a routine. The *restore* command restores the frame pointer.

Please note that a nonoptimized version of the object code is demon-strated—the delay slot after the *call* command is not filled out and is occupied by *nop* (no operation) command.

The *common* directive is used to allocate the global variable *a* in the *BSS* section of the ELF file.

In relation to each function, the *save/restore* pair of instructions *updates the frame pointer*. Please note that, if a function does not have arguments, local variables, or other calls, the update of the frame pointer is *not* needed (a possible kind of hardware-dependent optimization for SPARC).

The *call/ret* pair of instructions is supporting function calls and returns. When executing these commands, the hardware appropriately shifts the register windows.

The *sethi* and *or* pair of instructions demonstrates "the overhead of the RISC approach." Each instruction occupies a 32-bit word. So, to calculate the value of a 32-bit *address constant* in a register, SPARC hardware needs the two commands that, first, set the 12 higher bits of the register to higher 12 bits of the address, and then, set the remaining lower 20 bits.

As can be seen from the code, all arguments and local variables are addressed using %*fp* as the base. Arguments have positive offsets, local variables—negative offsets (the stack grows toward lower addresses).

7.9   GENERATION OF DEBUGGING INFORMATION

Each compiler generates *debugging information*, to enable the debugger during the program execution to work in terms of source code line numbers and names defined in the source code.

In Sun Studio compilers, generation of debugging information is controlled by the –*g* option.

Debugging information is a kind of back mapping from the executable code to the source, so its role is very important. The user should not lose this back mapping at runtime, when debugging the program, since the user should be able, at the debugging stage, to think about the program in terms of its source, rather than in some lower-level terms, like register numbers and offsets.

The format of debugging information in Microsoft.NET is *Program Data Base (PDB)*; in Shared Source CLI noncommercial version of .NET (also referred to as Rotor), the format is different—*Intermediate Language Data Base (ILDB)*. The latest version of Rotor (2.0) provides a converter from ILDB to PDB format. PDB and ILDB are stored in separate *.pdb* and *.ildb* files.

The format of debugging information for Sun platform is *STABS* (for *Symbol TABle entrieS*). Stabs are stored in a separate *(.stab) section* of the ELF file. We'll explain the structure of debugging information based on stabs. The *stabs* format specification is available for download from the Sun site [87].

Example. Here is a simple C program:

```
main ()
{
    int i = 5;
    {
        float i = 5.5;
        printf ("%f\n", i);
    }
    printf ("%d\n", i);
}
```

And here are the *stabs* generated by Sun Studio's C compiler for this application:

```
.stabs "main:F(0,3)",N_FUN,0,0,main
.stabs "main", N_MAIN, 0,0,0
.stabn N_LBRAC,0,1,.LL1-main
.stabs "i:(0,3)",N_LSYM,0,4,-4
.stabn N_SLINE,0,3,.LL2-main
.stabn N_LBRAC,0,2,.LL3-main
.stabs "i:(0,16)",N_LSYM,0,4,-8
.stabn N_SLINE,0,6,.LL4-main
.stabn N_SLINE,0,7,.LL5-main
.stabn N_RBRAC,0,2,.LL6-main
.stabn N_SLINE,0,10,.LL7-main
.stabn N_SLINE,0,11,.LL8-main
.stabn N_RBRAC,0,1,.LL9-main
```

Let's consider the principles and some details of stabs, based on this example.

The *main* pair of stabs provides a reference to the main function of the application, as a *function symbol*.

The *stabn* kind of stabs is used to represent *mapping from the object code to the lines of the source code*, line by line. This is especially important for the debugger, to be able to execute commands like "*stop in line N.*" The relative address of the start of the object code corresponding to each source code line is represented by the difference of the corresponding label symbol (marking the start of the line's object code) and the label symbol for the start of the whole *main* function.

The *N_LBRAC* and *N_RBRAC* pair of stabs specifies the start and the end of each scope of local declarations.

The *N_LSYM* stabs contain information on local definitions (symbols) for each scope. In the example, there is one local symbol only—the one for the *i* variable.

7.10 CODE GENERATION FOR DECLARATIONS (DEFINITIONS), EXPRESSIONS, AND STATEMENTS

Now let's discuss code generation principles for declarations, expressions, and statements—various kinds of programming language constructs. To illustrate these principles by concrete code, SPARC instructions will be used (see Sections 7.7 and 7.8 for more explanations of SPARC architecture).

Global declarations are mapped to *global symbols* (initialized or not). A Sun Studio compiler places the global symbol for each global variable to the appropriate section of the ELF code: initialized—to the *data* section—and noninitialized—to the *bss* section. An example of code generated for a global noninitialized variable *a* is given in Section 7.8:

```
.common    a,4,4
```

where *common* is the assembler instruction to allocate a new noninitialized global variable in the static *BSS* section; *a* is the name of the variable; the alignment (4) and the size (4) of the variable are specified as arguments of the instruction.

Automatic (local) variables, which are stored in stack activation records, may require initialization code (if any), or no code at all. In the example in Section 7.9, the local variable *y* is defined in the function *p*. According to SPARC ABI (see Section 7.7), the local variable *y* is addressed relative to the *frame pointer* (*%fp*), with negative offset, since the stack is growing "upward," to lower addresses; the offset of the first local variable is 20. So, the variable *y* is mapped by the code generator to *%fp-20*. For example, reading the value of the variable *y* to the register *%o0* can be implemented by the instruction:

```
ld    %o0, [%fp-20]
```

Assignment statements are compiled to commands of memory store or load to register, depending on the way how the variable is stored—in memory or in register. For example, the assignment statement *y* = 1 from the example in Section 7.8 (where *y* is a local variable) will be implemented as follows:

```
mov  1, %o0
st   %o0, [%fp-20]
```

where the first instruction assigns 1 to the working register *%o0*, and the second instruction stores this value from the register to *y* (mapped to *%fp-20*).

Code for *expressions* may be generated in different styles, depending on the object platform and its semantic model. The style of code generation for RISC architectures is explained by algorithm *D* in Section 7.2 and illustrated by an example (see Section 7.2).

In modern software platforms, .NET and Java, their stack-based virtual code—bytecode or Common Intermediate Language (CIL) code—is generated to evaluate the expression on the stack: All operands should be explicitly loaded onto the stack, and each operation (like *add*) should pop its operands from the stack and push the result onto the stack.

In *RISC* architecture, as shown in the above example of code generation for SPARC in Section 7.8, expressions are evaluated in *registers*. So, before each operation, its operands should be explicitly loaded to registers, and the result should also be found in a register.

For *compound statements*, the following code generation principles apply.

The code to be generated for an *if* statement is a sequence of *compares* and *conditional branches*. For example, the following source code in Pascal:

```
if a > b
then x:= a
else x:= b;
```

could be implemented on SPARC as follows:

```
     ld  %o0,  a
     ld  %o1,  b
     cmp %o0,  %o1
     ble .LL1
     st  %o0,  x
     b   .LL2
     nop
.LL1: st %o1,  x
.LL2:
```

Here, the values of *a* and *b* are loaded onto registers %*o0* and %*o1*, accordingly. Then, they are compared, and the *condition code* is generated. The synthetic *ble* (*branch lower or equal*) instruction enables control transfer to the *else* alternative. Please note that the *then* alternative, due to SPARC architecture delayed instructions, is started to execute *in parallel* to the branch itself; this helps to save one CPU cycle. However, we cannot place the second *st* instruction to the delay slot of the *b* instruction (that enables the branch to the end of the *if* statement), since, otherwise, the variable *x* would be incorrectly reassigned, so we have to fill out the delay slot for the *b* instruction by the *nop* instruction.

Case (or switch) statements, for example (in Pascal):

```
case X of
  C1:  S1;
  ...
  Cn:  Sn
end
```

can be implemented as efficiently as possible, depending on the values of the *case labels* that mark the alternatives.

If the case labels are *sparse* (i.e., their values occupy less that ½ of the range between their minimum and the maximum value), the case statement is implemented as a sequence of *if* statements.

If the labels are *dense* (occupy more than ½ of the range), the case statement is implemented via an *address switch array*: This array contains addresses of the code for all the alternatives, and the value of the case selector minus the minimum case label is used as an index to this array.

If the case labels are sparse, *hash function* may also be used for more optimal implementation of the *switch (case)* statement. The value of the selector is hashed and then compared only with those case labels whose hash values are the same. We used such technique in our Pascal compiler for "Elbrus" [2].

EXERCISES TO CHAPTER 7

7.1 Implement the algorithms of calculating sizes and alignments for different kinds of types described in Section 7.5.

7.2 Analyze the object (native or virtual) code generated by your commonly used compiler on your workstation, and try to understand how different kinds of language constructs are mapped to object code, based on the explanations of this chapter.

7.3 Implement the algorithm G of register allocation and code generation for an expression from Section 7.2.

7.4 Compile the C code example from Section 7.8 on your working machine (×86, ×64, Mac, etc.) using a GNU or Sun Studio compiler, analyze the assembler code generated, and compare it to the code generated for SPARC architecture.

Chapter *8*

Runtime, JIT, and AOT Compilation

This chapter covers runtime support—libraries and tools used to enable execution of a program compiled to native or virtual code.

As the novel material of this chapter, just-in-time (JIT) compilation architecture is discussed, based on the example of the fast just-in-time (FJIT) compiler for Shared Source Common Language Infrastructure (SSCLI)—academic version of .NET. Our research project on adding optimizations to FJIT is considered. Also, we describe ahead-of-time (AOT) compilation, since it enables faster execution of programs for Java and .NET.

8.1 THE TASKS OF THE RUNTIME

Runtime (support libraries) are inherent part of any *programming system*.

In general, programming system consists of the language + compiler + runtime. Runtime performs a variety of tasks.

> *Memory management.* There are two traditional ways of memory management based on *stack* (to store activation records for procedure calls) and *heap* (to store global objects). Runtime should support allocating, controlling, and freeing stack and heap memory.
>
> *Stack and procedures (methods) management.* The representation of stack and procedures is considered above in Chapter 7 (see Section 7.6).

Threads management. All modern software development platforms (.NET and Java in particular) support multi-threading. So, the runtime should support threading at the language and core API's level, as the Java Virtual Machine (JVM) and .NET Common Language Runtime (CLR) do. Thread support includes allocating a stack and per-thread storage and cache memory, thread scheduling, and so on.

Security checks. Modern software development platforms perform a lot of security checks, most of which should be done by the runtime. The set of runtime security checks includes security *stack walk* to determine if the method to be called has permissions to be executed in this dynamic environment; checking permissions to read and write files, and so on.

Garbage collection is actually part of the memory allocation task, but in modern platforms, it is so important that it should be considered separately. There are a lot of algorithms of garbage collection: *mark and sweep* (like in LISP), *copying* garbage collection, *conservative* garbage collection, and, the most popular now, *generational garbage collection*. The idea of the latter method is based on the heuristic principle that most of the objects die young, so the objects that have survived one or more garbage collections will most likely survive another one. So, separate heaps are used for young and old objects (two to three generations are considered), and after garbage collection all the objects that survived it are moved to the next generation.

Runtime type-checking is the most important part of what is now referred to as *managed execution*. Runtime type-checking mechanisms in .NET and Java enable that each operation is performed on the operands of correct (appropriate) types only; otherwise, an exception is thrown. In older programming systems like Pascal, runtime type-checking mechanisms were much simpler and included relatively easy checks prescribed by the language semantics specification, for example, *array index out of bounds* checks, and *subrange checks* in assignments (e.g., for a variable of type 1 ... 10, the runtime should check if the integer value to be assigned to this variable is within those limits). Such checks were performed if some specific options had been switched on at compile time. On the contrary, according to Java and .NET semantics, it is not possible to "switch off" managed execution mode, with intensive runtime type-checking, security checking, and so on. So, on the one hand, managed execution mode enables really trustworthy execution of the code, with all necessary checks in place. On the other hand, those checks cause runtime slowdown, so many software practitioners, especially those who are accustomed to programming in C and C++ in unmanaged and fast but risky environments, are still reluctant to use .NET, with its modern-style managed execution.

It should be noted that managed execution is not a brand new idea: Similar principles were followed by old hardware platforms, already mentioned above: Burroughs 5000 and "Elbrus" [2]. Those architectures of the 1960s–1970s enabled intensive runtime checks based on hardware-supported tags (in particular, checks for correct use of address information that excluded security attacks or occasional addressing out of memory bounds allocated for the program) and the use of metadata at runtime—typing information that was represented by special *object code extension files* linked to the object code and available to runtime diagnostics system. So, nowadays, in Java and .NET, very similar ideas based on object orientation are revived in worldwide use commercial systems (though not supported by hardware). It confirms the importance of the ideas of trustworthy code execution based on runtime typing.

Interoperability of languages. Runtime should support correct execution of mixed-language applications, which contains modules compiled from different languages. Such support may include appropriate data transformations (like marshaling, serialization, array relinearization from row-by-row to column-by-column form, etc.). In .NET, there is a special *Interop* class library to support language interoperability. In Java, interoperability of languages within one application is limited by the use of *native methods*—parts of Java application that can be written in C or C++, with some very specific runtime conventions and APIs to enable some very limited interoperability.

The ideas of multi-language interoperability at runtime, as well as the ideas of managed execution, are not novel: They were implemented in Burroughs 5000 and "Elbrus" architectures based on hardware support of typical mechanisms of data representation and language implementation (descriptors as universal trustworthy representation of addresses and arrays, stack and procedure calls with passing parameters, etc.) and on the runtime use of metadata (object code file extensions). Now, in .NET, the basis of multi-language interoperability is the Common Type System (CTS), a unified view on the types of all languages implemented for .NET.

8.2 THE RELATIONSHIP OF THE RUNTIME AND THE OPERATING SYSTEM (OS)

A very important problem related to runtime is the *interaction of runtime and the OS libraries*. The OS provides lower-level libraries for memory management, threading, file management, and so on, used by the runtime.

As for the interaction of *OS memory management and the language runtime memory management* mechanisms, there are a lot of interesting problems. The most important of them is as follows: whether the runtime can fully rely on the OS's memory allocation mechanisms, or not, that is, is it more efficient to avoid using OS memory allocation mechanism each time a piece of memory is needed for the runtime, by requesting a large memory area from the OS and allocating memory within that area, using language-specific efficient techniques. The solution of this problem in most cases is not in favor of OS memory management. For example, in older OSs like "Elbrus," a memory array request from the OS was as expensive as to require 100–150 machine cycles. In C++, on the contrary, it is quite possible to define one's own memory allocation mechanism, which may appear more efficient than the OS memory management mechanism and can be used by constructors and destructors.

As for *threading*, each modern OS provides its own threading libraries. So the authors of the programming system should adequately map the language threads to OS threads. One of the most enhanced and flexible threading mechanism is provided by Sun's Solaris. Java is the first programming system that supports threading at the language and core API level and, therefore, allows the programmers to abstract from the differences of threading libraries in various OSs, and work in the unified high-level Java threading environment. Similar principles of threading are followed by .NET.

> *Abnormal application result handling.* On the one hand, the OS provides its own ways to handle abnormal results, often too low level, like *signals*, *traps*, and *interrupts*. On the other hand, as the most contemporary high-level mechanism of error processing, appropriate for most languages, the runtime should support *exception handling*. So we think the right approach is to include basic support of exception handling into the OS libraries, as it was first done in Windows 2000, in object-oriented style. .NET offers a unified mechanism of exception handling suitable for all languages implemented for .NET; for example, it is possible to throw an exception from the module written in C# and catch and handle it in another module written, for example, in Visual Basic.NET.

8.3 JIT COMPILATION

JIT compilation is a very popular technology used in modern software platforms—Java and .NET—and originated in older software platforms and programming languages like Smalltalk (please see Section 6.5 for the history of JIT compilation).

The purpose of this section is to explain the basics of JIT compilation by the example of *FJIT*—shared-source JIT compiler, part of the academic version of .NET—SSCLI (Rotor) [88]. Also, in this section, we summarize our own JIT compiler research project—adding optimizations to FJIT [89].

Thanks very much to my PhD student Sophia Chilingarova whose dedicated work on implementing this project helped me a lot. Sections 8.3–8.5 are mostly based on her ideas, results, and examples.

Optimizing JIT compiler is an inherent part of any modern software development platform, like Java or .NET. In principle, many of the phases and tasks of a JIT compiler are similar to those of an ordinary compiler, since the goal of a JIT compiler is to generate a native object code.

The JIT compiler is called by the runtime system when some method (e.g., *M*) is first called. The JIT compiler compiles the method *M* from the bytecode (or Microsoft.NET Intermediate Language [MSIL]) to the native object code, and stores the native code into a runtime repository, so that during the next call of *M*, the runtime calls the native code version of *M*, which is much faster than interpreting the bytecode of the MSIL code of the method.

The above is just a general scheme of a simple JIT compiler. It should be taken into account that, as opposed to an ordinary "static" compiler, the JIT compiler has much more information about the whole program and the code to be compiled. It knows the specifics of the concrete CPU where the program is executed, all information on the execution environment, the *metadata*—repository that keeps all information on types defined and used in the program. What is the most important is that the JIT compiler can access execution profiling data for the program, if any. Due to all of that, a JIT compiler can perform full type-checking and verification of the bytecode (MSIL) and do many specific kinds of optimizations (see also Section 6.10).

The architecture of modern optimizing runtime compilation system (including optimizing JIT compiler) is depicted in Figure 8.1. It consists of:

- the *basic compiler/interpreter* to process each method to be called;
- the *controller* to make decisions on JIT compilation (recompilation) of particular methods;
- the *profiler* to collect data on program behavior during its execution (in particular, of special importance, on the number of calls of each method);
- the *profiling data repository*, used by the controller when necessary;

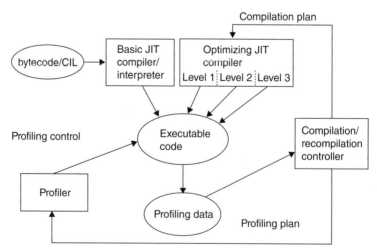

Figure 8.1. *The architecture of modern optimizing runtime compilation system, including JIT compiler.*

- the optimizing JIT compiler itself (with up to three levels of optimization, as explained below).

The *basic compiler/interpreter* is called automatically for each method to be called that hasn't yet been compiled. At the method entry point within the metadata structure, the method call *stub* is stored, which, initially, points to the basic compiler/interpreter and calls it. Then, the pointer in the stub is replaced to a pointer to the JIT-compiled native code of the method, so that it would be called during the next call of the method. So, the first call of a method takes longer than its other subsequent calls: The time of the first call includes the time of JIT compilation of the method. This fact is especially important to make decisions on high-level optimizations of the method: The time of JIT compilation shouldn't be too long for the user to feel it.

The *compilation/recompilation controller* tracks changes in the profiling data and makes decisions on compiling some definite methods with some definite optimization level. The first to be optimized are *hot* methods called maximal number of times, according to the profiling data. Optimizing JIT compilation is performed *in a separate thread*, that is, in parallel to the program execution, not to hold the program. Until the moment when the optimizing JIT compiler has finished optimizing the compilation of the method, the old (nonoptimized) version of the method is executed. When optimizing JIT compilation is finished, the pointer to the optimized code is stored in the method execution stub, to enable the call of the optimized code during next calls of the method.

The methods selected by the controller for compilation with high level of optimization are placed into the *optimization queue* and retrieved by the optimizing JIT compiler working in a separate thread (or several parallel threads, each running its "copy" of the optimizing JIT compiler).

The *profiler* controls collecting information on runtime behavior of the program. The initial version of nonoptimized code of each method contains specific instructions injected by the profiler to collect the necessary data (snapshots of the stack and of the registers). The collected profiling data are stored in the profiling data repository. The functioning of the profiler is managed by the controller that makes the *profiling plan*, in accordance with the current situation and with the options provided by the user.

The most popular kinds of optimizations performed by JIT compilers are *elimination of redundant assignments* and *inlining* of hot methods. As for redundant assignments, most of them are caused by the architecture of virtual machines (JVM or CLR) that requires for all of the operands to get loaded onto the *stack* before operating them.

Consider the following simple example in C#:

```
class Count
{ ...
  public int div10000(int a)
```

```
{
  int divisor = 3;
  int b = a;
  for (int j = 0; j < 10000; j++)
  {
    b = b / divisor;
  }
  return b;
}
}
```

Here is the MSIL code generated for this method by the C# compiler of SSCLI (Rotor):

```
.maxstack  2
  .locals init (int32 V_0,
          int32 V_1,
          int32 V_2)
  IL_0000:  ldc.i4.3
  IL_0001:  stloc.0
  IL_0002:  ldarg.1
  IL_0003:  stloc.1
  IL_0004:  ldc.i4.0
  IL_0005:  stloc.2
  IL_0006:  br.s       IL_0010
  IL_0008:  ldloc.1
  IL_0009:  ldloc.0
  IL_000a:  div
  IL_000b:  stloc.1
  IL_000c:  ldloc.2
  IL_000d:  ldc.i4.1
  IL_000e:  add
  IL_000f:  stloc.2
  IL_0010:  ldloc.2
  IL_0011:  ldc.i4     0x2710
  IL_0016:  blt.s      IL_0008
  IL_0018:  ldloc.1
  IL_0019:  ret
```

The nonoptimizing JIT compiler (FJIT) generates the following native code for this method (for the x86 hardware platform):

```
02D82EC4  mov    ecx,4
02D82EC9  push   0
02D82ECB  loop   02D82EC9
```

```
02D82ECD  mov    eax,3
02D82ED2  mov    dword ptr[ebp-14h],eax
02D82ED5  mov    eax,dword ptr [ebp+0Ch]
02D82ED8  mov    dword ptr [ebp-18h],eax
02D82EDB  xor    eax,eax
02D82EDD  mov    dword ptr [ebp-1Ch],eax
02D82EE0  mov    eax,dword ptr [ebp-1Ch]
02D82EE3  push   eax
02D82EE4  mov    eax,2710h
02D82EF2  pop    ecx
02D82EF3  cmp    ecx,eax
02D82EF5  jge    02D82F23
02D82EFB  mov    eax,dword ptr [ebp-18h]
02D82EFE  push   eax
02D82EFF  mov    eax,dword ptr [ebp-14h]
02D82F02  mov    ecx,eax
02D82F04  pop    eax
02D82F05  mov    edx,eax
02D82F07  sar    edx,1Fh
02D82F0A  idiv   eax,ecx
02D82F0C  mov    dword ptr [ebp-18h],eax
02D82F0F  mov    eax,dword ptr [ebp-1Ch]
02D82F12  push   eax
02D82F13  mov    eax,1
02D82F18  pop    ecx
02D82F19  add    eax,ecx
02D82F1B  mov    dword ptr [ebp-1Ch],eax
02D82F1E  jmp    02D82EE0
02D82F23  mov    eax,dword ptr [ebp-18h]
02D82F3A  mov    esi,dword ptr [ebp-4]
02D82F3D  mov    esp,ebp
02D82F3F  pop    ebp
02D82F40  ret
```

As can be seen from the above ×86 code, it contains a number of redundant operations, such as sending the same information back and forth. The code is obtained by a nonoptimizing version of Rotor's JIT compiler (FJIT). FJIT maps the stack top onto the *eax* register (this is the only hardware-dependent optimization JIT made). According to Common Intermediate Language (CIL) coding convention, the arguments of a method are passed via the stack, and the returned value is also saved on the stack. FJIT follows this convention for the method arguments, but, as for the returned value, it is passed via the *eax* register.

Now let's consider how this nonoptimal code can be optimized using elimination of redundant assignments and copy propagation (see Section 6.3).

We'll use a self-evident triple-like intermediate representation, to explain all the optimizations to be done. Let's denote the registers by *r1*, *r2*, ..., method arguments—by *a1*, *a2*, ..., and local variables—by *l1*, *l2*, ... Let *r1* be the register that stores the stack top (actually *eax*).

Using this intermediate representation, the nonoptimized native code generated by FJIT is as follows:

```
00   r1 <-  3
01   l1 <-  r1
02   r1 <-  a1
03   l2 <-  r1
04   r1 <-  0
05   l3 <-  r1
06   r1 <-  l3
07   s1 <-  r1
08 r1 <-  0x2710
09   r2 <-  s1
10   cmp r2,r1
11   jge 26
12   r1 <-  l2
13   s1 <-  r1
14   r1 <-  l1
15   r2 <-  r1
16   r1 <-  s1
17   idiv r1,  r2
18   l2 <-  r1
19   r1 <-  l3
20   s1 <-  r1
21   r1 <-  1
22   r2 <-  s1
23   add r1,  r2
24   l3 <-  r1
25   jmp 06
26   r1 <-  l2
27   ret
```

After deleting redundant assignments, the code takes the following form:

```
00   l1 <-  3
01   l2 <-  a1
02   l3 <-  0
03 r1 <-  0x2710
04   r2 <-  l3
05   cmp r2,  r1
06   jge 16
```

```
07   r2 <- l1
08   r1 <- l2
09   idiv r1, r2
10   l2 <- r1
11   r1 <- 1
12   r2 <- l3
13   add r1, r2
14   l3 <- r1
15   jmp 03
16   r1 <- l2
17   ret
```

Then, let's apply constant propagation to the above version of the code. The resulting code is given below:

```
00   l2 <- a1
01   l3 <- 0
02   r2 <- l3
03   cmp r2, 0x2710
04   jge 13
05   r2 <- 3
06   r1 <- l2
07   idiv r1, r2
08   l2 <- r1
09   r2 <- l3
10   add r2, 1
11   l3 <- r2
12   jmp 02
13   r1 <- l2
14   ret
```

Then, let's allocate the local variables *l2* and *l3* on registers. The code will become much shorter:

```
00   r3 <- a1
01   r4 <- 0
02   cmp r4, 0x2710
03   jge 08
04   r2 <- 3
05   idiv r3, r2
06   add r4, 1
07   jmp 02
08   r1 <- r3
09   ret
```

Finally, let's rename *r3* to *r1*, and *r4* to *r3*, and we'll save one more operation:

```
00   r1 <- a1
01   r3 <- 0
02   cmp r2,0x2710
03   jge 08
04   r2 <- 3
05   idiv r1, r2
06   add r3, 1
07   jmp 02
08   ret
```

So, we now have the code whose size is just 9 instructions, instead of 28 instructions in the original versions.

Just to compare, the optimizing JIT compiler of the Microsoft.NET Framework 1.1 (the commercial version of .NET) generates the following optimized code for the method above:

```
06CC00C5   mov        ecx,3
06CC00CA   cdq
06CC00CB   idiv       eax,ecx
06CC00CD   inc        esi
06CC00CE   cmp        esi,2710h
06CC00D4   jl         06CC00C5
06CC00D6   pop        esi
06CC00D7   ret
```

Such optimizations as *redundant assignments elimination*, *constant propagation*, and *constant folding* don't require a long time, so they are usually performed by the JIT compiler. Also, *inlining* is performed by JIT compilers for *short* methods—the method is considered to be short if its size (without prologue and epilogue) is less than the size of the code of the call of the same method.

Also, *devirtualization* of virtual method calls (see Section 6.10) is performed by optimizing JIT compilers, if the object whose virtual method is called is known without any runtime analysis.

Also, the following optimizations are performed by optimizing JIT compilers at the first optimization level:

- elimination of redundant checks for *null* pointer;
- elimination of redundant checks for array index out of bounds;
- elimination of redundant checks for possible exceptions;
- elimination of redundant type casting operations.

Inlining of other methods and other higher-level optimizations are performed, based on the profiling data.

Examples of JIT optimizations at higher levels are:

- *on the second level*—dead code elimination; loop-invariant code motion (see Section 6.3);
- *on the third level*—loop unrolling (see Section 6.3).

For methods that appeared to be not so hot, based on the results of dynamic profiling of the program, *de-optimization* is made.

8.4 THE ARCHITECTURE OF FJIT—JIT COMPILER FOR SSCLI/ROTOR

The runtime compilation system in SSCLI (Rotor) is designed and implemented to be the most general possible. The basic interpreter/compiler works in a separate dynamically linked library, so it is quite possible to plug in the other JIT compiler, or several JIT compilers, without any changes in the interface with the core of the virtual machine.

The major components implementing a call of JIT compiler in SSCLI are depicted in Figure 8.2.

From the virtual machine side, the *JIT compilation manager* is responsible for the interaction with the JIT compiler. According to SSCLI architecture, there can be several JIT managers. Each JIT manager enables the call of the corresponding JIT compiler and reads the information stored by the JIT compiler for the garbage collector. The latter function is performed by the *code manager*. According to the basic architecture concept, for each type of the JIT manager, the corresponding type of the code manager should be defined. The *execution manager* component calls the appropriate JIT

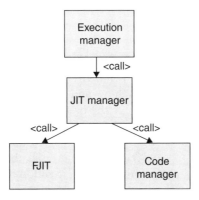

Figure 8.2. *The major runtime components implementing a call of the JIT compiler in SSCLI.*

manager, determined using the variable *code type* whose value is passed to the execution manager.

The *FJIT* compiler is the basic JIT compiler in SSCLI. It is a one-pass JIT compiler that doesn't perform any hardware-independent or complicated hardware-dependent optimizations, and doesn't use any intermediate representations. It analyzes the input CIL instructions and translates each CIL instruction to native machine code. The virtual stack of execution of SSCLI is mapped onto the hardware stack. For the ×86 architecture, the stack top is stored in the *eax* register, which allows us to reduce the number of redundant copying (the operand on the stack top, for many kinds of operations, works as accumulator, keeping the result of the operation).

The FJIT compiler saves information for the garbage collector in its own format understandable by the code manager. Information for the garbage collector and information on guarded blocks and exception handlers in the method is passed to the virtual machine via the API presented by the virtual machine kernel to the JIT compiler. The same API is used by the JIT compiler to get any necessary information.

The call of the basic JIT compiler during the first call of a method of the target application is implemented as follows. In the metadata representation for the class, the virtual machine keeps the table of methods containing executable code for each method. Such reference is initialized by the address of a stub that calls the function initiating the JIT compiler for the method processed. This function calls the execution manager, which transfers control to the JIT manager associated to the FJIT compiler. The JIT manager calls the FJIT compiler. If the compilation succeeded, the reference from the metadata is replaced by the reference to the compiled native code. Next, the target method is called.

The next section will explain how we modified this scheme to enable the call of optimizing JIT compiler for the selected methods.

8.5   THE ARCHITECTURE OF OPTIMIZING JIT COMPILER FOR SSCLI/ROTOR

This section describes the architecture and implementation of optimizing JIT compilation system for SSCLI (Rotor) [89] developed as a research project at St. Petersburg University. The original version of SSCLI implements only basic features of the virtual machine and does not include an optimizing JIT compiler (see Section 8.4). Since the first version of SSCLI was shipped in 2002, there were several attempts of the implementation of optimizing JIT compilation system for SSCLI (Rotor) [90,91]. In those projects, optimizing JIT compilers were completely independent from the basic one, with their own JIT managers and code managers (see Section 8.4). The code manager reads the information on the objects for the garbage collector recorded by the optimizing JIT compiler [90]. In spite of the fact that initially the architecture of SSCLI JIT compilation system was designed keeping in mind the above scheme of plugging in extra JIT compilers (see Section 8.4), its practical implementations discovered a lot of issues related to incompleteness of the API [90].

In our project, the optimizing JIT compiler is more tightly integrated with the basic JIT compiler—part of the proginal version of Rotor. It is located in the same dynamically linked library (DLL) as the basic JIT compiler, stores the data for the garbage collector in the same format as the basic compiler, and uses the same JIT manager and code manager classes as the basic compiler.

Now let's consider the architecture of our optimizing JIT compilation system for SSCLI, the structure and principles of the profiler and the optimizing compiler, and their integration with the existing elements of SSCLI.

The basic principle of the architecture of the optimizing JIT compilation system for SSCLI is the principle of *selective multilevel JIT compilation* that was successfully used in other projects [78,83,92]. Since optimizing transformations slow down the JIT compiler, compilation of all methods with full optimizations is not an efficient decision for a JIT compiler [78]. As explained above in this chapter, optimization will be beneficial if it is applied to more often called (hot) methods only.

To collect information on hot methods, a profiler is used, which either injects into the code the calls of its tools [78] or collects statistical information on program execution [78,92]. The latter alternative is used only for interpreted or nonoptimized code.

In our system, we implemented a *sampling* (statistical) *profiler*, since it allows us to collect profiling information, which is representative enough, without substantial performance decrease. This profiler is the only profiler in our system. It collects information on all methods optimized at different levels. Its implementation is described below.

The major parts of optimizing JIT compilation system for SSCLI and their interaction are shown in Figure 8.3.

The basic one-pass JIT compiler (FJIT) is part of the original shipped version of Rotor (see Section 8.4). In our system, the basic compiler (that compiles methods during their first calls) is augmented by our two-level optimizing JIT compiler. Methods of optimization for the selected methods are chosen by the controller, based on the profiling data.

Information on the frequency and structure of method calls is collected by a sampling profiler [89] that interacts with managed threads of SSCLI, makes regular snapshots of the stack, analyzes them, and stored the information collected in the profiling data repository. To make a stack snapshot, the existing SSCLI stack walk mechanism is used that is intended for stack demo in debugging, and for stack unwinding in case of exceptions.

The controller regularly checks the profiling data repository to select methods whose call counter is exceeding some threshold value. The selected methods compiled without optimization by the basic JIT compiler, are put into the first-level optimizing compilation queue. Methods already compiled with the first level of optimization are put into the second-level optimizing

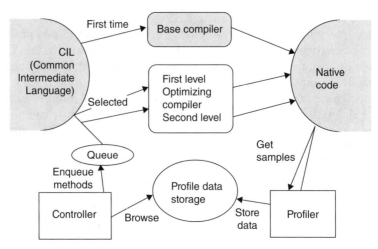

Figure 8.3. The major parts of optimizing JIT compilation system for SSCLI and their interaction.

compilation queue, if the threshold for the second-level optimization is exceeded (in other words, if they become "too hot"). Methods already compiled with the second optimization level are not put into any queue and can be recompiled, in case the decisions on devirtualization or inlining optimizations taken for those methods have become obsolete, due to changes in statistical information. On recompiling the methods, the controller replaces the reference to executable native code from the method metadata and sets the optimization level in the profiling data.

We have chosen and implemented a sampling profiler [89] as a tool that, on the one hand, allows us to collect precise and complete enough statistical data on the frequency and the context of method calls, and, on the other hand, is "lightweight" enough, not to overload the program with extra work. The profiler collects the data on the number of calls for each method from the sample (to select candidate methods for level one optimization), as well as the data on the *context* of method calls (i.e., which methods are the callers of the sample methods), necessary to determine the candidate methods for devirtualization and inlining at the second level of optimization.

The profiler collects the data using a compact structure referred to as *Call Context Map (CC-Map)*, which allows us to quickly retrieve the data on possible call contexts of a given method, as well as on the methods called from the given method [89].

A fragment of the *CC-Map* structure is depicted in Figure 8.4. Arrows denote reference from one node to the other. The *MethodProfile* nodes store the *absolute call counter* for each method, the references to the other nodes describing calls of the other methods from the given method, and information on the call context of the given method. The CC-Map structure is implemented

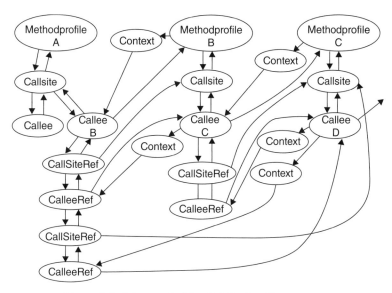

Figure 8.4. *A fragment of the Call Context Map structure.*

as a hash table that keeps references to *MethodProfile* nodes. As the hash key, the code of description of the method in the metadata is used.

Each *Callee* node contains the counter of calls of one method by the other in the given concrete point of the code. A *Callee* node refers to the *MethodProfile* node related to the method being called. Using those references, it is possible to get information on the other contexts of a given method calls.

CallSite nodes contain information on the point of the call. Their role is to represent information on the number of methods actually called in the given point of the program as a virtual method (of a descendant class of the given base class). Based on this information, the controller can make a decision on devirtualization or inlining of the method. From each *Callee* node as the root, a tree of nodes of the types *CallSiteRef* and *CalleeRef* is built. Those nodes contain call counters of methods in the given context, and provide information on the number of different methods called in the given point of the program in the given context. For example, the leftmost tree in Figure 8.4 specifies the following sequence of calls: A->B->C->D, and the middle tree—the sequence of calls B->C->D. If the *Callee* node for the method C in the middle tree stores information on all detected calls of the method C from the method B, then the *CalleeRef* node in the leftmost tree contains only information on the calls of the method C from the method B for the cases when the method B was called from the method A. So such information structures allow us to easily find the most often repeated sequence of method calls of any size and don't contain any redundant data (we avoided storing the counters of calls for each call chain detected).

CC-Map accumulates total call count for every caller–callee pair, and at the same time, it allows retrieving information concerning calls in the specific context. This information is easily available: The compilation controller can look up contexts by the *Context* references when some counter exceeds a threshold, as well as move up and down through a call chain.

From the *CallSite* and *CallSiteRef* nodes the controller can know if there is, probably, only one target (and so consider devirtualization) or not. *CallSite* provides this information for all calls from the specified site, *CallSiteRef*—only in a given context.

CC-Map is a compact structure. Nodes don't store duplicate data. It allows quick updating, as well as rather quick removal of nodes, which appear "cold." Compilation controller need not perform additional analysis of trees to get the information necessary for good decision: It may only follow references.

Filing and updating the CC-Map. When a sample is being taken, all the data are initially written into a buffer. Then, at the start of the buffer, we have a reference to the method corresponding to the activation record at the top of the stack (i.e., the most inner call), and at the end of the buffer— the outer call reference.

The pseudocode for the sample buffer processing algorithm looks as follows:

```
for (int i = 0; i < end_of_sample; i++)
{
   update MethodProfile(buf[i]);
   if (i > 0)
   {
      update Callee(buf[i], buf[i - 1]);
   }
   for (j = i - 2; j >= 0; j-)
   {
      update CalleeRef(buf[j]);
   }
}
```

The real code is a little more optimized and a little more complicated, but the underlying algorithm is the same.

The profiling algorithm. Maintaining such a complex structure as the CC-Map requires some effort. Algorithm described in the previous section may take a long time to complete. But we cannot afford to pause user threads for observable intervals because of profiling.

The solution we have chosen is to separate taking sample from thread stack and storing the sample data in the CC-Map. For this purpose, we use two profiling threads and queues for the samples waiting for processing and storing.

Profiling job is launched by the *MarkThreadsWorker* system thread, which marks every live managed thread, so have it learn that it should take a sample when reaching a safe point. Every live managed thread has its own sample buffer and its own short sample queue. The sample is written into the thread local buffer and pushed into the thread local queue. When local queue length exceeds a threshold (which is low enough, currently 10), all its contents is pushed to the global queue. This scheme is aimed to decrease the need to grab a global queue lock and, thus, to decrease possible pauses caused by waiting for the lock. Little delay in sample processing is not critical because only large numbers are considered when making compilation decisions.

The CC-Map manager thread periodically grabs the global queue lock, takes out a bunch of samples, and puts them into its own queue. Then, it releases the lock and proceeds with processing samples without hurry. The global queue hashes samples by the thread *id*, so the CC-Map manager thread can return the processed sample buffers back to their thread, so as not to allocate new memory. Local thread buffer grows automatically when needed; the queued samples buffers grow as they need, to adapt to local buffer size. So when threads get back their own buffers, previously queued, these buffers are likely to have an appropriate size. If the thread is already finished, when the CC-Map manager returns processed sample buffers for it, this chain of buffers is put aside to be used by next new thread.

Tuning sampling interval. The profiler is *self-tuning*. It chooses an interval of taking samples, depending on the characteristics of the environment where it runs. Namely, it tracks how often the same activation records appear on the top of the stack. There are two threshold values defined: maximum percentage of repetitions and minimum percentage of repetitions. The CC-Map manager thread evaluates the actual percentage of repetitions (of activation record appearance on the top of the stack) every 1000 samples (more precisely, than processed samples portions is more than 1000, because the manager thread handles a bunch of samples in every pass). If percentage of repetitions is lower than the minimal threshold, it is considered too low, and sampling interval decreases. If the percentage of repetitions is higher than the maximum threshold, the sampling interval increases.

Integration with SSCLI. Rotor has a built-in mechanism for walking the stack, which is used for such purposes as exception handling and security checks [88]. It involves several methods and functions of virtual machine, among them, the *StackWalkFrames* method of the virtual machine (VM) *Thread* class, which we use to take samples. *StackWalkFrames* takes a function to execute on every encountered stack frame as a parameter, so its work is easily customizable. The advantage of using such technique is that it's already known how to distinguish between managed method frames and unmanaged method frames, and we can recognize context transitions (e.g., across application domain boundaries), encapsulate calls to Rotor facilities to get metadata references and offsets, and use convenient API to perform jobs on the stack.

We have managed threads call *StackWalkFrames* method at, so called, "safe points," building upon the other intrinsic Rotor mechanism—trapping threads when they know it's safe to suspend. This mechanism has been originally used to trigger garbage collection. Checks for a suspend request have been inserted by the JIT compiler at back edges and everywhere the next piece of code may take a long time to execute [88]. Such checks are also performed by some of the runtime helper functions extensively used in Rotor. We utilize this mechanism and add additional check points at the entry of every method. At that new checkpoints, we test only for the need to take samples.

We also use the SSCLI core *HashMap* class to construct the CC-Map in Rotor. SSCLI *HashMap* class implements a hash table used by VM for its internal needs. It hashes pointer type values by the pointer type keys (so allows storing profile objects by the pointer-to-metadata keys); implements locking for insert, delete, and lookup; and takes care of cleaning up itself. It is just what we need. So, we have chosen *HashMap* as a hash table to store *MethodProfile* references at the highest level of CC-Map and as a hash table to hold queues of samples waiting for processing in the global samples store.

Profiling results. We tested our profiler on SSCLI 1.0. To measure overhead and accuracy of profiling, we used tests from a suite supplied with SSCLI. To estimate the overhead, we chose a set of base tests from *bcl\system* and *bvt* subdirectories and tests from *bcl\threadsafety* subdirectory of the Rotor *tests* directory. To estimate the accuracy, we used tests from *bcl\ threadsafety* subdirectory, where multiple threads execute the same code. For measurement, we used statistical correlation of the total executions counters stored in *MethodProfile* nodes and Arnold & Ryder overlap percentage [92] for the whole tree comparison. The overlap percentage of trees *T1* and *T2* is computed as follows:

$$\Sigma_{N \ in \ T1,T2} \ [\min \ (\text{Weight} \ (N_{T1}), \text{Weight} \ (N_{T2}))]$$

where:

Weight (N_{Tx}) = value$(N_{Tx})/\Sigma_{N \ in \ Tx}$value(N);
N is a node holding a counter;
value is the value of the counter.

When N is not found in Tx (though it exists in Ty and thus in the $TxTy$ set), it is assumed that value(N_{Tx}) = 0.

For the performance test, the low threshold for repetitions (cases when the same method appears on the top of the stack) was set to 1%, high threshold for repetitions was set to 15%. For the correlation and overlap measurement of tests, self-tuning was turned off, because it can affect the correlation results distinctly for short-running tests, such as those we used. However, the great deal of these differences is produced at the interval when the profiler is tuning, so such results do not reflect the real picture in stable state. Logging sample interval changes in the process of tuning revealed that the sample interval becomes stable after one to two changes. We measured correlation and tree overlap with different sample intervals (with self-tuning turned off), and the best results (95–99%) were obtained with the same interval that the profiler found automatically.

In the accuracy test, we recorded and compared executions counters and the whole CC-Maps from 10 subsequent runs. The results of every run were compared with the results of every other and an average value was computed.

To make the CC-Map accessible even after the VM has stopped running, we dumped the CC-Map (in the *fastchecked* mode) to an XML file at VM shutdown. Then, original CC-Maps were restored from XML representation and compared (in the XML dump of the CC-Map, managed methods are identified by the full name and signature to make comparison possible, though at runtime, they are identified only by pointer to the metadata).

Table 8.1 shows the average correlation for 10 subsequent runs of the same test and average tree overlap percentage. All the tests are from *bcl\ threadsafety* suite.

We can see that, though the correlation of simple execution counters is always good (98–99%), the overlap percentage sometimes appears

TABLE 8.1. Average Correlation for Total Executions Counters and Overlap Percentage Extracted from the Comparison of Results of 10 Subsequent Runs

Test Name	Correlation (%)	Overlap (%)
co8545int32	99	97
co8546int16	99	92
co8547sbyte	99	94
co8548intptr	99	98
co8549uint16	99	95
co8550uint32	99	95
co8551byte	99	97
co8552uintptr	99	97
co8553char	99	96
co8555boolean	99	96
co8559enum	98	75
co8788stringbuilder	99	67
co8827console	99	77
co8830single	99	98

lower than 80%. We think, however, this can be explained probably by the fact that the tests themselves were very short.

Tests were run on Celeron433 processor, 256M RAM. Sampling interval was set to 10 ms. This is a rather short interval for this hardware configuration, and for long-running programs, it may be longer. However, the tuning mechanism can adjust the interval well. When testing, we started from interval 50 ms, and for the tests that performed bad with such an interval, the profiler made it shorter. For the tests that performed well, the interval remained unchanged. We can also see in Table 8.1 that for some tests, the accuracy is even redundant. Ninety-five to ninety-seven percent would be enough to consider results statistically significant. For the cases when we can get such accuracy with longer interval, it will not decrease (or it can even increase if the initial interval appears too short).

The profiling overhead was measured on the free build against unchanged Rotor free build, on the same hardware configuration, on the tests from *bcl\system*, *bvt*, and *bcl\threadsafety* subsets of Rotor core test suit. Initial sampling interval was set to 50 ms. Tuning was turned on. Tests were run two times, and the total overhead did not exceed 3%. In the future, we intend to consider automatic turning off tuning after a certain period of time so as to lower overhead.

8.6 AOT COMPILATION

From the previous sections, we can see how ingenuous JIT compilation can be. The purpose of JIT compilation is to improve runtime performance by dynamically tuning to the target application.

AOT compilation is yet another technique to improve runtime performance. When we first got acquainted to this term, it looked as if it was taken from science fiction—as if it meant compiling the program that is not yet written. In reality, AOP compilation means a very simple thing—*precompilation* of the .NET assemblies or Java class files to native code before the execution of the program. As can be seen from comparison with the previous sections related to JIT compilation, AOT compilation does make sense if the behavior of the programming module represented in the intermediate code (.NET CIL/MSIL code, or Java bytecode) is stable, well studied, and predictable, and if the program will not be reconfigured at runtime. Though, theoretically, dynamic reconfiguration is quite possible for Java and .NET applications, due to their built-in mechanisms of dynamic class loading. So, when the user knows that his or her application is not changeable, and would like to achieve maximal efficiency, based on that fact, AOT compilation techniques are recommended for use.

Of modern software development platforms, .NET offers a comfortable opportunity to do AOT compilation—by the *ngen* (*native code generator,* actually *native precompiler*) utility built into the .NET Framework and Visual Studio.NET. The native assembly generated by the *ngen* utility will be marked by special attributes as *native* and will be executed as a native code, though, containing all necessary runtime checks required by managed execution policy.

As for Java, there is no built-in AOT compilation utility in Sun's Java Development Kit (JDK), though most integrated development environments (e.g., Borland JBuilder) contain native precompilation option that can be used to perform AOT compilation, similar to using .NET's *ngen*.

Both JIT and AOT compilations, used when needed, are the two state-of-the-art compilation techniques aimed at increasing runtime performance of the applications written for Java or .NET.

EXERCISES TO CHAPTER 8

8.1 Compare .NET CLR and JVM features in relation to our considerations in Section 8.1.

8.2 Compile simple .NET and Java applications to intermediate code (MSIL or Java bytecode) and to native code (by JIT and AOT compilers available). Compare the performance of the application AOT compiled versus JIT compiled.

8.3 Study the sources of FJIT compiler for SSCLI/Rotor, and try to understand how to build optimizations into this compiler using methods described in this chapter.

8.4 What kind of optimizations are performed by a JIT compiler, in which cases, and why?

Chapter *9*

Graph Grammars and Graph Compilers

This chapter may seem unusual for a compiler book, more associated with traditional compilation methods, phases, and algorithms. While traditional compilers are still very important, another hot area closely related to compilers has been originated and is developing rapidly—*graph compilers*.

Although our personal research interests are not closely related to graph grammars and graph compilers, we decided to include an overview of graph compilers into our book, as an introductory material for students to get interested in graph grammars and graph compilers. We think it is worth doing, since graph compilers are now widely used in science and in industry, especially in the electronics industry, for very large scale integration (VLSI) circuit design and development. Another area of application of graph grammars is visual programming languages, in particular, domain-specific languages (DSL). Also known are applications of graph grammars to knowledge management, to image recognition, and to IT teaching.

For a deep study of graph grammars, of various approaches to graph transformations, of graph compilers and graph compiler construction tools, we recommend the papers in References 93–107. The material of the chapter is based on these papers and on several dozen of other graph grammar papers not explicitly included in the reference section.

Please consider this chapter an introduction, which we hope can help somebody to get interested in this topic, and an attempt of summary of the current state of the art in graph compilers area from the viewpoint of an experienced developer of traditional compilers.

Trustworthy Compilers, by Vladimir O. Safonov
Copyright © 2010 John Wiley & Sons, Inc.

9.1   BASIC CONCEPTS OF GRAPH GRAMMARS AND GRAPH COMPILERS

Graph compilers is a general concept to unite all kinds of software tools dealing with analysis of graphs, their visualization, and transformations to other graphs or to some code in high-level language or machine (assembly) language.

Graphs are well known as a general-purpose self-evident visualization mechanism to display wide spectrum of entities and relationships, in particular:

- electronic circuits;
- chemical formulas;
- business activity diagrams;
- program schemes and structures, in particular, as applicable for visual programming languages;
- diagrams of any kinds of entities and their relationships;
- abstract machines and their states and state transitions;
- live systems in biology.

As compared with the textual form of representing information (processed by traditional text compilers, the subject of all the rest of the book, except for this chapter), the graph form is, on the one hand, very general, and on the other hand, clear and self-explanatory.

It should be noted, however, that expressing anything by graphs may reflect the specifics of the way of reasoning by the researcher, teacher, or student, rather than a real need of graphs versus texts to make some specifications or designs in the problem area. Graphs are convenient and elegant, but it takes very long to draw them, even using such comfortable tools as DiaGen/DiaMeta [96,99] and AGG [97]. Also, as compared with texts, it takes very long to parse them—many of the general graph parsing and transformation algorithms appear to be NP-complete. For example, to express the idea of sequence of statements, it is quite enough to formulate it in traditional textual form:

$$S1; S2$$

rather than to draw a graph representing this trivial "block scheme." As for our personal experience, we have developed a lot of complicated programs and tools in many areas but have not ever used the "block schemes" or "program schemes" technique, even at the design stage, due to "text-processor" style of individual reasoning. However, we do know there are a lot of researchers and especially engineers who are thinking by drawings, graphs, and diagrams, and cannot even write a simple program without prior graphical modeling of its structure. Besides that, in many scientific and engineering areas, like the above-mentioned electronics design and chemistry, graph-like representations are used as essential tools and methods.

A *graph* is a (visually displayable) construct consisting of finite set of *vertices* connected by *edges*. Usually, the edges are directed (this fact is represented by arrows), and both the vertices and the edges are *labeled* by some textual information.

More formally, as the simplest formal definition, a (directed) graph is a pair:

$$G = <V, E>$$

where V is a finite set of *vertices*, and E (a subset of Cartesian product $V \times V$) is the set of *edges* of the graph. Each edge is characterized by a pair (x, y), where x is the source vertex, and y is the target vertex. A *labeled* graph is a graph, with each vertex and each edge labeled by some text. A *multigraph* is a graph that can contain more than one edge connecting any two vertices x and y—either in one direction, or in both directions, or loops (like an edge from x to x).

Another definition of a graph, in more algebraic style, and for this reason, more widely used in graph grammar theory, is as follows. A *graph* G is a tuple:

$$G = (V, E, s, t)$$

where V is the set of *vertices*, E is the set of *edges*, and s (for *source*) and t (for target) are mappings: $s, t: E \rightarrow V$. So, for each edge e, $s(e)$ is the source of the edge, and $t(e)$ is the target of the edge.

A *labeled* graph is a graph whose vertices and edges are marked with labels from some alphabet. More formally, a labeled graph is a tuple:

$$G = <V, E, s, t, l_V, l_E>$$

where V, E, s, and t are already defined; l_V is the *vertices labeling* function: $l_V: V \rightarrow \Sigma$; l_E is the *edges labeling* function: $l_E: E \rightarrow \Sigma$; and Σ is the alphabet of labels to mark each vertex and each edge of the graph. In some papers, only labeling the edges is considered; however, it is clear that labeling vertices is equally important (see Fig. 9.1 as an example).

To study the similarity of structures of graphs (important for graph transformations), the concept of *graph morphism* is considered.

Informally, a graph morphism is a mapping to represent one graph as a subgraph of another one.

More formally, graph morphism $f: G_1 \rightarrow G_2$ is a pair of mappings: $f = (f_V, f_E)$ where $f_V : V_1 \rightarrow V_2$ and $f_E: E_1 \rightarrow E_2$ such that:

$$f_V \circ s_1 = s_2 \circ f_E$$

and:

$$f_V \circ t_1 = t_2 \circ f_E$$

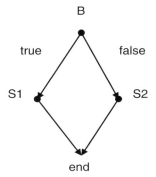

Figure 9.1. *Directed labeled graph visualizing the control structure of the conditional statement if B then S1 else S2 end.*

The two above conditions mean that the functions f_V and f_E of the morphism *f* preserve sources and targets of the edges when mapping one graph to another: The source of an edge in G_1 is mapped to source of the corresponding edge in G_2; the target of an edge in G_1 is mapped to the target of the corresponding edge in G_2. In our opinion, this intuitively clear concept is not well explained in graph transformation papers (even in tutorials), and a variety of denotations, without clear explanation, may mislead the readers.

It is very important that the *composition*:

$$g \circ f = (g_V \circ f_V \,, g_E \circ f_E) : G_1 \to G_3$$

of the graph morphisms:

$$f : G_1 \to G_2$$

and:

$$g : G_2 \to G_3$$

is also a graph morphism.

It is possible to define a graph morphism for labeled graphs: In this case, the morphism will preserve labels, as well as incidence.

To be more close to programming and compilers, the graph example in Figure 9.1 depicts a directed labeled graph visualizing the control structure of the conditional statement *if B then S1 else S2 end* (the *end* terminator is added for more clearance and to be used as connector in further graph transformations). The vertices corresponding to condition *B* and alternatives *S1* and *S2* are labeled with their names; the exit vertex is labeled by *end*; the edges corresponding to the alternation of control flow are labeled with *true* and *false*—the corresponding values of *B*.

To be able to formalize graph transformations, similar to text transformations during compilation and any other kind of text processing, it appeared necessary to define the concept of a *graph grammar*.

Formal grammars introduced by Chomsky, widely used in compilers and in natural language processing, are intended for transformations of *texts*—linearly ordered sequences of characters (symbols). Any *grammar rule* of a Chomsky-type grammar describes some rule of *text rewriting*, that is, replacing, in the input text string x, any text *pattern* y found in x to the other text z:

$$y \to z$$

As opposed to formal (text) grammars, a *graph grammar* is a set of *graph grammar rules*. More formally, a graph grammar is a pair (G_0, P) where G_0 is the *initial (starting) graph*, similar to the starting symbol in text grammars; P is a set of *graph transformation rules*. Each of the rules describes a rule of transformation of a host graph G by replacing each graph pattern l to the graph r:

$$B^l \to B^r$$

However, a question arises how to identify the patterns in the host graph G. For text processing grammars, it is very simple, since the text is linearly ordered, and each text or subtext has the only start symbol and the only end symbol, so a replacement of one text to another is easy.

For graph grammars, there appears to be a variety of approaches to the ways how to represent graphs, their vertices and edges, how to apply graph transformation rules, how to specify *constraints* on graphs, and how to parse graphs. This is quite natural at the current initial state of this new area. We think, in the near future, many more approaches and tools based on those are likely to appear. The most popular of the existing approaches are summarized below in the subsequent sections.

9.2   CATEGORICAL APPROACH TO GRAPH TRANSFORMATIONS

Categorical approach to graph transformations [93] is based on considering the notion of a graph as an instance of a more general concept—*category*. Informally speaking, a category is a formal structure consisting of a *class of objects*, a set of *morphisms* defined for any two objects (including the *identity* self-morphism for each object), with the operation of a *composition* and the property of *associativity* for the composition of three morphisms. Particular instances of categories are *sets*, *graphs*, and *multi-sorted algebras* (see Chapter 2 for an overview of the concept of multi-sorted algebra used for formal specifications of program semantics).

In the categorical approach, to define a transformation rule from one graph to another, an *interface (gluing)* graph I is considered. It is used as a graph connector (which becomes part of the graph grammar rule). The interface graph I is mapped to the *context graph* C, part of the host graph G to which the transformation rule is applied, and to the parts of the rule B^l and B^r.

A graph grammar rule in the categorical approach takes a more complicated form: B^l <- I -> B^r, and such transformation is formally described as a category theory operation referred to as *pushout*. Two kinds of pushouts are used—*single pushout* and *double pushout*.

In the *double-pushout* approach, the rules of a graph grammar take the form:

$$p : L \xleftarrow{l} K \xrightarrow{r} R$$

where L, K, and R are graphs; l and r are two morphisms matching K, respectively, in L and R.

Derivation with double pushout approach proceeds as follows.

Given a graph G, a production p: $L \xleftarrow{l} K \xrightarrow{r} R$, and a graph morphism $\mu : L \to G$, the following two steps of a derivation are performed:

1 The *context graph* is obtained by deleting from G all images of elements in L but not of elements in K (this operation is referred to as *pushout complement*).

2 The *final graph* is obtained by adding to the context graph all elements of R that don't have a pre-image in K (this operation is referred to as *pushout*).

Informally, the morphism μ enables the mapping of the left-hand part of the rule *(pattern L)* to the host graph G. The graph K "keeps" the context of the transformation and does not allow us to delete any necessary parts from the graph G as the result of the transformation.

A popular "toy" example considered in many papers on graph grammars is the "Pacman's game," which moves the figure of Pacman as follows. The current position is that there are two vertices connected to each other. Initially, the Pacman points by an edge to the left vertex of them. The transformation rule of the "Pacman's game" graph grammar enables that, as the result of the transformation, the Pacman moves its "looking" edge from the left vertex to the right one. The left part of the rule L depicts Pacman "looking" at the left vertex; the right part depicts Pacman "looking" to the right vertex. The graph K—"save context" part of the rule—depicts the figure of Pacman and the two connected vertices. Figures 9.2–9.5 demonstrate the host Pacman graph, the transformation rule (referred to as *movePacman*), the match found in the host graph, and the resulting graph after the transformation, with the found edge's target moved from one vertex to another (source: Reference 101).

In our opinion, the most critical part of this process is to find the morphism μ for each derivation step. This task actually means finding a subgraph in a graph and, in the general case, this problem is known to be NP-complete. That's the real issue of the practical use of graph grammars, even if they are very practically important.

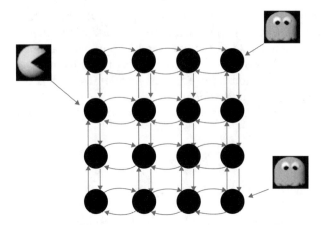

Figure 9.2. The host Pacman graph.

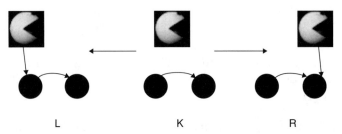

L   K   R

Figure 9.3. The double-pushout style graph transformation rule (movePacman) for the Pacman graph.

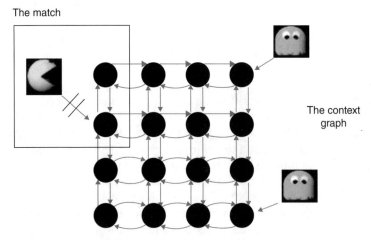

Figure 9.4. The match found in the Pacman graph.

The match

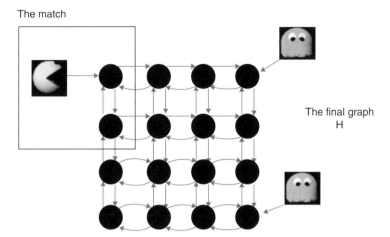

The final graph
H

Figure 9.5. *The resulting Pacman graph after the transformation.*

Another remark we should make is, in our opinion, the algebraic terminology and system of notions used for graph transformations is too general for software engineers. In our humble opinion, there is no need to consider such general (almost philosophical) concepts as categories, morphisms, and pushouts to explain and justify a simple self-evident transformation of the graph. Our version of the terms to be used is as follows: While protecting the graph context K (some important neighbor vertices and edges) of the transformation, not-to-be-deleted, delete in G the subgraph similar to L and draw a new subgraph similar to R. We think such terminology is more intuitive and much clearer.

As we remember, there is yet another form of the derivation in graph grammars—*single pushout*. With this form, a rule of a graph grammar is of the following (much simpler) kind:

$$p : L \to^r R$$

where r is a partial graph morphism. As stated by graph grammar theorists, the single-pushout approach can model more situations than the double-pushout approach.

Figure 9.6 illustrates a single-pushout style graph transformation rule for the same example as above—the Pacman graph, and the task of moving one arrow (source: Reference 101).

Again, we do think the terminology already accepted in this approach (category, pushout, etc.) is too general. It may confuse software engineers who are eager to learn and use a tool based on this approach.

So, in our opinion, this approach is very interesting and general from a theoretical viewpoint but looks complicated for practical software engineers.

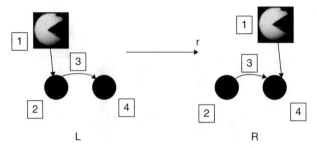

Figure 9.6. *The single-pushout style graph transformation rule for the same Pacman graph.*

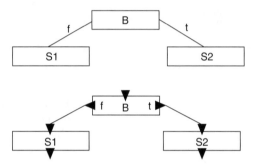

Figure 9.7. *Two graphs representing the structure of the if statement in two variants—ordinary graph (above) and reserved graph (below).*

However, the algebraic approach is used as a solid theoretical basis for most of the known graph grammar approaches and tools.

9.3 RESERVED GRAPH GRAMMARS (RGGs)

RGGs approach [94] is based on some specific extended form of graphs—*reserved* graphs, that, in addition to ordinary vertices, have *super-vertices* (consisting of several labels and their related input and *output* connections to other vertices) convenient to specify the *type* of the vertex and all its *connections*. A *node* in RGGs may have a complicated structure and consist of vertices and super-vertices. The difference between ordinary graphs and reserved graphs is illustrated by a simple example of a graph representing the structure of the conditional (if) statement, depicted in Figure 9.7 in two variants—ordinary (above) and reserved (below). Figure 9.8 illustrates more clearly the difference between a vertex and a super-vertex in a reserved graph [102].

From the above examples, it can be seen that the reserved graph is much more expressive and self-evident: In Figure 9.7, the super-vertex represents

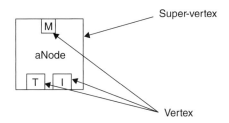

Figure 9.8. *Vertices and super-vertices in a reserved graph.*

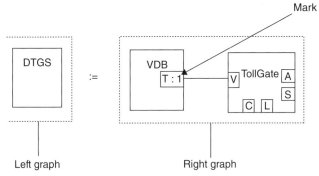

Figure 9.9. *Example of a reserved graph transformation rule. DTGS, a kind of infrared defector (made of deuterated triglycine sulfate); VDB, Video Data Base.*

the information that the condition is the entry vertex of the construct (it has one *in* connection), and the information that the connection vertices (labeled *S1* and *S2*) is reached, accordingly, if the condition is true (the connector labeled *t*) and if the condition is false (the connector labeled *f*). RGGs define transformations of reserved graphs based on super-vertices and their edges. This approach is implemented in the visual programming language generator VisPro [94]. In our opinion, this approach is more appropriate for engineers, and reserved graphs are quite suitable for drawing technical schemes.

Figure 9.9 depicts an example of a reserved graph transformation rule [102].

To be more formal, a *node* in an RGG on a label set L is defined to be a tuple:

$$n = (s, V, l)$$

where:

- V is a set of vertices;
- s in V is a super-vertex;
- $l: V \rightarrow L$ is an injective mapping from V to L.

A *reserved graph* over a label set L is defined to be a pair:

$$G = (N, E)$$

where:

- N is a finite set of nodes over L;
- $E = \{ (id(v1), id(v2)) \}$ is a finite set of edges, where $v1$ and $v2$ are vertices; $id(v)$ is the (unique) *identity* of the vertex v; and the edge $(id(v1), id(v2)) = (id(v2), id(v1))$, that is, the edges are nondirected.

In general, the problem of parsing a graph to find a subgraph isomorphic to the left-hand part of a graph grammar production (*redex*, in terms of Reference 94) is NP-complete. So, the researchers seek partial solutions to this problem. As for RGGs, the authors of this approach [94] have found an efficient polynomial-complexity parsing algorithm referred to as *selection-free parsing algorithm (SFPA)*, which only tries *one* parsing for each reserved grammar rule $P = (L, R)$ where L and R are reserved graphs. For the SFPA algorithm to be applicable, the RGG should satisfy the following condition [94]: *if any graph merged from two productions' right graphs has two redexes r1 and r2 corresponding to the productions, and any of such graphs can be applied, with the R-application, first by r1, then by r2, and vice versa, and the result graphs are the same, then we say the RGG satisfies the SFPA constraint.*

Since RGGs, under certain conditions, enable efficient parsing, they become probably the most attractive approach to graph transformations.

9.4 LAYERED GRAPH GRAMMARS

Layered graph grammars approach [95] is based on traditional graphs, with one important addition—*layering of labels* of the edges and the vertices of the graphs.

The main ideas of layered graphs and layered graph grammars are as follows. The sets of labels for vertices (L_V) and edges (L_E) of the graph are split into disjoint sets of *layers*: $L_0, ..., L_n$, and, for each x, an element of the graph G (x is a vertex or an edge), the function *layer(x)* is defined such that $layer(x) = i \iff l(x)$ is in L_i, where $l(x)$ is the label of the element x.

Each rule (L, R) of a layered graph grammar is defined such that $L < R$ in the following sense: There exists k such that L and R contain the same number of labels of all levels less than k, but L has less labels of the level k than R has. In other words, as the result of applying each rule to a layered graph, the number of labels of higher levels should increase. So, when the rules are applied in reverse order (right-to-left) to reduce the graph into the initial (*lambda*) vertex during bottom-up parsing, the process of parsing should terminate in a finite time. So layering of labels is introduced to enable a decidable

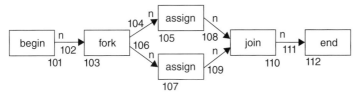

Figure 9.10. *Example of a simple layered graph of a process flow diagram describing fork/join statements.*

parsing algorithm. The parsing algorithm works bottom-up, that is, finds right-hand parts in the current working graph, and replaces them to left-hand parts. Due to the above properties of labels, this process should terminate in finite time, since the layering of graph elements is decreased during parsing and cannot decrease less than to 0.

In the parsing algorithm [95], to specify the states of the analysis, the authors of the approach use the intermediate notion of a *dotted rule* similar to the concept of the *LR(0) item* used in LR parsing for text grammars (see Chapter 4).

Figure 9.10 depicts an example of a simple layered graph of a process flow diagram describing fork/join statements. Please see Reference 95 for more details.

To summarize this section, layered graph grammars are well organized and very expressive, but the algorithms of their parsing are of exponential complexity.

9.5   META-MODELING APPROACH TO GRAPH GRAMMARS AND DIAMETA EDITOR

Meta-modeling approach [98,99] is used to specify visual (graph-like) languages. Each of visual languages is based on its *model—abstract syntax* specification (see Chapter 4 for the definition of abstract syntax). Such models are visually represented as *class diagrams* (e.g., *UML diagrams*). Since the syntax of models is also specified by models (the latter should be, therefore, called *meta-models*), this approach to visual languages definition is referred to as *meta-modeling*.

In visual tools based on meta-modeling, two approaches to creating and editing visual diagrams are used: *structured editing* and *freehand editing* [99]. With *structured editing*, the user is provided with a set of legal operations, which allow him or her to transform correct diagrams into other correct diagrams. *Freehand editing* allows the user more freedom—to choose and use for drawing diagrams any kind of diagrams from a given visual language-specific set of diagrams represented on the screen, without any restrictions. So, it is the task of the editor to analyze the diagram freely constructed by the user and determine whether it is correct and what is its meaning.

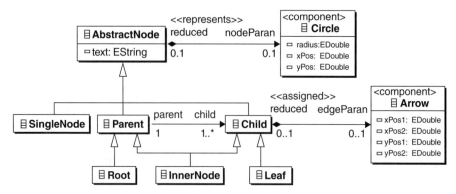

Figure 9.11. *The class diagram specifying the structure of trees.*

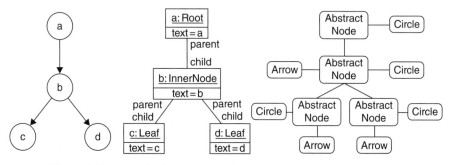

Figure 9.12. *Example of a tree complying the class diagram in Figure 9.11.*

An example of a class model (actually, a *meta-model*) is given in Figure 9.11. This class diagram specifies the structure of trees [99]. The abstract class *AbstractNode* is used as an abstract class for tree nodes. Each tree node has a member attribute *text*. The classes *Parent* and *Child* are specifying parent–child relationships. The concrcte classes *Root*, *InnerNode*, and *Leaf* specify all possible kinds of nodes of a tree (*InnerNode* is a descendant of both *Parent* and *Child*). The cardinalities in the class diagram specify that any child must have exactly one parent, and each parent must have at least one child. The classes *Circle* and *Arrow* specify elements of concrete syntax of visualizing trees. This diagram is simplified. It doesn't completely specify the trees: It doesn't impose additional restrictions that there should be no cycles in a tree.

Figure 9.12 shows an example of a tree complying the class diagram in Figure 9.11, a UML object diagram of the tree, and its *instance graph* [99].

When analyzing such visual diagrams as the example of a tree, the freehand editor checks its syntax correctness and binds the appropriate internal representation to each visual component. For the above example, the freehand editor, as the result of analyzing the visual image of the tree, constructs its *instance graph* containing instances of the used model classes, without indicat-

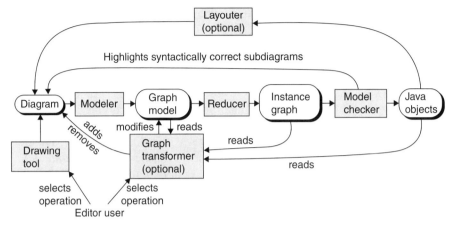

Figure 9.13. *The architecture of the DiaMeta editor.*

ing any concrete types. The concrete types are deduced by the freehand editor, which actually solves the *constraint satisfaction problem* during the analysis of the instance graph.

The *DiaMeta* diagram editor [99] is based on the above outlined meta-modeling approach. The architecture of the editor is depicted in Figure 9.13. DiaMeta editor is an extension of the diagram editor *DiaGen* [96]. The editor works as follows. First, the diagram created by the user is transformed by a *modeler* into the *graph model*. Then, the *reducer* creates the *instance graph* (see above), and the *model checker* analyzes the instance graph for correctness. The model checker also generates a *Java code* to represent the structure of the diagram drawn. In case of errors, the editor shows to the user (by a specific color) the *maximal correct subdiagram* of the diagram drawn and indicates the errors. The *layouter* modifies the diagram's layout, in accordance with the attributes of the recognized syntactically correct subdiagrams.

DiaMeta uses the following three *stereotypes*: <<vcomponent>>, <<vrepresents>>, and <<vassigned>>, to annotate class diagrams and to control its code generator. The meanings of the stereotypes are self-evident from their names. All of them are used in the above example.

So, DiaMeta editor, from the viewpoint taken in our book, can actually be considered as a *trustworthy graph compiler*, in our understanding, one of the first yet implemented.

Please find more details about DiaMeta in Reference 99.

9.6 HYPERGRAPH APPROACH TO GRAPH GRAMMARS IN DIAGEN

Hypergraphs approach [100,103,104] is a generalization of the concept of a graph by *hyperedges*. The formal definition of a hypergraph is as follows. A hypergraph H is an ordered pair (V, E) where V is a set of vertices and E is a set of edges such that E is a subset of $P(V)$—the powerset of V. A context-free hypergraph grammar consists of two sets of *hyperedges*, one for nonterminal and the other for terminal nodes, and the starting hypergraph that contains nonterminal hyperedges with labels only. Each rule of a hypergraph grammar is a pair $L ::= R$ where both L and R are hypergraphs. The grammar defines the *set* of all hypergraphs with terminal nodes only that can be derived from the starting hypergraph.

Hypergraph grammars are used in *DiaGen* [96] diagram editor. DiaGen uses hypergraph grammars with *embeddings*: A special kind of *embedding* productions is possible to use, with an additional hyperedge at the right-hand side.

DiaGen (Diagram Editor Generator) [96] uses language specifications based on labeled hypergraphs and hypergraph grammars. DiaGen consists of two parts: *designer* and *editor framework*. The designer is a GUI tool to specify the language. The specification visualized as a graphical diagram is internally represented as an XML document. This document is converted to Java code by the DiaGen's *code generator*. This generated Java code, together with the *editor framework*, implements a graphic editor for a specific language.

A diagram modeled in an editor is translated into its *hypergraph model*.

Here is an example how to represent simple state machine diagram in DiaGen [104]. The state machine consists of two states and the transitions from one state to another. Figure 9.14 represents a simple state machine diagram (upward), and its *hypergraph model* (middle) and *reduced hypergraph model* (downward). The diagram represents two states with two transitions.

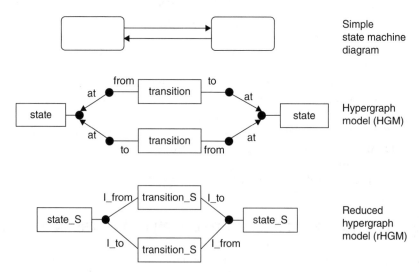

Figure 9.14. *A simple state machine diagram (up), its hypergraph model (middle), and reduced hypergraph model (down).*

The hypergraph model illustrates it with four *hyperedges* (represented by rectangles), one for each graphical object. Each of the two states has an *attachment area* represented as a *node* (filled dot). Each transition has two attachment areas. The arrows connecting the attachment areas are special relationship edges to represent *spatial relationship* between visual objects. In the example, both the spatial relationships are *at*-relationships. They indicate that the transition's end point (its correct attachment point) is connected *at* the *state* border (its correct attachment area). The labels *to* and *from* of the transitions indicate the two ends of the transition.

The hypergraph model in DiaGen is *reduced* to enable its more efficient handling. In the example, reduced hypergraph model is represented in terms of larger groups of *structured components*. In the reduced model, all spatial information is removed, and the graphical objects are replaced with equivalent *terminals* (as shown in the example). The attachment areas are replaced by links acting as nodes.

As can be seen from the example, this approach is very expressive. On the other hand, it has to deal with too low-level elements, such as spatial representations, which have to be reduced during graph transformations.

9.7 GRAPH COMPILER GENERATION TOOLS

In spite of the complexity of the problems of graph transformations, there are a variety of practically used tools for generating graph compilers, visual editors, and domain-specific visual programming languages. Here, we briefly summarize the most widely known of them.

DiaGen/DiaMeta (considered in Sections 9.5 and 9.6) is a framework for diagram editor generation, probably the most widely used now. Its theoretical basis is formed by *meta-model language specifications* and *hypergraph grammars*. From the practical side, it is a Java tool, with a convenient installer, designer, editor, and generator. Especially important are its trustworthiness features (see Sections 9.5 and 9.6).

AGG [97] is an interpreter for attributed graph transformations. The AGG language is a rule-based *visual language* to support algebraic approach to graph transformations. The main feature of AGG is the ability for the user to define an attributed graph and graph transformation, based on *layered graph transformations* and *node type inheritance*. The latter term means that, to pass attributes from one node to another, it is possible to define inheritance relations between nodes. This functionality makes AGG a very helpful tool for transformation of *attributed abstract syntax trees*, to be used for graph compilers. AGG can also be used without GUI as a general-purpose graph transformation engine in Java.

MOFLON [105] is a meta-modeling framework used to specify tools for domain-specific software architectures. The goal of this project is to combine MOF 2.0 meta-modeling language as graph schema language with Fujaba [106] graph transformation rules. MOFLON generates Java code using the

MOMoC code generator. *Fujaba* is a toolkit to generate Java prototype code, given UML class of activity diagrams.

GenGED (Generation of Graphical Environment for Design) [107] supports generic description of visual modeling languages for generating graphical editors and simulation of behavior models. GenGED is based on AGG as a tool for algebraic graph transformations. It provides features for checking graphical constraints. It has been applied to generating a number of visual languages. Its visual environment supports generation of visual editors working in structured or freehand mode.

To summarize the features of the above tools, they support syntax definition and model transformation for visual languages. Using these tools, the user can easily generate a graphical editor or compiler for a visual language. Moreover, some visual modeling tools already provide analysis and verification functionality, which is especially important for trustworthy use of visual modeling and visual languages technologies—the main area of application of graph grammars and graph transformations.

Graph compilers have become an inherent part of many programming systems to support various fields of activity.

As a perspective for future development, in our opinion, the challenge of trustworthy integration of graph compilers and traditional compilers should be considered, since there are real tasks whose parts can be solved either by graphical or by traditional algorithmic methods. In this relation, developing graphic extensions for the most popular and powerful software development languages and platforms, Java and C#, could be an interesting task.

EXERCISES TO CHAPTER 9

9.1 Design an appropriate representation of a graph grammar, and implement single-pushout and double-pushout approaches described in Section 9.1.

9.2 Try to clearly formulate the differences between various approaches to graph transformations (categorical, layered graph grammars, RGGs, hypergraphs, meta-models) summarized in Section 9.2 and the advantages and drawbacks of each approach.

9.3 Why do you think graph grammars are not so widely spread as might be expected? What are the problems of graph grammars?

9.4 What is typical of RGGs? What is a super-vertex and a node in graph grammars? What are the advantages of RGGs?

9.5 What is the characteristic feature of layered graph grammars? Why is the layering defined?

9.6 What is meta-model approach to graph grammars?

9.7 What is a hypergraph and a hyperedge? Why are they introduced?

9.8 Please formulate the major features of DiaGen/DiaMeta diagram editor.

Chapter 10

Microsoft Phoenix, Phoenix-Targeted Tools, and Our Phoenix Projects

This chapter, the last one in the book, is fully devoted to Microsoft Phoenix [3]—a new toolkit for developing optimizing compiler back-ends and various program analysis and transformation toolkits for an extensible set of target platforms.

Phoenix is a collection of a variety of compiler development technologies and features we already covered in the previous chapters—internal representations and their transformations, multilayered optimization techniques, code generation, support of compiler drivers, passes and phases, and so on.

So, we consider Phoenix a state-of-the-art toolkit in compiler area. We have special interest to Phoenix, and a number of important results in our Phoenix projects, as will be seen from the chapter.

In the chapter, we outline the history of our Phoenix projects and our relationships with the Phoenix team. Then, we consider Phoenix basic concepts, architecture, features, and use cases. Finally, we describe our latest Phoenix projects developed at St. Petersburg University and analyze the perspectives of Phoenix.

Trustworthy Compilers, by Vladimir O. Safonov
Copyright © 2010 John Wiley & Sons, Inc.

10.1   HISTORY OF PHOENIX AND OF OUR PHOENIX PROJECTS

Phoenix is the result of a joint project of Microsoft Research and Microsoft Visual Studio product team. History of its use outside Microsoft starts in 2003 when the first public version, *Phoenix Research Development Kit (RDK)*, was issued as a research product to be assessed by the academic community.

Due to a kind proposal by the Microsoft Research Phoenix manager John Lefor (now the head of the European Microsoft Innovation Center in Aachen, Germany), in September 2003 I was honored to become the first academic user of Phoenix outside Microsoft. Figure 10.1 is a photo of this memorable moment taken at Microsoft Redmond in September 2003—John Lefor hands me the first public CD of Phoenix.

In 2003, Microsoft announced the Phoenix Academic Program. Due to that, several hundred compiler developers worldwide got access to Phoenix for its assessment and use for education and research.

Our first, and now the most widely known, Phoenix project is Aspect.NET [1]—aspect-oriented programming (AOP) toolkit for Microsoft.NET based on Phoenix and integrated to Microsoft Visual Studio. Our book [1] covers Aspect.NET in detail. Besides that, our Aspect.NET project site [108] contains the code of examples from the book [1] illustrating the use of Aspect.NET for trustworthy software development. For our considerations in this chapter, the most important is the fact that Aspect.NET *weaver* (the component of our toolkit responsible for injecting aspects into target application) uses Phoenix. In early 2005, a new version of Phoenix RDK was issued that could really handle Microsoft.NET assemblies. In a few weeks, the first working prototype

Figure 10.1. *Microsoft Redmond, September 2003: John Lefor, Microsoft Research Phoenix manager (left) hands Vladimir Safonov (right) the first academic CD of Phoenix.*

Figure 10.2. *Microsoft Academic Days 2005, Moscow: Shahrokh Mortazavi, Microsoft Phoenix manager, with Vladimir Safonov and his team after the successful demonstration of the first version of Aspect.NET. Left to right: Maxim Sigalin, PhD student; Alexey Smolyakov, PhD student; Shahrokh Mortazavi, Microsoft Phoenix manager; Professor Vladimir O. Safonov; and Dmitry Grigoriev, PhD student.*

of Aspect.NET was developed, on the base of that new version of Phoenix, by a team of our PhD students—Dmitry Grigoriev, Mikhail Gratchev, and Alexander Maslennikov. Figure 10.2 is a picture of our team together with Shahrokh Mortazavi, Microsoft Phoenix manager, in April 2005, at the Microsoft Academic Days Conference in Moscow, after the successful demonstration of Aspect.NET. This project was so fortunate as to receive three Microsoft Research grant awards—in 2002, 2004, and 2006. It is now used in 25 countries. Please find more details on Aspect.NET in References 1 and 108. The project is actively developing and attracting yet more attention worldwide.

Our next Phoenix project was *St. Petersburg University (SPBU) for Phoenix (SPBU4PHX)* started in 2006, due to a grant award by Microsoft Research Redmond. This project is aimed at the development of complex of AOP and compiler development tools based on Phoenix. The project includes enhancement of Aspect.NET and two new parts: *Phoenix-FETE* [60]—a compiler front-end development toolkit and environment targeted to Phoenix (covered in Section 10.11)—and *Phoenix high-level abstract syntax tree (HL-AST)* [109]—high-level language-agnostic abstract syntax trees architecture targeted to Phoenix. Both Phoenix-FETE and Phoenix HL-AST projects are still being developed by our PhD student teams.

We also use Phoenix in a number of other compiler development projects performed by our PhD students and graduate students of St. Petersburg University. One of such PhD projects is a toolkit for visualization and editing Microsoft.NET assemblies based on Phoenix and integrated to the Microsoft Visual Studio.

Phoenix is an important part of our university course on trustworthy compiler development [4]. Students demonstrate a keen interest to Phoenix, many of them have already used Phoenix in their term and graduate projects under our supervision.

So, we have integrated Phoenix into our research and educational process, and this chapter is a kind of summary of our activity in this direction.

10.2 OVERVIEW OF PHOENIX ARCHITECTURE

Phoenix is Microsoft's prospective platform for building compilers (just-in-time [JIT] compilers, ahead-of-time [AOT] compilers, native compilers) and a wide spectrum of code analysis tools (code browsers, profilers, etc.).

Figure 10.3 depicts the Phoenix logo.

Phoenix works with Windows XP, Windows 2003, and Windows 2008 operating systems.

Phoenix brings together skills and results of Microsoft Visual C++ product team and Microsoft Research Phoenix team.

The latest version of Phoenix right now (July 2009) is the Phoenix Software Development Kit (SDK) issued September 2008 [3]. It is integrated with Visual Studio.NET 2008 and available for free download. The installation contains a variety of samples and detailed documentation.

Speaking allegorically, the role of Phoenix is similar to the role of the foundation and to the body of a rostral column (please recall the allegorical picture on the front cover and see its explanation in the Preface).

In developing a compiler based on Phoenix, Phoenix takes on the responsibility on the optimizing back-end, and on the total framework and function-

Figure 10.3. The Phoenix logo.

ing of the compiler. Phoenix supports concepts of *pass* and *phase*, and helps to organize a compiler as a sequence of *passes*. Each of the passes can have one or more *phases*. Phoenix "understands" a *high-level intermediate representation (HIR)*, to be generated by a third-party compiler front-end that should be implemented as one or several subsequent passes of the Phoenix-based compiler. Internally, Phoenix uses two more, lower-level kinds of intermediate representation (IR)—*middle-level intermediate representation (MIR)* and *low-level intermediate representation (LIR)*, more close to machine code. Phoenix provides a wide scale of optimizations at the IR level. Finally, Phoenix supports the code generation phase and contains optimizing code generators for one of the following target platforms: ×86, IA64, AMD64, and .NET (Microsoft Intermediate Language [MSIL] code). The set of the target platforms can be extended using the target platform specification language *GURL* (Grand Unified Retargeting Language), which is especially important for prospective compiler projects and their porting to novel target platforms. So, to be brief, Phoenix is a realization of dreams of compiler developers of previous generations for dozens of years (including those of them who implemented DELTA, SUPER, ALPHA, BETA, and other compiler development toolkits discussed in the previous chapters). These dreams have come true in a product by Microsoft.

Our personal opinion, based on the Sun compiler experience, is that Phoenix architecture and design have experienced deep influence of the architecture of Sun's Scalable Processor ARChitecture (SPARC) compilers. However, Phoenix has a lot of original ideas implemented.

We should caution those readers who would like to learn Phoenix deeply and use it in your projects: Learning Phoenix is not easy, cannot be done just by one hello world style example, and requires step-by-step "immersion," since Phoenix is a very complicated product. So, we'll try to provide a kind of incremental learning Phoenix in this chapter. However, for an experienced compiler developer, all Phoenix's numerous features, structures, and options are intuitively clear, since they are based on many years of compiler development experience by the Phoenix key architects. The next steps in learning Phoenix for the readers after studying this chapter should be to try Phoenix samples and to attempt to develop your own Phoenix tool.

What Phoenix does not support (and is not intended for) is the development of a compiler *front-end*. The front-end should be developed separately and should generate Phoenix HIR. One of the possible solutions for compiler front-end developer is to use, together with Phoenix as the basis for the compiler back-end, our Phoenix-FETE compiler front-end development toolkit (see Section 10.11) that supports several parsing strategies, and is specially targeted to Phoenix—provides easy-to-use high-level API to generate the elements of Phoenix HIR, to be called from semantic actions of the compiler's source language-attributed grammar.

For a developer of any kind of programming language-related tool (e.g., a code browser or a profiler), Phoenix provides a variety of opportunities to analyze, optimize, or generate a code.

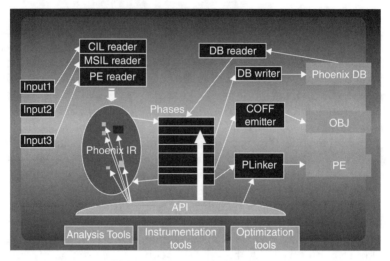

Figure 10.4. *Phoenix infrastructure.*

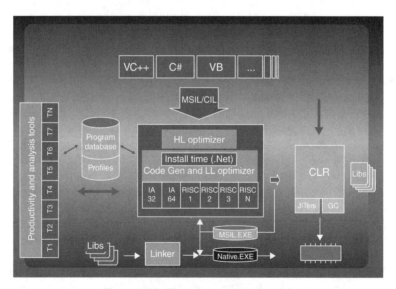

Figure 10.5. *Phoenix compilation model.*

Now let's consider Phoenix architecture, using the schemes of Phoenix infrastructure (Fig. 10.4), Phoenix compilation model (Fig. 10.5), and Phoenix architecture layers (Fig. 10.6) [3].

Phoenix provides significant flexibility to build various types of compilers and tools. Phoenix supports the list of *passes* and *phases* of a tool, two-level IR very comfortable to process an application, and a mechanism to easily define and use a *plug-in* to Phoenix, or a Phoenix-based tool.

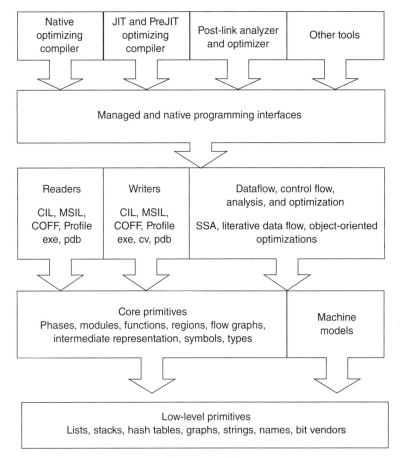

Figure 10.6. *Phoenix architecture layers.*

Core primitives of Phoenix are hardware platform independent.

The central platform building block is a multilevel IR. It can be either generated by a front-end of a Phoenix-based compiler, or generated by one of the *readers* shipped with Phoenix, for example, as the result of reading MSIL code.

Phoenix is available in dual mode (either in managed and unmanaged versions). So, there are two quite common ways of Phoenix use: from C#, in managed mode, or from C++, in unmanaged mode.

The managed version is more suitable for debugging and can be used together with Microsoft Visual Studio.NET 2008. Phoenix supports a special kind of Visual Studio projects—*Phoenix projects*, both for C# and for C++ languages.

The unmanaged version is faster and can be used in the release versions of Phoenix-based products.

The inputs of code for Phoenix can be provided as Microsoft.NET portable executable (PE) file, Microsoft.NET MSIL code, and CIL code. Please note that in this context and in this chapter, the *CIL* acronym means *Visual C++ Intermediate Language* used by the Microsoft Visual C++ product team. So the readers shouldn't get confused and mix up C++ intermediate language with the Common Intermediate Language of .NET; the latter is referred to as *MSIL* (Microsoft Intermediate Language) in this chapter.

For each of the above listed forms of code, Phoenix provides a *reader*—a component that reads that form of code and generates Phoenix IR.

In particular, in our Aspect.NET project, we use Phoenix for reading .NET assembly code. But, due to Phoenix, we can process application code at the much more comfortable layer—Phoenix IR. For example, we can comfortably seek in the generated Phoenix HIR a call of the method whose name satisfies the aspect's name wildcard, which is much easier than directly parse.NET assembly with its complicated structure [1].

We hope the set of Phoenix *reader* components will be extended, due to implementation of new target platforms.

Phoenix IR is passed to a Phoenix-based tool, separated to a list of *passes* and *phases*. Those tools can be code *analysis* tools, code *instrumentation* tools, and code *optimization* tools.

A compiler or source code browser, in particular, can be built as a Phoenix tool.

The Phoenix tool can use and update the Phoenix IR of the target application using Phoenix API, and can also use *Phoenix writers*—components to produce the desirable output form of the code—a common object file format (COFF) object file that can contain ×86, or AMD64, or IA64 code, or .NET PE code (assembly).

Figure 10.6 demonstrates Phoenix architecture layers.

Phoenix-based compilers and other Phoenix-based tools (JIT compilers, pre-JIT compilers, etc.) use the highest layer—Phoenix managed or unmanaged API.

The Phoenix API, in its turn, calls Phoenix *readers* (for CIL, MSIL, .exe, and Program Data Base [PDB] formats), writers (for CIL, MSIL, .exe, and PDB formats), and also *Phoenix data flow and control flow analysis and optimization tools*.

In their turn, the above Phoenix high-level tools use *Phoenix core primitives*—phases, modules, IR, symbols, and types—and also machine (target platform) models described in a special language.

Phoenix core primitives use various Phoenix *collections*—stacks, lists, tables, and so on.

10.3 PHOENIX-BASED TOOLS, PASSES, PHASES, AND PLUG-INS

Phoenix allows the users to develop *Phoenix-based tools* (e.g., compilers). Each of the Phoenix tools should be organized as a sequence of *passes*. Each pass is a sequence of one or more *phases*. For example, *c2*—the Visual C++ compiler back-end shipped with Phoenix—has got *two* passes; the actual code generation is performed at the second pass.

It is also possible to write a *plug-in* for Phoenix. A plug-in is an external module executed by a Phoenix-based compiler or by a Phoenix-based code analysis tool. Each plug-in should implement extra passes, or extra phases, which can be inserted into the appropriate list of the passes (*PassList*) or the phases of each pass (*PhaseList*) of the compiler or tool. *Phase* and *Pass* are classes of the Phoenix API. Each phase can have a *pre-phase event* and *post-phase event* (e.g., dumping some intermediate structures).

Phoenix-based tool or plug-in operates with the most basic structure Phoenix constructs for the source program—the *call graph* of *units*, mostly *functional units* (*functions*). A typical action to be implemented by a Phoenix tool or plug-in is an extra dump of some structure (e.g., the IR) of the unit, or some transformation of the unit's code (e.g., inserting the *nop* operation after each instruction, implemented by the *addnop_tool* and *addnop_plugin* samples from the Phoenix SDK shipment).

Other examples of Phoenix plug-ins are as follows:

- an alternative, experimental, register-allocation phase that replaces the one built into the *c2* compiler;
- injection of extra (instrumentation, traceback, etc.) code into each function being compiled;
- dump of a view of the IR for a function as it is compiled, showing how it evolves during successive optimizations and transforming to LIR;
- dump of the information about the operation of *c2*, such as CPU and/or memory use.

So, the developer of a Phoenix-based tool or a plug-in that implements an extra pass should implement the *Execute* method that actually performs the traversal of the units call graph and applies the phases to each unit of the graph.

We don't provide here the code of examples of Phoenix-based tools and plug-ins, since it's too early—Phoenix is a complicated API, and first, we need to consider its basic concepts. Such example is given in Section 10.10. The readers are also recommended to study and run Phoenix samples [3].

10.4 PHOENIX PRIMITIVES: STRINGS AND NAMES

All Phoenix types are members of the *Phx* namespace.

The most primitive types in Phoenix are *strings* (*Phx.String*) and *names* (*Phx.Name*). Strings in Phoenix are represented as managed wide-character strings.

Names should be used when Phoenix API expects the *Name* type. Names in Phoenix are *interned* (hashed), so there is only one name with a given string, for example, "St.Petersburg."

Example in C++:

```
String ^spbStr = L"St.Petersburg Russia";
String ^spbflStr = L"St.Petersburg FL";
Phx::Name spb = Phx::Name::New(nullptr, spbStr);
Phx::Name spbfl = Phx::Name::New(nullptr, spbflStr);
Phx::Output::WriteLine(L"spb name string is \"{0}\"",
    spb.NameString);
Phx::Output::WriteLine(L"spbfl name string is \"{0}\"",
    spbfl.NameString);
```

To compare Phoenix names, the *Name.Equals* method should be used:

```
if (Phx::Name::equals(spb, spbfl)) {
  Phx::Output::WriteLine(L"There is only one St.
      Petersburg");
} else { // this is actually true
    Phx::Output::WriteLine(L"No, there are two St.
        Petersburgs!");
}
```

The implementation of this method is more efficient than compare strings character-by-character: Since names are optimized, the identity of the string objects is checked.

Strings and names are Phoenix *primitives*. Among the Phoenix primitive types are also:

- *controls*—Phoenix primitives to manage program behavior, for example, *dump* or *trace* (i.e., various *options*);
- *collections*—provided to handle compound data structures—lists, hash tables, vectors, etc.).

10.5   PHOENIX INTERMEDIATE REPRESENTATION (IR)

As already noted, IR is the main structure of Phoenix.

The Phoenix framework uses single, strongly typed, linear IR.

The IR represents a function at multiple levels of abstraction, from very high-level, machine-independent representation to very low, machine-dependent levels (HIR and LIR).

The Phoenix framework stores the IR of a function as a doubly linked list of instructions.

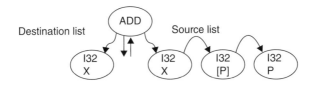

HIR view of a simple C++ statement

X = ADD X, *P

Figure 10.7. *Example of Phoenix high-level IR (HIR) for the statement x = x + *p.*

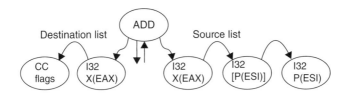

LIR view of a simple C++ statement
ADD X(EAX), [P(ESI)]

Figure 10.8. *Possible Phoenix low-level IR (LIR), targeted to ×86 architecture model, for the same construct x = x + *p.*

Each instruction has its *operator*, an *input list* of source operands, and *output list* of destination operands.

Phoenix IR is designed in such a way to make data flow analysis easier.

For any Phoenix IR instruction, it can be easily found out which operands are used and which operands are updated by the instruction. This is the key point for data flow-based optimizations.

In our Aspect.NET experience [1], Phoenix IR is very comfortable to find join points in a target application and weave the aspect into these join points. It would be noncomfortable if we had to handle PE file and MSIL instead, by our own hands.

Figure 10.7 shows an example of Phoenix *HIR* for the statement $x = x + *p$.

Figure 10.8 depicts possible LIR (targeted to ×86 architecture model) for the same construct.

All in all, Phoenix provides the following kinds of IR:

- *HIR*—architecture-independent and runtime-independent;
- *MIR*—architecture-independent but runtime-dependent;
- *LIR*—architecture-dependent and runtime-dependent;
- *encoded intermediate representation (EIR)*—architecture-dependent and runtime-dependent.

During compilation, IR is transformed from one layer to another. For example, the *Lower* phase in the *c2* C++ compiler back-end shipped with Phoenix transforms MIR to LIR. In general, generation of lower-level IR from high-level one is referred to as *lowering*, the backward process is referred to as *raising*.

To better feel the style of the Phoenix HIR, consider an example in Visual C++ [3]:

```
#include <stdio.h>
int main(int argc, char** argv)
{
   int x = 5;
   int y = 3;
   int* p = &y;
   x = x + *p;
   printf("%d\n", x);
}
```

The *c2* Visual C++ compiler back-end shipped with Phoenix generates the following HIR for this program (the format of IR shown below is the standard format of IR dump in Phoenix):

```
$L1: (refs=0)
   {-4}, {-7}         = START _main(T)
_main: (refs=1)
   _argc, _argv       = ENTERFUNCTION
   _x                = ASSIGN 5
   _y                = ASSIGN 3
   _p                = ASSIGN &_y
   t275              = ASSIGN _p
   t276              = ADD _x, [t275]*
   _x                = ASSIGN t276
   {-9}              = CALL* &_printf,&$SG3674,_x, {-9},
                        $L5(EH)
                      RETURN 0, $L3(T)
$L5: (refs=1)
                      UNWIND
$L3: (refs=1)
                      EXITFUNCTION
$L2: (refs=0)
                      END {-4}
```

Most of the above HIR instructions are self-evident. We only comment those that need explanations.

Some of the IR instructions, if necessary, are labeled. Each label (e.g., *$L2*) is accompanied by a counter of references to that label in the program.

The general format of an IR instruction is similar to a triple (see Chapter 5). Most of the instructions can be represented in the form:

out_operands = OPCODE in_operands

where *out_operands* are operands (there can be one or more) that are updated as the result of the operation represented by its *OPCODE*.

The asterisk (*) after the operation code means that the instruction can throw exceptions. Phoenix provides a mechanism for exception handling. In the above example, it is the *CALL** instruction. In such cases, one of the *in* operands of the instruction contains a reference to the *exception handler*. In the example, this is the operand *$L5(EH)*. The IR instruction labeled as *$L5* is the *UNWIND* operation that performs *stack unwinding* if an exception is thrown.

Also important is the use of temporary variables (like *t275* and *t276*) during the evaluations of the expressions. In further lowering the IR, those temporary variables can be mapped to registers if possible.

As the result of the lowering phase targeted to ×86 architecture model, the *c2* compiler back-end will generate the following LIR for this program:

```
$L1: (refs=0)
   {-4}, {-7}         = START _main(T)
_main: (refs=1)
  _argc, _argv       = ENTERFUNCTION
  [ESP], {ESP}       = push EBP
  EBP                = mov ESP
  ESP, EFLAGS        = sub ESP, 12(0x0000000c)
$L9: (refs=0) Offset: 6(0x0006)
                     ENTERBODY
  _x[EBP]            = mov 5
  _y[EBP]            = mov 3
  tv279-(EAX)        = lea &_y[EBP]
  _p[EBP]            = mov tv279-(EAX)
  tv275-(EAX)        = mov _p[EBP]
  tv276-(ECX)        = mov _x[EBP]
  tv276-(ECX), EFLAGS = add tv276-(ECX), [tv275-(EAX)]*
  _x[EBP]            = mov tv276-(ECX)
  [ESP], {ESP}       = push _x[EBP]
  [ESP], {ESP}       = push &$SG3674
  {-9}, {EAX ECX EDX ESP EFLAGS MM0-MM7 XMM0-XMM7
         FP0-FP7 FPUStatus} =
                     call* &_printf, $out[ESP],
                     $out[ESP]+32, {-9},
                     {EAX ECX EDX ESP EFLAGS MM0-MM7
                      XMM0-XMM7
                      FP0-FP7 FPUStatus}, $L5(EH)
```

```
ESP, EFLAGS       = add ESP, 8
tv283-(EAX)       = mov 0
$L3: (refs=0) Offset: 58(0x003a)
                  EXITBODY
ESP               = mov EBP
EBP, {ESP}        = pop [ESP]
{ESP}             = ret {ESP}, $L10(T)
$L5: (refs=1) Offset: 62(0x003e)
                  UNWIND
$L10: (refs=1) Offset: 62(0x003e)
                  EXITFUNCTION tv283-(EAX)
$L2: (refs=0) Offset: 62(0x003e)
                  END {-4}
```

In the above LIR code, we emphasize the use of ×86-specific registers to represent the operands and the implicit side effects of the instructions.

The above IR examples are the visual representation of the IR. In its internal binary representation, the IR is a double-linked list, which makes any insertions into IR or deletions from IR easier.

To navigate across the program structure, Phoenix HIR provides the concept of *units*—parts of the program tree. The following categories of units are supported:

- *GlobalUnit*—corresponds to the concept of *compilation unit* traditional for compilers. This is the outermost unit in the units hierarchy;
- *ProgramUnit*—the next (lower) layer of the unit hierarchy. A global unit can have one or more program units (since a compiler can compile several programs as one compilation unit);
- *AssemblyUnit*—the next (lower) layer of the unit hierarchy after the *ProgramUnit*. The concept of *assembly* in Phoenix is similar to that in .NET. An assembly is a group of modules and resource files and is a fundamental unit of versioning, security, and reuse. A program unit can have one or more assembly units, as well as a number of individual *module units*;
- *ModuleUnit*—the next layer of the hierarchy after the assembly unit. An assembly consists of module units (representing a set of *functions*) and may contain *data units* (representing groups of data);
- *FunctionUnit* is the basic unit of compilation and program transformations in Phoenix. A function unit contains *IR instructions stream* (see the examples above), *symbol table* (representing the symbols defined in the function), *flow graph* (representing control and data flow in the function), and *aliasing information* for the function. Function unit is the basic unit to which a sequence of phases of a Phoenix-based tool is applied;
- *DataUnit*—a collection of related data, for example, a set of initialized variables;

- *PEModuleUnit*—the result of compilation for .NET platform, a PE file image represented by an *.exe* file (executable .NET application), or a *.dll* file (dynamically linked library).

10.6 PHOENIX SYMBOL SYSTEM

Phoenix *symbol* is an abstraction of a *named entity* in a programming language. Symbols in Phoenix can denote the following entities: *types*, *labels*, *function names*, *variables*, *addresses*, *metadata entities*, and *module exports/ imports*. However, there can be *unnamed* symbols.

Symbols are used to refer to the above entities in the Phoenix IR.

Symbols are stored in *symbol tables*.

Actually, in our opinion, the concept of a symbol and symbol table in Phoenix is close to treatment of symbols by assemblers and linkers.

Symbols, symbol tables, and *symbol table maps* provide an abstraction of the concrete *lookup* mechanisms of a variety of programming languages (see Chapter 5).

> *Symbol table maps.* A *symbol table map* is essentially a mapping of some *key* to a symbol or multiple symbols. A map is bound to the concrete symbol table and provides a way to lookup symbols. A map can be *full* (i.e., relate to *all* symbols in a table) or *partial* (relate to only a *subset* of symbols in the symbol table). A map can be *single* (refer to only one symbol with a given key value) or *multiple* (refer to multiple symbols with the same key value). There can be several maps (i.e., several ways of lookup) related to the same symbol table.
>
> These are the following kinds of maps:
>
> - *LocalIdMap*—a full, single map whose key is the value of the *LocalId* property that each symbol has. A local id of the symbol is an unsigned integer value, unique for a map. The *LocalId* map is implicitly created with each symbol table by default;
> - *ExternIdMap*—a partial, single map whose key is the *external id* of the symbol. Not each of the symbols has external ids: Symbols introduced and used by the back-end don't have them. An external id for the symbol can be introduced by the compiler front-end;
> - *NameMap*—a partial, multiple map whose key is the *name* of the symbol. Since names can be repeated (i.e., several symbols can have the same name), this kind of map is multiple.
>
> The relationship of the concepts of symbol, symbol table, and symbol table map is illustrated in Figure 10.9 [3]. The symbol table in Figure 10.9 contains three global variable symbols (*GlobalVarSym*), named x, y, and again, y, and two function symbols—one named f, and the other with no name. The latter is a common situation, since anonymous functions are

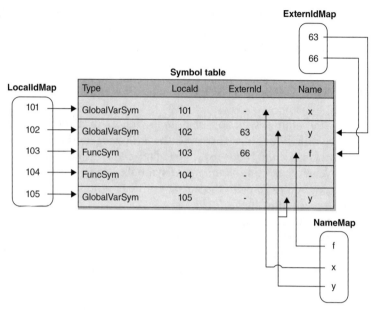

Figure 10.9. *Relationship of the concepts of symbol, symbol table, and symbol table map in Phoenix.*

typical for many programming languages since ALGOL-68; in particular, there are anonymous methods in .NET 3.5. In spite of the fact that some names are repeated and some symbols have no names, symbol table maps based on local or external ids enable different ways to lookup symbols in the table.

Creating a symbol table. Below is an example of creating a symbol table (in Visual C++):

```
// Create a unit for the table
Phx::Name unitName = Phx::Name::New(lifetime,
      "unit");
Phx::ModuleUnit ^ moduleUnit =
  Phx::ModuleUnit::New
    (lifetime, unitName, Phx::GlobalData::GlobalUnit,
    Phx::GlobalData::TypeTable, runtime->
        Architecture, runtime);
// Construct a table
Phx::Symbols::Table^ moduleSymbolTable =
  Phx::Symbols::Table::New(moduleUnit, 1000, true);
// The table is now linked with the unit.
Assert(moduleUnit->SymbolTable ==
        moduleSymbolTable);
Assert(moduleSymbolTable->Unit == moduleUnit);
```

First, a name for the module unit (*"unit"*) is created. Then, the *moduleUnit* is created, and, finally, the table is constructed.

The table constructor allocates a *lifetime* to hold the table and all maps and symbols. The concept of a lifetime in Phoenix is close to that in some programming languages, for example, in ALGOL-68. In the simplest case, a lifetime can be *null*: It means that an entity lives forever. There is a way to explicitly manipulate *lifetime* objects: When such an object is deleted, all entities with this lifetime are deleted also.

Next, the table constructor in our example creates the table and allocates, by default, a *LocalId* map with the initial capacity for 1000 symbols.

Let's continue our example: Imagine that, next to creating a symbol table, we need to add a *NameId* map to it. That can be done by the following Visual C++ code:

```
// Add a name map to the table so we can look up
symbols by name
Phx::Symbols::Map ^ moduleNameMap =
  Phx::Symbols::NameMap::New(moduleSymbolTable,
1000);
moduleSymbolTable->AddMap(moduleNameMap);
```

So now there are *two* symbol table maps related to our symbol table— a *LocalId* map and a *NamedId* map, similar to the table depicted in Figure 10.9.

Adding symbols to the symbol table. Now it's time to add symbols to our sample symbol table. There is no limit on the number of the symbols in a table. We'll add to our symbol table a symbol describing a global function declaration with the prototype:

```
int gcd (int x, int y)
```

Please note that creating a symbol in the symbol table automatically assigns to the new symbol a *unique LocalId* to be used for lookup the symbol.

Adding the symbol is performed by the following Visual C++ code:

```
// Create the type for the symbol
Phx::Types::FunctionType ^ gcdType =
  moduleUnit->TypeTable->GetFunctionType(
    Phx::Types::CallingConventionKind::CDecl,
    0,
    moduleUnit->TypeTable->Int32Type,
    moduleUnit->TypeTable->Int32Type,
    moduleUnit->TypeTable->Int32Type,
    nullptr, nullptr);
// Now create the symbol in the symbol table
```

```
Phx::Name gcdName = Phx::Name::New(lifetime, "gcd");
Phx::Symbols::FunctionSymbol ^ cgdSymbol =
  Phx::Symbols::FunctionSymbol::
    New(moduleSymbolTable, 0,
    gcdName, gcdType,
    Phx::Symbols::Visibility::GlobalDefinition);
// Note that symbols refer back to the tables that
  contain them.
Assert(gcdSymbol->Table == moduleSymbolTable);
// Now create a reference to a global variable, as
  follows:
// extern float a;
Phx::Types::Type ^ floatType =
  moduleUnit->TypeTable->Float32Type;
Phx::Name aName = Phx::Name::New(lifetime, "a");
Phx::Symbols::GlobalVariableSymbol ^ aSymbol =
  Phx::Symbols::GlobalVariableSymbol::New
    (moduleSymbolTable, 100, aName,
    floatType, Phx::Symbols::Visibility::
    GlobalReference);
aSymbol->Alignment =
  Phx::Alignment(Phx::Alignment::Kind::
    AlignTo4Bytes);
```

Each symbol is *typed*, so the first action to do is to create a *type* for the function declaration symbol. Phoenix type system is covered in Section 10.7. The sample type above is self-evident.

Each symbol created in a symbol table refers back to its table.

In the above example, on creating a symbol for the function declaration, we also created a symbol for the global variable *a* declaration.

Symbol lookup. Let's continue our example by performing a lookup in our table of the symbol for the *gcd* function declaration:

```
// We can look up symbols either by name or by LocalId
Phx::Symbols::Symbol^ sym1 =
  moduleSymbolTable->NameMap->Lookup(gcdName);
Phx::Symbols::Symbol^ sym2 =
  moduleSymbolTable->LocalIdMap->Lookup(gcdSymbol
  ->LocalId);
Assert (sym1 == gcdSymbol);
Assert (sym2 == gcdSymbol);
```

Please note that we've used two ways to look up the symbol—via the *LocalId* and via the *name*.

Hierarchy of symbol tables. Symbol tables in Phoenix automatically form a hierarchy, based on static nesting of the modules in a program. There is yet another method, *ScopedLookup* (in addition to the "local" *Lookup* method considered above), that performs *scoped lookup* in traditional style used in many compilers, and is summarized in Chapter 5. If the symbol is not found on the local unit's symbol table, the search is continued in the parent (enclosing) unit's symbol table and so on.

Our point regarding Phoenix scoped lookup is as follows. We think it is quite suitable for Phoenix-based back-ends and other tools, and don't slow down their work, since back-ends typically use a lot of other algorithms of high complexity. But, as for lookup performed by Phoenix-based compiler front-ends, we do recommend our efficient methods of symbol table organization and symbol lookup presented in Chapter 5, rather than the Phoenix symbol lookup.

Here is a list of some more kinds of *basic symbols* in Phoenix:

- *GlobalVarSym, LocalVarSym, TypeSym, FuncSym,* and so on, are used to represent language-specific entities such as local variables, types, and functions;
- *PE Module Symbols* provide a way to describe the structure of .NET PE file at a somewhat higher abstract layer; for example, *ImportSym, ExportSym,* and *ImportModuleSym* are enabled to represent export/import lists for a module;
- *Metadata symbols,* for example, *AssemblySym* and *PermissionSym,* support the analysis of .NET *metadata*—language-agnostic information on the assembly (.NET's binary code), its security permissions, and the types defined and used in the assembly.

To summarize this section, the symbol table system in Phoenix is convenient, expressive, and flexible, and is suitable for compiler back-ends of a variety of programming languages with static-type identification (see Chapter 5).

10.7 PHOENIX TYPE SYSTEM

The Phoenix *type system* provides different kinds of types and a way of building rules for type-checking.

Semantic specification of Phoenix types is independent of the source language.

The Phoenix type system represents both high-level and machine-level types.

The role of the Phoenix type system is comparable to the role of .NET's Common Type System (CTS), in the sense that Phoenix type system is to be general and unified enough to represent types of different languages. Moreover, the Phoenix type system is to be even more general than .NET's CTS, since

Phoenix types should also cover *unmanaged* types, for example, the types of "unmanaged" Visual C++ of "pre-.NET" age. For the .NET (MSIL) target platform, Phoenix maps CTS types to Phoenix types.

Please compare the content of this section to our overview of programming language types and typing given in Chapter 5.

Here are some major kinds of Phoenix types whose names may look self-explanatory for the readers:

- *Phx.Types.PrimitiveType*—Phoenix primitive type. These are the following kinds of primitive types in Phoenix: *Boolean*, *character*, *integer*, *floating-point*, and *void*;

- *Phx.Types.PointerType*—pointer type representing managed pointers, native pointers, and references. The pointer type contains its *referent* type—the type of data to that the pointer refers. If the IR is not strongly typed (e.g., mid-level or lower-level IR), the referent type may be *unknown*, which covers traditional nontyped (unrestricted) pointers;

- *Phx.Types.AggregateType*—aggregate type, except arrays. Aggregate types have *members* (fields and methods). Examples of aggregate types are classes, interfaces, and structures (in .NET);

- *Phx.Type.EnumerationType*—enumeration type. Enumeration types in Phoenix are considered a kind of aggregate types (so this class is a subclass of *AggregateType*), since in modern languages and platforms (Java, .NET), enumerations (unlike Pascal-like old languages) are aggregates with their own operations implemented by methods, even if all the objects (values) of any enumeration types are statically known;

- *Phx.Types.TypeVariableType*—*type variable* type. In .NET and Java terms, *type variable* means *formal parameter type* in a *generic* class or interface;

- *Phx.Types.ManagedArrayType*—managed array type. In Phoenix, this class is a subclass of *AggregateType*. The characteristic features of managed array types is that the element type is strictly defined, and the runtime system should explicitly check that the array indexes and within the array bounds; otherwise, an exception is thrown;

- *Phx.Types.UnmanagedArrayType*—unmanaged (native) array types;

- *Phx.Types.FuncType*—function type. This contains the types of the function's arguments and results, and the calling convention for the function. See the example in the previous Section 10.6 for the use case of function type.

Type equality (in our terms, *type identity/equivalence*, cf. Chapter 5) in Phoenix is close to *name equivalence*; however, type name aliases themselves are not related to Phoenix type equivalence.

Two aggregate types are always considered different, which corresponds to the most secure treatment of types.

As for nonaggregate types, their equivalence is compared structurally, since it is important for the Phoenix optimizer and code generators to work with those types in terms of their sizes and alignments. So, for example, any primitive type with the *kind SignedInt* and the size of 32 bits is considered equal to any other primitive type with the same type kind and size.

The instantiations of *generic types* are compared structurally (see Chapter 5); for example, two types defined (at the language layer) as *Stack<int>* are considered equal in Phoenix.

Two *managed array* types in Phoenix are considered equal if they have equivalent element types, and the same number of dimensions.

Example. We already provided an example of defining a function type in the previous section. As another example of defining a nonprimitive Phoenix type, let's consider representation in Phoenix of a C structure type with two integer fields *re* and *im* (typically used for representing a complex number).

The code of the structure definition in C is as follows:

```
struct Complex
{
   int re;
   int im;
};
```

Here is a C# method code to define the same type in terms of Phoenix type system. The example can serve as a code pattern to create Phoenix structure types (since their creation is a nontrivial process):

```
public Phx.Types.AggregateType
CreateComplexStructType
(
   Phx.Lifetime lifetime, // the lifetime of the tables
        defined
   Phx.Types.Table typeTable, // the unit's type table
   Phx.Symbols.Table symbolTable // the unit's symbol
        table
)
{
   // Create the type Complex
   Phx.Symbols.TypeSymbol cTypeSymbol =
      Phx.Symbols.TypeSymbol.New(symbolTable, 0,
         Phx.Name.New(lifetime, "Complex"));
   Phx.Types.AggregateType cType =
      Phx.Types.AggregateType.New(typeTable, 64,
            cTypeSymbol);
   // Set meta-properties for the type Complex
   cType.IsOnlyData = true;
```

```
    cType.IsSealed = true;
    cType.HasCompleteInheritanceInfo = true;
    cType.HasCompleteOverrideInfo = true;
    // Create the re and im integer fields for the type
        Complex
    Phx.Symbols.FieldSymbol reFieldSymbol =
        Phx.Symbols.FieldSymbol.New(symbolTable, 0,
            Phx.Name.New(lifetime, "re"), typeTable.
Int32Type);
    Phx.Symbols.FieldSymbol imFieldSymbol =
        Phx.Symbols.FieldSymbol.New(symbolTable, 0,
            Phx.Name.New(lifetime, "im"), typeTable.
                Int32Type);
    // Evaluate the offsets of the fields (cf. Chapter 7)
    reFieldSymbol.BitOffset = 0;
    imFieldSymbol.BitOffset = (int)
        Phx.Alignment.NaturalAlignment(reFieldSymbol.Type).
            BitSize;
    // Append the fields to the struct type representation.
    Phx.Types.Field reField =
        cType.AppendFieldSymbol(reFieldSymbol);
    Phx.Types.Field imField =
        cType.AppendFieldSymbol(imFieldSymbol);
    // Now all the fields of the type are specified.
    cType.HasCompleteMemberInfo = true;
    return cType;
}
```

10.8 DATA FLOW ANALYSIS, CONTROL FLOW ANALYSIS, GRAPHS, AND STATIC SINGLE ASSIGNMENT (SSA) IN PHOENIX

Since Phoenix supports optimization, it has extensive support of data flow and control flow analysis. Phoenix allows the users to construct data flow and control flow graphs, and analyze them to obtain information for the optimizer.

The Phoenix *Phx.DataFlow* framework (namespace) contains the *Data* and the *Walker* abstract classes to support data flow analysis.

The *Data* class operates with data flow nodes represented as *basic blocks* (see Chapter 6). A basic block starts with a *label* instruction (i.e., has its own label), ends with a conditional or unconditional branch, or with the end of a function, and does not contain any "side entrances" inside the basic block, or any branch statements between its start and its end.

The *Walker* class performs the traversal of the basic blocks of a function. It can create new *Data* nodes and perform any user-defined analysis of basic blocks.

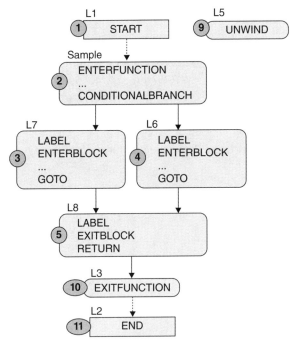

Figure 10.10. *The flow graph for the C function sample constructed by the c2 compiler in Phoenix.*

For example, consider a data flow graph of the following C++ function:

```
int sample(int x, int y)
{
    int s;
    x = x * y;
    y = x - y;
    if (x > y)
        s = x;
    else
        s = y;
    return s;
}
```

The flow graph for this example is depicted in Figure 10.10. Each node in the data flow graph represents basic blocks. So, in this very simple function, it appears to be eight basic blocks, labeled with *L1–L8* labels.

Built-in data flow analysis features in Phoenix enable to perform *live variable* analysis. A live variable is a variable that is assigned in one basic block of a function and is used later in the function. For example, for the "concluding" basic blocks *L2* and *L3* in the above example, the variable *s* is a live-out variable, since it is used to return the result of the function.

Phoenix allows the users to construct the following *graphs*:

- *flow graph* (already considered above)—determines the possible order of execution in terms of Phoenix IR; each flow graph is associated with some *function*, that is, with a *FunctionUnit*;
- *inheritance graph*—specifies the inheritance relationships between classes;
- *interference graph*—specifies the dependencies between variables and registers;
- *call graph*—specifies caller/callee relationships between methods or functions.

Phoenix also contains a package to support *SSA* discussed in Chapter 6. As an example, consider the following C code [3]:

```
#include <stdio.h>
int main(int argc, char ** argv)
{
    int a;
    int c = function();
    if (c < 33) {
        a = 11;
    } else {
        a = 22;
    }
    printf("%d\n", a);
}
```

The basic block layout of this program (in SSA format) is shown in Figure 10.11. As we remember from Chapter 6, according to the principles of SSA representation, each occurrence of the variable *a* is renamed if needed,

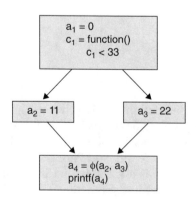

Figure 10.11. *The basic block layout for the sample C program in SSA format.*

to enable the property of *single assignment*: Each uniquely denoted variable should be assigned once only. The φ function represents the fact that the variable may have either of the two values assigned in different branches (basic blocks) of the program.

Here is the dump of the Phoenix IR generated for this example by the *c2* compiler:

```
$L1: (references=0)
   {*StaticTag}, {*NotAliasedTag}, {*UndefinedTag}<1> =
     START _main(T)
_main: (references=1)
   _argc<2>, _argv<3> = ENTERFUNCTION
                     ENTERBLOCK ScopeSymbol267
                     ENTERBLOCK ScopeSymbol269
                     ENTERBLOCK ScopeSymbol272
   t274, {*CallTag}  = CALL* &?function@@YAHXZ,
{*CallTag}, $L10(EH)
   _c<4>             = ASSIGN t274
                       ENTERBLOCK
   t275              = COMPARE(LT) _c<4>, 33(0x00000021)
                       CONDITIONALBRANCH(True) t275, $L7,
                       $L6
$L7: (references=1)
                       ENTERBLOCK
                       ENTERBLOCK
   _a<5>             = ASSIGN 11(0x0000000b)
                       EXITBLOCK
                       EXITBLOCK
                       GOTO $L8
$L6: (references=1)
                       ENTERBLOCK
                       ENTERBLOCK
   _a<6>             = ASSIGN 22(0x00000016)
                       EXITBLOCK
                       EXITBLOCK
                       GOTO $L8
$L8: (references=2)
   _a<7>             = PHI _a<6>, _a<5>
                       EXITBLOCK
   {*CallTag}        = CALL* &_printf, &$SG3677, _a<7>,
                       {*CallTag}, $L10(EH)
                       EXITBLOCK ScopeSymbol272
                       EXITBLOCK ScopeSymbol269
                       EXITBLOCK ScopeSymbol267
                       RETURN 0, $L11(T)
```

```
$L10:  (references=2)
                        GOTO {*StaticTag}, $L5
$L5:  (references=1)
                        UNWIND
$L11:  (references=1)
                        GOTO {*StaticTag}, $L3
$L3:  (references=1)
                        EXITFUNCTION
$L2:  (references=0)
                        END
```

The elements of SSA representation—different "incarnations" of the variable *a* with different indexes (represented in angular brackets) and the *Phi* function—are clearly seen in the IR code.

SSA can be used for a variety of optimizations, for example, constant propagation and copy propagation. Examples how to implement those optimizations using SSA are provided in Phoenix documentation [3].

10.9   OVERVIEW OF OTHER PHOENIX FEATURES

Phoenix is so multifunctional that it deserves a whole separate book to cover all its features. We only considered the most important of them, the supporting core features, and those related to the rest of our book content.

Here is an overview of the other features of Phoenix.

Alias analysis. Phoenix provides the *Alias* package to analyze the aliases of the variables and all kinds of overlaps for the variables. For example, a common way to create an alias to a variable is to create a pointer to it, or to its part. Higher-level optimizations can be based on alias analysis.

Safety. Phoenix provides a *safety package* to represent language features that cannot be explicitly represented in the Phoenix IR. For example, the safety package allows the users to represent C/C++ *volatile* variables. Also, the safety package provides an opportunity to formulate *constraints* on the pieces of IR, such as "forbid code motion and dead code elimination for this IR fragment." Such functionality allows us to solve the problems like buggy deletion of useful assignments to the uplevel variables (see Chapter 6).

Extension objects. Phoenix allows us to define *extension objects* that can be added to any program unit. This is helpful to store user- or language-specific information in Phoenix objects.

Phoenix support for static analysis. Static analysis is the analysis of a program without its execution. Here are typical kinds of static analysis performed by compilers or static code checkers, with the appropriate Phoenix features that can be used to implement those kinds of static analysis:

- *unused variables*—supported by Phoenix SSA;
- *unnecessary object creation*—supported by Phoenix SSA;
- *hidden members of types*—supported by Phoenix type system;
- *noninitialized variables*—supported by Phoenix SSA;
- *empty catch blocks* in try/catch statements—supported by Phoenix graphs;
- *security validation*—supported by Phoenix SSA;
- *memory leak detection*—supported by Phoenix SSA.

So, we can conclude that Phoenix is a good basis for developing *trustworthy compilers* and *code checkers* (see Chapter 5).

Exception handling. Phoenix supports in its IR a variety of exception handling mechanisms accepted in different languages and platforms, in particular, .NET-style *try/catch/finally* blocks. For each IR instruction, it is possible to indicate that it can throw exceptions and provide a reference to the corresponding exception handler. This greatly improves the trustworthiness of the code generated by Phoenix.

Simulation-based optimization. Phoenix provides a framework for analysis a function by *symbolic interpretation (simulation)* of the IR. The abstract interpreter of the IR is referred to as *lattice*. The users can derive their own lattices from that abstract framework. The built-in lattices enable *global conditional constant propagation*, *determination of the set of dead definitions*, *determination of the variables that contain null values*, and a number of other optimizations and trustworthiness checks.

10.10 EXAMPLE OF A PHOENIX-BASED PLUG-IN

As an example of a Phoenix-based plug-in, let's consider a plug-in [3] that sets the *Inlineability* property before code generation, to prevent inlining of functions. The plug-in adds an extra phase to the *c2* C++ compiler back-end before the code generation pass. The C# code of the plug-in is given below:

```csharp
using System;
using System.Collections.Generic;
using System.Text;
namespace InlineabilityTest
{
  public class MyPlugIn : Phx.PlugIn
  {
    public override void RegisterObjects() { }
    public override void BuildPasses
    ( Phx.Passes.PassConfiguration passConfiguration )
    {
      Phx.Passes.Pass pass =
```

```
         passConfiguration.PassList.FirstPass;
      Phx.Phases.PhaseConfiguration phaseConfiguration =
         pass.PhaseConfiguration;
      phaseConfiguration.PhaseList.FindByName
         ("CxxIL Reader").
            InsertAfter(UninlinePhase.
New(phaseConfiguration));
      } // BuildPasses
      public override string NameString
      {
         get {
            return "MyPlugIn";
         }
      } // NameString
   } // MyPlugIn
   public class UninlinePhase : Phx.Phases.Phase
   {
      public static UninlinePhase New
      ( Phx.Phases.PhaseConfiguration config )
      {
         UninlinePhase phase = new UninlinePhase();
         phase.Initialize(config, "Uninline");
         return phase;
      }
      protected override void Execute ( Phx.Unit unit )
      {
         Phx.FunctionUnit func = unit as Phx.
FunctionUnit;
         if (func == null) {
            return;
         }
         func.FunctionSymbol.Inlineability =
            Phx.Inline.Inlineability.Never;
      }
   }
}
```

The architecture of the plug-in is as follows. The plug-in is defined as a subclass of the class *Phs.PlugIn*. Three methods are overridden in the *MyPlugIn* class:

- *RegisterObjects* (with empty implementation, since the plug-in is stateless, and all information is passed to its method as arguments);
- *BuildPasses* (which finds the phase of CIL reading and inserts after that phase our new phase *UninlinePhase*);

- *NameString*—a read-only property whose value is the name of our plug-in—"*MyPlugIn.*"

The new phase is defined as a subclass of *Phx.Phase*. The most important method overridden in the phase class is the *Execute* method that processes each function of the source program, and sets its *Inlineability* property to *Never* (to switch off inlining of this function).

While the architecture of this plug-in is relatively simple, we (following the authors of Phoenix) highly recommend the readers to use the existing Phoenix samples as code patterns for creating your own Phoenix plug-ins and tools. In this way, the risk to forget anything is minimized.

To conclude our Phoenix overview in this chapter, we emphasize again the importance of the *samples* and *walkthroughs* shipped with Phoenix. The full list of samples is provided in Phoenix documentation. Studying the samples and the walkthroughs, and using samples as the starting point for your own Phoenix projects is the best way to learn Phoenix deeply. Otherwise, the complexity of the Phoenix API and a variety of its features may prevent the readers from learning Phoenix "from scratch" using its documentation only.

Among the Phoenix samples, there are two sample compilers—*Pascal* and *LISP* (the name of the latter sample is *Lispkit*). One of the simplest examples in Phoenix sample set is *addnop_tool*, a Phoenix tool that reads in a .NET assembly (whose name is passed as argument) and inserts a *nop* instruction after each MSIL instruction found.

We wish interesting and productive work with Phoenix to the readers interested in state-of-the-art compiler development tools.

Based on the interest to Phoenix within the academic community, the success of the Phoenix Academic Program, and the progress of our own Phoenix projects, we do believe that Phoenix is very prospective and will be soon shipped together with one of the newer versions of Microsoft Visual Studio, and the *c2* C++ compiler back-end shipped with Phoenix will be taken as the product's back-end of the Visual C++ compiler, part of the Visual Studio.

10.11 PHOENIX-FETE—A COMPILER FRONT-END DEVELOPMENT TOOLKIT AND ENVIRONMENT TARGETED TO PHOENIX

The goal of our project Phoenix-FETE (*Phoenix compiler Front-End development Toolkit and Environment*) [60] is twofold. On the one hand, we intend to fill the gap of lacking such a toolkit targeted to Phoenix and provide the users with such necessary addition to Phoenix as a front-end development tool. On the other hand, we would like to share our compiler development experience (in particular, our original parsing techniques) with the Phoenix users. The author of the implementation of Phoenix-FETE and of many important ideas of its design is our PhD student Daniel Vassilyev.

This project was supported by Microsoft Research in 2006, as part of the "SPBU for Phoenix (SPBU4PHX)" granted project.

The purpose of the Phoenix-FETE project is to develop a Phoenix-oriented compiler front-end tool and environment based on syntax-directed translation schemes, similar to *yacc*, *bison*, and other compiler generation tools, but intended to use with Phoenix. It should take as input an attributed LL or operator precedence grammar of a programming language and generate a compiler front-end for this language that issues either Phoenix HIR, or our HL-AST [109] (the latter plan will work when the HL-AST project is completed). The purpose of the tool is to make easier compiler front-end development for Phoenix.

Here are the features to be implemented in Phoenix-FETE (the project is still in progress, and some of the features below are already implemented in the prototype):

- the ability to process either LL or operator precedence grammars and to generate a purely recursive descent, or *combined* recursive descent parser (for statements) and operator precedence parser (for expressions), since in real compilers, including our experience [2], such combined forms of parsers are often used for efficiency reasons;

- the ability to define and process LL or operator precedence conflicts, similar to other modern compiler development tools—ANother Tool for Language Recognition (ANTLR) [22] and Coco/R [23];

- support of our efficient parsing and semantic evaluation techniques covered in Chapter 5 (storing synthesized attributes in the HL-AST attributed syntax tree during LR parsing, lookup of identifiers using current effective definition [CED] pointers, etc.);

- support of visualization and control over the process of generation of a Phoenix-FETE-based compiler front-end and over the process of work of the generated front-end;

- adequate support of generation of both HL-AST (whose architecture should be developed as another part of our project) and direct Phoenix HIR generation by a Phoenix-FETE-generated compiler front-end;

- implementing add-in for Phoenix-FETE to work as part of the Visual Studio.NET.

10.11.1 Architectural Specifics of Phoenix-FETE

Several parsing techniques are used in Phoenix-FETE:

- *Recursive descent* (see Chapter 4) is the basic parsing method. It was chosen due to its simplicity and readability of the generated parser's code (unlike LR parsers generated by *yacc* and similar tools).

- *Operator precedence* [26] is an alternative, more efficient bottom-up parsing method for expressions based on *precedence relations* against the grammar symbols. Using this technique for parsing expressions, while the rest of the syntax is parsed by recursive descent, allows us to make the parsing more efficient, as compared with purely recursive descent analysis of the whole program. We developed and used such mixed-strategy parsers in our compilers for the "Elbrus" system [2] and practically proved its efficiency, as compared with pure recursive descent parsing.

In the input grammar definition language of our tool, the constructs to be parsed by a method different from the basic one are marked by a special keyword in the input grammar. In further versions, automatic selection of parsing techniques will be implemented.

Another important point is the error recovery mechanisms to be used, as follows:

- "intelligent" panic mode (see Chapter 4)—a modification of basic error recovery strategy common for recursive descent. In the smart panic mode, the set of synchronizing tokens is changed according to the current context of parsing. In particular, nested constructs (like *if … then … else* and left/right bracketed expressions) are all taken into account in error recovery.
- Weak token-based error recovery. Weak tokens are those often missed or misspelled. Example: semicolon after a statement. The parser inserts such token as a recovery action. A similar technique is implemented in CoCo/R [23].

In the current version, *panic mode* error recovery is implemented. When generating the parser code, Phoenix-FETE constructs the set of synchronizing tokens for each input grammar rule. In case a severe syntax error occurs, the generated parser skips the input text until a token that belongs to the synchronizing set. Then, parsing continues as usual.

10.11.2 The Input Grammar Meta-Language

The input grammar definition language in Phoenix-FETE is a superset of the grammar definition meta-language of the most popular parser generator ANTLR [22]. This decision was made intentionally, to keep compatibility with a widely spread tool, and to be able to use ANTLR input grammars for generating Phoenix-based compilers.

Each rule consists of Extended Backus–Naur Forms (EBNF) syntax definition and a set of related semantic actions. In common compiler terms, it is a kind of *syntax-directed translation schemes*.

The meta-symbols and constructs of our meta-language are explained in Table 10.1.

**TABLE 10.1. The Constructs of the Grammar Definition
Meta-Language of Phoenix-FETE**

Symbol	Description
(...)	*Subrule*
(...)*	*0 or more times*
(...)+	*One or more times*
(...)?	*0 or 1 time*
{...}	*Semantic action*
[...]	*The arguments of the rule*
|	*The «or» (alternative) operator*
..	*The «subrange» operator*
~	*The «not» operator*
.	*Wildcard*
=	*The «assignment» operator*
:	*The label and rule start operator*
;	*The rule end operator*
<...>	*Choice (alternatives)*
class	*A class of the grammar*
extends	*Inheritance of another class of the grammar*
returns	*The type returned by the rule*
options	*The options section*
header	*The header section*
tokens	*The tokens definition section*

The input file with the grammar definition consists of the following sections:

- **header**—defines the code to be added to the header of each generated compilation unit source code (the list of namespaces used, the list of header files, comments, etc.);
- **options**—defines the tool options;
- **tokens**—defines the tokens and the string literals that can be assigned a corresponding label;
- the rest of the grammar—its mandatory main part.

As a working example, let's consider the following grammar (the specification of the parser and the lexical analyzer) for arithmetic expressions in Phoenix-FETE meta-language:

```
class ExpressionParser extends Parser;
atom     : INT ;
powExpr  : atom (POW atom)? ;
prodExpr : powExpr ((MUL|DIV|MOD) powExpr)* ;
sumExpr  : prodExpr ((PLUS|MINUS) prodExpr)* ;
```

```
expr    : sumExpr SEMI ;
class ExpressionLexer extends Lexer;
PLUS  : '+' ;
MINUS : '-' ;
MUL   : '*' ;
DIV   : '/' ;
MOD   : '%' ;
POW   : '^' ;
SEMI  : ';' ;
LRAREN: '(' ;
RPAREN: ')' ;
protected DIGIT : '0'..'9' ;
INT   : (DIGIT)+ ;
```

The first line defines the name of the parser class and indicates its inheritance from the predefined *Parser* class. Then the syntax rules are defined. The left-hand part of each of them contains a nonterminal symbol, the right-hand part—list of the alternatives and iterations that constitute the syntax of the corresponding construct.

10.11.3 The Current Status of the Implementation

Currently, a fully functioning prototype of Phoenix-FETE is developed. The following features are implemented:

- rich subset of the grammar definition meta-language;
- generation of C# code of the parser based on the input grammar;
- generation of C# кода of the lexical analyzer based on the input grammar;
- use of recursive descent in the currently generated version of the parser;
- use of panic mode (see Chapter 4) is used as the syntax error recovery mechanism;
- high-level API for generating Phoenix IR. It is much more convenient than the direct use of the Phoenix API for IR generation. The calls of our high-level Phoenix IR generation API can be used in the semantic actions of the input grammar.

Besides that, a tree-like IR of the input grammar is implemented. The IR tree is unified both for representing the parser grammar and for representing the lexical analyzer grammar. The tree is constructed in the process of parsing the input grammar definition. On the completion of constructing the intermediate tree, Phoenix-FETE starts generating the output C# code of the lexer and the parser.

Phoenix-FETE is integrated with Microsoft Visual Studio 2005, so it can be used as part of the Visual Studio integrated development environment. A special *add-in* module is developed for the purpose of integration. So, there are two ways of using Phoenix-FETE: in command-line mode or within the Visual Studio.

We have already provided above a working example of the Phoenix-FETE input grammar for arithmetic expressions (see Section 10.11.2).

On processing the above input file, Phoenix-FETE will generate two output files, *ExpressionParser.cs* and *ExpressionLexer.cs*, to implement the C# classes for the parser and the lexical analyzer.

The next step is to obtain a full compiler of the input language for some platform. A straightforward approach could be to update the source code of the parser and lexer classes manually. But the second, more comfortable approach is to insert the API calls to generate Phoenix IR as the semantic actions of the input grammar rules, using our high-level Phoenix IR generation API. In the latter case, the updated input grammar file will be as follows:

```
class ExpressionParser extends Parser;
atom     : {Token lexem = LA();} INT
{
     AppendImmediateInt32Operand(lexem);
};
powExpr  : atom {Phx.IR.Operand op1 = lastOpnd;} (POW
           atom
{
     Phx.IR.Operand op2 = lastOpnd;
     Phx.IR.VariableOperand varOpnd =
          NewInt32VariableOperand();
     MakeLastInstruction(NewInstruction
          (Phx.Common.Opcode.Pow, varOpnd, op1, op2));
     lastOpnd = varOpnd;
}
)? ;
prodExpr : powExpr
{
     Phx.IR.Operand op1 = lastOpnd;
     Token a = LA();
     Phx.Common.Opcode opcode =
          ((a.TType==MUL)?(Phx.Common.Opcode.
                         Multiply):
          ((a.TType==DIV)?(Phx.Common.Opcode.Divide):
          ((a.TType==MOD)?(Phx.Common.Opcode.
                         DivideWithRemainder):
     Phx.Common.Opcode.Add))));
}
((MUL|DIV|MOD) powExpr
{
```

```
        Phx.IR.Operand op2 = lastOpnd;
        Phx.IR.VariableOperand varOpnd =
        Phx.IR.VariableOperand.NewTemporary
                (mainFunc.AsFunctionUnit, typeTable.
                 Int32Type);
        MakeLastInstruction(NewInstruction(opcode,
                             varOpnd, op1, op2));
lastOpnd = varOpnd;
}
)* ;
sumExpr  : prodExpr
{
        Phx.IR.Operand op1 = lastOpnd;
        Token a = LA();
        Phx.Common.Opcode opcode =
                ((a.TType==PLUS)?(Phx.Common.Opcode.Add):
                ((a.TType==MINUS)?(Phx.Common.Opcode.
                                   Subtract):
        Phx.Common.Opcode.Add));
}
((PLUS|MINUS) prodExpr
{
        Phx.IR.Operand op2 = lastOpnd;
        Phx.IR.VariableOperand varOpnd =
                NewInt32VariableOperand();
        MakeLastInstruction(NewInstruction
        (opcode, varOpnd, op1, op2));
        lastOpnd = varOpnd;
}
)*;
expr    : sumExpr
{
        Phx.IR.VariableOperand varOpnd =
                NewInt32VariableOperand();
        MakeLastInstruction
                (NewInstruction(Phx.Common.Opcode.Assign,
                 varOpnd,
lastOpnd));
}
SEMI;
class ExpressionLexer extends Lexer;
PLUS  : '+' ;
MINUS : '-' ;
MUL   : '*' ;
DIV   : '/' ;
```

```
MOD    : '%' ;
POW    : '^' ;
SEMI   : ';' ;
LRAREN : '(' ;
RPAREN : ')' ;
protected DIGIT : '0'..'9' ;
INT    : (DIGIT)+ ;
```

Using this input grammar, Phoenix-FETE will generate C# code for a full-fledged compiler of the language of arithmetic expressions—an executable file. Phoenix is used for generating Phoenix IR, and then, to generate the .exe file from the IR. The compiler can take as input a correct arithmetic expression and generate the corresponding executable binary code.

The current results on the Phoenix-FETE project, though it is not yet completed, practically confirm the consistency of the taken approach to implementing the system. Even the first developed prototype demonstrates that developing of a compiler prototype is simple enough with Phoenix-FETE.

We hope that the use of a superset of ANTLR meta-language as input, as well as the high-level API for generating Phoenix IR, will attract the attention of compiler developers.

Further plans on the project are as follows:

- extension of the meta-language of the input grammar definition;
- extension of the high-level API for Phoenix IR generation;
- publication of Phoenix-FETE distribution on the Microsoft academic Web site;
- development of a visualizer of the grammar;
- development of a visual debugger;
- development of the wizard for input grammar definitions.

So, to summarize this section, currently, Phoenix-FETE is a prospective project targeted to simplify the process of compiler development using Phoenix. We hope it will attract more attention from Microsoft.

EXERCISES TO CHAPTER 10

10.1 Download the latest Phoenix SDK from the Web site [3], install it, and run the samples.

10.2 What, in your opinion, are the specifics of Phoenix, as compared with the other compiler development toolkits you know and have ever used?

10.3 What are the major features of Phoenix?

10.4 What is the difference between names and symbols in Phoenix?

10.5   Summarize the kinds of types in Phoenix type system and explain for what kind of programming language types they are introduced. In your opinion, what kind of types in your favorite programming languages will be problematic to map to Phoenix type system?

10.6   What kind of graphs and other program analysis structures does Phoenix construct, and for what kind of optimizations can they be used?

10.7   Write and run a simple Phoenix plug-in using the Phoenix samples and our sample in this chapter: The plug-in should dump the IR before the code generation. Use the "Phoenix projects" type of project in Visual Studio 2008. Develop the plug-in in two variants: in C# (in managed mode) and in C++ (in unmanaged mode).

10.8   Develop a front-end of a compiler from your favorite programming language (or its subset) targeted to Phoenix that generates Phoenix HIR as its output.

Conclusions

In our book, we have considered many traditional, as well as novel, approaches to trustworthy compiler development and to compiler development tools.

We have covered all known kinds of compilers, including traditional (native) compilers, just-in-time (JIT) compilers, and graph compilers. We hope the readers will appreciate these and the novelty of our book as a whole.

We have considered in detail all phases of compilation and the related methods, both classical and our original methods, more efficient than those described in classical compiler textbooks.

Our main goal in this book is for the readers to get a clear understanding of what a trustworthy compiler is, how to make a compiler trustworthy, and what kind of tools can be used to make the process of compiler development easier and more trustworthy.

We have not considered *all* topics related to compilers—it would require a series of books, since the history of compiler development originated more than 50 years ago. In particular, we didn't cover interesting topics such as *interpreters*—we do have interesting methods and results in this area [2]. Also, the methods of optimization we summarized in Chapter 6 deserve a series of monographs. We didn't consider specific code generation and optimization techniques for highly parallel target hardware platforms, such as Very Long Instruction Word (VLIW), Explicit Parallelism Instruction Computer (EPIC), multi-core, and so on. This is for our further publications and for other compiler authors to consider, since all of those topics are also very interesting and important for studying compiler development.

In case we just summarized some topics, like graph compilers, we provided a variety of references for further reading.

At the end of each chapter, the readers can find a number of *exercises*. Some of them are simple and require just attentive reading of the chapter. Others are more difficult, but we hope interesting to do. The set of exercises and other supplementary materials for the book will grow and will be uploaded to our book companion Web pages: http://www.vladimirsafonov. org/trustworthycompilers.

We are eager to receive feedback from the readers. Please contact us by e-mail at vosafonov@gmail.com.

We do believe that the area of trustworthy compilers is very prospective, and there are a lot of things for the readers to design, develop, and implement. Perspectives of trustworthy compilers are outlined at the end of Chapter 2.

As we have seen in this book, many vitally important problems, such as how to make a compiler *verified* and *verifying*, how to have the compiler provide recommendations to the users and code patterns of trustworthy programming, and many other problems of trustworthy compilers, are being investigated. For more than 50 years, after the invention of the first programming language, we have been learning and investigating how to make our programs and our compilers really trustworthy, rather than only "efficient."

Of special importance are novel areas such as graph compilers and JIT compilers. Graph compilers are very helpful in making the use of computers wider, due to visual programming languages they support. JIT compilers help in making the platform-independent code (Microsoft.NET Intermediate Language [MSIL], Java bytecode, etc.) generated by compilers of modern software development platform faster. All these areas, as well as the traditional compilers area, are waiting for your novel ideas, your efficient compilation methods, and your novel compiler development tools, which will make compilers yet more and more trustworthy.

We hope that our modest contribution to the compiler development area described in this book—efficient methods of lexical analysis, parsing, semantic analysis, and typing; implementing trustworthiness checks of the customer's source programs; optimizing JIT compilers development and compiler development tools for Phoenix—will attract the interest of the readers and will be helpful to them.

Also, we hope that this book, together with our trustworthy compilers course [4], will be used as curriculum for university study of trustworthy compiler development worldwide.

Thanks a lot for your attention, and good luck in learning and developing trustworthy compilers.

References

1. Safonov VO. Using aspect-oriented programming for trustworthy software development. Hoboken, NJ: Wiley; 2008.

2. Safonov VO. Programming languages and techniques for the "Elbrus" system. Moscow: Science; 1989 (in Russian).

3. Microsoft Phoenix. Available at http://connect.microsoft.com/phoenix. Accessed June 9, 2009.

4. Safonov VO. Trustworthy compilers. Graduate university course curriculum. Available at http://www.facultyresourcecenter.com/curriculum/pfv.aspx?ID=7698. Accessed June 9, 2009.

5. Aho AV, Lam MS, Sethi R, Ullman JD. Compilers: Principles, techniques, and tools. 2nd ed. Reading, MA: Addison-Wesley; 2007.

6. Leroy X. Formal verification of a realistic compiler. Communications of the ACM 2009;51(7):107–115.

7. Hoare CAR. Verifying compiler: A grand challenge for computing research. Journal of the ACM 2003;50(1):63–69.

8. Mac R. Writing compilers and interpreters. 2nd ed. Hoboken, NJ: Wiley; 1996.

9. Katzan H. Batch, conversational, and incremental compilers. AFIPS Joint Computer Conference, Boston. New York: ACM. May 14–16, 1969.

10. Knowledge.NET Web site. Available at http://www.knowledge-net.ru/en/index.htm. Accessed June 9, 2009.

11. Barnett K, Leino RM, Schulte W. The Spec# programming system: An overview. Workshop on construction and analysis of safe, secure, and interoperable smart

devices, Marseille, France, March 10–14, 2004. Lecture Notes in Computer Science, 3362, New York: Springer; 2004.

12. Meyer B. Object-oriented software construction. 2nd ed. Upper Saddle River, NJ: Prentice Hall; 1997.

13. Muchnick S. Advanced compiler design and implementation. San Francisco, CA: Morgan Kaufmann; 1997.

14. Sun Studio compilers Web site. Available at http://developers.sun.com/sunstudio/. Accessed June 9, 2009.

15. Myers G. Software reliability: Principles and practices. New York: Wiley; 1976.

16. Knuth D. Semantics of context-free languages. Mathematical Systems Theory 1967;2(2):127–145.

17. Lecarme O, Bochmann G. A (truly) usable and portable compiler writing system. In: Rosenfeld JL, editor. Information Processing '74, Amsterdam, August 1974. Amsterdam: North-Holland; 1974:218–221.

18. Bezdushny AN, Luty VG, Serebriakov VA. Compiler development in the SUPER system. Moscow: Computing Centre of the Academy of Sciences of the USSR; 1991 (in Russian).

19. Johnson S. YACC: Yet Another Compiler Compiler. Computing Science Technical Report 32, Murray Hill, NJ: AT&T Bell Laboratories; 1975.

20. Bison Web site. Available at http://www.gnu.org/software/bison/JavaCC. Accessed June 9, 2009.

21. JavaCC Web site. Available at https://javacc.dev.java.net/. Accessed June 9, 2009.

22. Parr T, Quong R. ANTLR: A predicated-LL(k) parser generator. Journal of Software Practice and Experience 1995;25(7):789–810.

23. Wöß A, Löberbauer M, Mössenböck H. LL(1) conflict resolution in a recursive descent compiler generator. Joint Modular Languages Conference (JMLC'03), Klagenfurt, 2003. Lecture Notes in Computer Science, 2789, New York: Springer; 2003.

24. SableCC Web site. Available at http://sablecc.org/. Accessed June 9, 2009.

25. Safonov VO, inventor; Sun Microsystems, Inc., assignee. TIP technology and its application to SPARCompiler Pascal. US patent 6,305,011. October 16, 2001.

26. Gries D. Compiler construction for digital computers. New York: Wiley; 1971.

27. Popov VP, Stepanov VA, Stisheva AG, Travnikova NA. A programming program. Journal of Computing Mathematics and Mathematical Physics 1964;4(1):78–95 (in Russian).

28. Ershov AP, editor. ALPHA—A system of programming automation. Novosibirsk: Computing Centre of the Siberian Branch of the USSR Academy of Sciences; 1965 (in Russian).

29. Ershov AP. The BETA system—A comparison of the requirement specification to the prototype implementation. Proceedings of the USSR symposium on methods of implementation of new algorithmic languages, Novosibirsk, 1975. Novosibirsk: Computing Centre of the Siberian Branch of the USSR Academy of Sciences; 1975 (in Russian).

30. Tseytin G, editor. ALGOL 68: Methods of implementation. Leningrad: Leningrad University Publishers; 1976 (in Russian).

31. Turchin VF. REFAL-5 programming guide and reference manual. The City College of New York, Holyoke: New England Publishing Co.; 1989.

32. Lavrov SS, Kapustina EN, Selyun MI. The extensible algorithmic language ABC. Symbolic Information Processing 1976;3(1):5–53 (in Russian).

33. Pentkovsky VM. The programming language EL-76. Moscow: Science; 1989.

34. Trustworthy computing initiative Web site. Available at http://www.microsoft.com/mscorp/twc/default.mspx. Accessed June 9, 2009.

35. Shaw M. APLHARD: Form and content. New York: Springer; 1981.

36. The VCC verifying compiler Web site. Available at http://research.microsoft.com/en-us/projects/vcc/. Accessed June 9, 2009.

37. Bradley AR, Manna Z. The calculus of computation: Decision procedures with applications. New York: Springer; 2007.

38. Verifying compilers Web site. Available at http://www.verifyingcompiler.com. Accessed June 9, 2009.

39. Hoare CAR. An axiomatic basis for computer programming. Communications of the ACM 1969;12(10):576–580, 583.

40. Plotkin GD. The origins of structural operational semantics. The Journal of Logic and Algebraic Programming 2004;60–61:3–15.

41. Scott D, Strachey C. Toward a mathematical semantics for computer languages. Oxford Programming Research Group Technical Monograph. PRG-6; 1971.

42. Goguen JA, Thatcher JW, Wagner EG, Wright JB. Initial algebra semantics and continuous algebras. Journal of the ACM 1977;27(1):68–95.

43. Gurevich Y, Kutter PW, Odersky M, Thiele L, editors. Abstract state machines. Theory and applications. International Workshop, ASM 2000, Monte Verita, Switzerland, March 2000. Proceedings. Lecture Notes in Computer Science, 1912, New York: Springer; 2000.

44. Milner R, Torte M, Harper R. The definition of standard ML. 2nd ed. Cambridge, MA: MIT Press; 1997.

45. The Caml language Web site. Available at http://caml.inria.fr/. Accessed June 9, 2009.

46. The objective Caml language Web site. Available at http://caml.inria.fr/ocaml/index.en.html. Accessed June 9, 2009.

47. The F# language Web site. Available at http://msdn.microsoft.com/en-us/fsharp/default.aspx. Accessed June 9, 2009.

48. van Wijngaarden A, Mailloux BJ, Peck JEL, Koster CHA, Sintzoff M, Lindsey CH, Meertens LGT, and Fisker RG, editors. Revised report on the algorithmic language ALGOL 68. New York: Springer; 1973.

49. Aho AV, Ullman J. The theory of parsing, translation, and compiling. Englewood Cliffs, NJ: Prentice Hall; 1972.

50. Van den Brand MGJ, Klusener S, Moonen L, Vinju JJ. Generalized parsing and term rewriting: Semantic driven disambiguation. Electronic Notes in Theoretical Computer Science 2003;82(3):575–591.

51. Wirth N. Compiler construction. Indianapolis, IN: Addison-Wesley; 1996.

52. Ziegler C. Programming system methodologies. Upper Saddle River, NJ: Prentice Hall; 1982.

53. Knuth DE. On the translation of languages from left to right. Information and Control 1965;8:607–639.

54. Johnson SC. A portable compiler: Theory and practice. Proceedings of the 5th ACM SIGACT-SIGPLAN symposium on principles of programming languages, Tucson, AZ, 1978.

55. Tomita M, editor. Generalized LR parsing. Boston: Kluwer Academic Publishers; 1991.

56. Tomita M. Efficient parsing for natural languages. A fast algorithm for practical systems. Boston: Kluwer Academic Publishers; 1985.

57. Fernandes J. Generalized LR parsing in Haskell. Available at http://wiki.di. uminho.pt/twiki/pub/Personal/Joao/-TwikiJoaoPublications/technicalReport.pdf. Accessed June 9, 2009.

58. YACC++ and the Language Objects Library. Available at http://world.std. com/~compres/. Accessed June 9, 2009.

59. Parr TJ. Language translation using PCCTS and C++. San Jose, CA: Automata Publishing Company; 1997.

60. Safonov VO, Vassilyev DA. Phoenix front-end toolkit and environment. Microsoft Research Phoenix Academic Program. Phoenix booklet. Available at http:// research.microsoft.com/en-us/collaboration/focus/cs/phoenix_booklet_0625_ ebook.pdf. Accessed June 9, 2009.

61. Safonov VO, inventor; Sun Microsystems, Inc., assignee. Method and apparatus for compiler symbol table organization with no lookup in semantic analysis. US patent 5,701,490. December 23, 1997.

62. Safonov VO, inventor; Sun Microsystems, Inc., assignee. Method and apparatus for efficient evaluation of semantic attributes in LALR parsing. US patent 5,892,951. April 6, 1999.

63. Safonov VO, inventor; Sun Microsystems, Inc., assignee. Method and apparatus for record fields usage checking at compile time. US patent 5,758,163. May 26, 1998.

64. Knuth D. Semantics of context-free languages. Theory of Computing Systems 1968;2(2):127–145.

65. Biryukov AN, Kurochkin VM, Serebriakov VA. Global attributes and their use in programming languages definitions. Journal of Computing Mathematics and Mathematical Physics 1980;20(5):1284–1293 (in Russian).

66. Bochmann GV. Semantic evaluation from left to right. Communications of the ACM 1976;19(2):55–62.

67. Hoare CAR. Proof of correctness of data representations. Acta Informatica 1972;1:271–281.

68. Dynamic Language Runtime (DLR) Web site. Available at http://www.codeplex. com/dlr. Accessed June 9, 2009.

69. Johnson S. Lint, a C program checker. Computer Science Technical Report 65, Bell Laboratories, December 1977.

70. Muchnick S. Optimizing compilers for SPARC architecture. Sun Technology Papers; 1989.

71. Wirth N. Algorithms + data structures = programs. Englewood Cliffs, NJ: Prentice Hall; 1976.

72. FORTH language Web site. Available at http://www.forth.org. Accessed June 9, 2009.

73. Ershov AP. On the essence of translation. Programmirovanie 1977;1(6):10–20 (in Russian).

74. Cooper KD, Torczon L. Engineering a compiler. San Francisco, CA: Morgan Kaufmann; 2005.

75. Kennedy K, Allen R. Optimizing compilers for modern architectures: A dependence-based approach. San Francisco, CA: Morgan Kaufmann; 2001.

76. Cierniak M, Li W. Optimizing Java bytecodes. Concurrency: Practice and Experience 1997;9(6):427–444.

77. Lunev S. Programmatic methods of performance increase for picoJava-II architecture. Candidate of Sciences dissertation, Moscow, Moscow State University, 2002 (in Russian).

78. Suganuma T, Yasue T, Kawahito M, Komatsu H, Nakatani T. A dynamic optimization framework for a Java just-in-time compiler. ACM Conference on Object-Oriented Programming Systems, Languages, and Applications (OOPSLA), October 2001.

79. Suganuma T, et al. Evolution of a java just-in-time compiler for IA-32 platforms. IBM Journal of Research and Development 2004;48(5/6):767–795.

80. Dwyer MB. Compiler bytecode optimization. Available at http://projects.cis.ksu. edu/.../scmsvn/?action=browse&path=%2F*checkout*%2Fcompiler%2Fslides %2FADVANCED-bytecode. Accessed June 22, 2009.

81. Alpern B, et al. The Jalapeno Virtual Machine. IBM Systems Journal 2000;39(1): 211–238.

82. VisualWorks Tutorial. ParcPlace Systems, Inc. Part Number DS20002002. Revision 2.0, October 1994 (Software Release 2.0).

83. Grove D, Hind M. The Design and Implementation of the Jikes RVM Optimizing Compiler. OOPSLA '02 Tutorial, November 5, 2002.

84. Gough J. Compiling for the .NET common language runtime. Englewood Cliffs, NJ: Prentice Hall; 2001.

85. SPARC Architecture Manual. Version 9. Available at http://developers.sun.com/ solaris/articles/sparcv9.html. Accessed July 21, 2009.

86. Patterson DA, Ditzel DR. The case for the reduced instruction set computing. SIGARCH Computer Architecture News 1980;8(6):25–33.

87. STABS. Available at http://sourceware.org/gdb/current/onlinedocs/stabs.html. Accessed July 21, 2009.

88. Stutz D, Neward T, Shilling G. Shared source CLI essentials. Sebastopol, CA: O'Reilly; 2003.

89. Chilingarova S, Safonov VO. Sampling profiler for rotor as part of optimizing compilation system .NET technologies 2006. Pilzen, Czech Republic, 2006. Short papers conference proceedings. Pilzen: West Bohemia University; 2006:43–50.

90. Anderson T, Eng M, Glew N, Lewis B, Menon V, Stichnoth J. Experience integrating a new compiler and a new garbage collector into rotor. Journal of Object Technology 2004;3(9):53–70.

91. Vaswani K, Srikant YN. Dynamic Recompilation and Profile-Guided Optimizations for a .NET JIT Compiler. IEEE Software 2004.

92. Arnold M. Online profiling and feedback-directed optimization of Java. PhD thesis, Rutgers University, October 2002.

93. Schneider H. Graph transformations. An introduction to the categorical approach. University of Erlangen—Nürnberg, 2008.

94. Zhang DQ, Zhang K. Reserved graph grammar: A specification tool for diagrammatic visual programming languages. *Proceedings of the 1997 IEEE Symposium on Visual Languages.* Washington, DC: IEEE Computer Society; 1997:284–291.

95. Rekers J, Shurr A. Defining and parsing visual languages with layered graph grammars. Technical Report 96-09, Leiden University, 1996.

96. Minas M. Syntax definition with graphs. Electronic Notes in Theoretical Computer Science 2006;148(1):19–40.

97. Kühne T, Girschick M, Klar F. Tool support for architecture stratification. In: Mayr RC, Brew R, editors. Proceedings of the Modellierung 2006. LNI(82), Innsbruck, Tirol, Austria: Küllen Druck Verlag GmbH; 2006:213–222.

98. Clark T, Sammut P, Willans J. Applied metamodeling—A foundation for language driven development. Ceteva; 2008. Available at http://itcentre.tru.ac.uk/~clark/docs/Applied%20Metamodelling%20%28Second%20Edition%29.pdf. Accessed November 30, 2009.

99. Minas M. Generating meta-model-based freehand editors. Proceedings of the Third International Workshop on Graph-Based Tools; 2006.

100. Drewes F, Kreowski H-J, Habel A. Hyperedge replacement graph grammars. In: Rosenberg G, editor. *Handbook of Graph Grammars and Computing by Graph Transformation.* River Edge, NJ: World Scientific Publishing Co, Inc.; 1997:95–162.

101. D'Antonio F. Introduction to graph grammars. LEKS, IASI-CNR, Rome, October 14, 2003. Available at http://www.dsi.uniroma1.it/~estrinfo/sws/2003_10_14/Introduction%20to%20Graph%20Grammars%20-%20DAntonio.ppt. Accessed July 15, 2009.

102. Zhang K, Song GL, Kong J. Rapid software prototyping using visual language techniques. RSP'04, Geneva, Switzerland, June 29, 2004. Available at http://www2.computer.org/portal/web/csdl/doi/10.1109/IWRSP.2004.1311106 Accessed July 8, 2009.

103. Maneth S, Vogler H. Attributed context-free hypergraph grammars. Technical University Dresden Technical Report TUD/FI 97/12, October 1997.

104. Tveit MS. Specification of graphical representations—Using hypergraphs or meta-models? Proceedings of the NIK-2008 Conference, Oslo, Norway. Available at http://www.nik.no. Accessed July 9, 2009.

105. Object Management Group (OMG). OMG's MetaObjectFacility, 2006. Available at http://www.omg.org/mof. Accessed July 9, 2009.

106. Richters M. A precise approach to validating UML models and OCL constraints. PhD thesis, Universität Bremen, Logos Verlag, Berlin, BISS monographs, No. 14, 2002.

107. GenGED Web site. Available at http://user.cs.tu-berlin.de/~genged/. Accessed July 15, 2009.

108. Aspect.NET project site. Available at http://www.aspectdotnet.org. Accessed July 15, 2009.

109. Safonov VO. High-level language abstract syntax tree for Phoenix (Phoenix HL-AST). Microsoft Research Phoenix Academic Program. Phoenix booklet. Available at http://research.microsoft.com/en-us/collaboration/focus/cs/phoenix_booklet_0625_ebook.pdf. Accessed June 9, 2009.

Index

ABC, programming language, compiler
    for "Elbrus," 14
Action, semantic, 11
ActionScript, 48, 92
Ada, programming language,
    implementation for "Elbrus," 15
Addressing
  variables of different types, 181–186
  uplevel, 19, 157
Address, pair, 189
  level of, 189
  offset of, 189
Algebra, formal structure
  carrier of, 23
  equate(s) in, 23
  multi-sorted, 23
  signature of, 23
  sort of, 23
ALGOL, 13. *See also* ALGOL-60
ALGOL-60, 13–14, 32
  spelling of keywords in dialects of, 32
  use of display in the implementation,
    116, 189

ALGOL-68
  formal definition by Van Wijngaarden
    two-level grammars, 54
  mode (type) definitions in, 104, 120
  Soviet implementation for IBM-360, 14
  structural type identity in, 121
  user-defined keywords and indicators,
    40, 44
ALPHARD, 18
Analysis
  control flow, 131, 158, 162, 246, 260
  data flow, 157, 162, 249, 260, 261
ANTLR, compiler development tool, 2,
    11, 45
  input grammar file structure, 48–49
  lexical analysis specification and
    generation, 48–51
  lookahead buffer, 49
  nextToken method, 50
  parser specification and generation,
    92–93
ArrayIndexOutOfBoundsException, 32,
    173

Trustworthy Compilers, by Vladimir O. Safonov
Copyright © 2010 John Wiley & Sons, Inc.